FIRST HAND

FIRST HAND:
The Unland Diaries and Memoirs of the Revolutionary War, World War II, and Watergate
***
John Unland

***

© 2020 by John Unland
All rights reserved. This book or any portion thereof may not be reproduced or used in any manner whatsoever without the express written permission of the author except for the use of brief quotations in a book review.

Printed in the United States of America
First Printing, 2020
ISBN 978-1-7361584-0-1

John Unland
P.O. Box 711
Driggs, ID 83422
Email: junland@mac.com

Cover photo credits:
Revolutionary War/World War II image courtesy of Boston Public Library
White House photo courtesy of David Everett Strickler (davidestrickler.com)

Contents

About the Author ix
Preface x
Acknowledgements xiii
Prologue xiv
    My Unusual Political Upbringing xv
Introduction xxiv
Chapter One: Lt. McDowell's Role in the Battle at Stony Point 1
    Orders Given to the Light Infantry before the Battle at Stony Point ~ July 14, 1779 2
    Letters Regarding the Battle at Stony Point 7
    Excerpt from "Decisive Battles of the American Revolution" by Lt. Col. Joseph Mitchell 24
Chapter Two: The Beginning of Lt. William McDowell's Actual Diary 27
    May 1781 ~ Pennsylvania to Virginia 27
    June 1781 ~ Leesburg, Virginia to near Williamsburg, VA 28
    July 1781 ~ Near Williamsburg, VA to Jamestown and the Battle of Green Spring 34
Chapter Three: Rejoining My Brothers in Arms 41
    October 1781 ~ Philadelphia to Baltimore to Yorktown 41
Chapter Four: "Brought from Journal #1" 51
    Number of miles 1384— 51
Chapter Five: March 1782 59
    After Special Duty 59

Chapter Six: "Brought from Journal #2" 85
    Number of miles brought from No. 2—2071 85
Chapter Seven: History of the McDowell Family 89
Chapter Eight: World War II Memoir of James M. Unland 107
Chapter Nine: Off to Join the War 119
Chapter Ten: July, 1944 133
Chapter Eleven: Coming Home 147
Chapter Twelve: A Few More Stories 179
Chapter Thirteen: My Time at the White House During Watergate and Beyond 199
    An Internship to Remember 199
Chapter Fourteen: My Personal Diary of My White House Days 203
    The Proposal 324
Chapter Fifteen: Some Final Stories 327
Epilogue: What We Did in Our 20s 367

About the Author

John Unland and his wife of 44 years (and counting), Linda, met in the summer of 1974 while working in the White House.

They live on the Idaho side of the Teton Mountains in a yurt and small cabin with their Newfoundlands and are very involved in non-profit work within the community.

Houser, Aggie, and Yogi

Preface

Why did I do this book and how did I piece it together? Well, having moved my belongings at least 15 times over the past 45 years or so from Illinois, to Washington, D.C., to New York, to Philadelphia (five different homes), to Colorado, to Idaho, and probably other places I have forgotten—almost every move entailed not only moving furniture, but of course, personal items. Among those personal items are five or more large boxes of material relating to my White House days, plus boxes from my career, etc. There were also boxes that always followed me with every move which were labeled simply: "Alice's." Until a few years ago, I didn't pay much attention to them—just shuffled them from place to place, shelf to shelf, storage unit to storage unit. I only knew vaguely that what was contained in those "Alice" boxes were documents related to a distant relative who fought in the Revolutionary War—as well as some family lineage documents, etc.

Then, on a beautiful day in Idaho back in 2019, I sat down and opened these boxes up and found a literary treasure from 1781 about the Revolutionary War that had been painstakingly transcribed by an old typewriter—as if my Aunt Alice had wanted it to be preserved for future generations to read and learn from. And after digging a bit further into some nearby boxes, I also found my father's World War II memoir. Then, low and behold, when I stumbled across the diary I kept during my White House/Watergate years, it dawned on me—looking at this veritable treasure trove of information in one room—that not many families in the United States have relatives who kept either daily diaries or memoirs of their lives during such historic eras of our country's history. And there I sat looking at three significant documents written by members of my family. So, I decided to put them all together into one book.

Let's call it a commemoration of history if you will, but I believe it's also an overall lesson in obtaining, fighting for, and then protecting, freedom.

Regarding Lieutenant McDowell's diary of his time in the Revolutionary War, this came about from a relative on my grandmother's side; my grandmother, Rachel McDowell Unland. Alice Brants was related to my grandmother and was deeply, deeply involved in the state of Illinois' chapter of the Daughters of the American Revolution (DAR) and was also very involved at the national level.

There were both regional and national conventions every year and I don't think she missed a single one during her adult life. In fact, the era of the American Revolution was her passion largely due to a distant relative of ours, Lieutenant (later Captain) William McDowell, who fought in the war

My Aunt Alice Brants (circa 1968)

and kept a daily diary throughout much of his enlistment period. Alice spent many, many months transcribing Lt. McDowell's hand-written diary into a type-written format on her Smith Corona typewriter.

In the pages that follow, you will see the transcription of McDowell's original handwritten diary, as well as some examples of his handwritten pages. We were also able to track down where pages of this diary can be viewed by the public in the library at the National Society of the Sons of the American Revolution (SAR)[1] located in Louisville, Kentucky. In the late 60s, after she finished her transcription and research, Alice asked my Mom and Dad to drive her down to Louisville to deliver the original McDowell diary to the library, which they did.

Obviously, no pictures of Lieutenant McDowell exist, but in going through Aunt Alice's boxes that held his diary, I did find a photo of his tombstone that she must have taken on a trip to Mercersberg, PA in the 1950's or so.

This is the gravestone of William McDowell who was born sometime in 1749 or 1750 and died on June 19, 1835 at the age of 86.

Regarding the World War II memoirs of my father, unlike so many of his generation who fought in that war, my dad had no hesitation of talking about it and telling my brother and me stories about it (other than gruesome details which I'm certain existed). The one thing I do remember where he was bothered by his memories of the war was at the Fourth of July firework displays. We would go out to the hillside in our town and watch the fireworks. I remember a couple of times when the fireworks were really

---

[1] Sons of the American Revolution https://www.sar.org/

loud, he would just quietly leave our family and drive back to our house a few miles away and go into our basement where he couldn't hear them. At the time I didn't know why he left, but my mom told me later that it was because it reminded him of being in the infantry and being in the war.

When he was in his 70s, I realized that he was aging and that those of his generation who fought in the war were passing away rapidly, so I asked him to write his memoirs for me; which he did without hesitation. During the process of him writing his memoirs I never asked him how he was doing, but I could tell that this effort was therapeutic for him. He enjoyed reaching back to his youth, recalling his college years and also recalling the major events of his time in the war—some which seemed to be quite painful.

For me, keeping a daily diary during my White House years, I felt it was something that should be documented because I knew that history was unfolding right before me. I knew I was incredibly fortunate to be there, and again, being interested in history and politics, I wanted to chronicle my days there—not knowing that when I began my diary that I would be witnessing a major event in our country's history.

My goal here was to put all three of these uniquely historic documents together for me; my wife, Linda and our two sons, Logan and Tyler; my brother, Jim; and anyone else who might be interested in history and in particular these three eras of our American past.

This project took nearly a year to complete after going through many, many boxes and sorting through literally hundreds of documents and photos—all of which have now been edited down to this one book. I appreciate the time you are dedicating to read it and I do hope you enjoy it.

Sincerely,

John Unland

Acknowledgements

There is but one person who I must acknowledge in putting this book together in all facets: organizing, editing, helping in the design and, as you will see, paying attention to every detail of these eras of our nation's history. That person is Shanlynn Rabenda, who has been my friend and outstanding assistant for nearly 14 years. She is spectacular!

As far as sparking my interest in history, I want to give a nod to my high school history teacher, Burdett A. "Bird" Loomis, Professor Emeritus at the University of Kansas, who as much as anyone in my life taught me to think on my own and always wanted us to ask the questions "why."

Prologue

As I mentioned, this is a trilogy of diaries; one written during the Revolutionary War by Lieutenant William McDowell (who was later elevated to Captain); the second is a memoir of recollections written by my father, James Maxwell Unland (who was also a Lieutenant in the Army and later elevated to Captain) about his experiences in combat during World War II, which took him from Normandy across Europe in General Patton's 3rd Army; and the third is my own diary during my days in the White House from Watergate through the first year of President Ford's presidency.

As a relative, as distant as I might be from Lt. McDowell, (I discovered we are actually eight generations removed!) it's quite rare, I think, that a family has diaries and memoirs giving a firsthand account of these poignant eras in American history.

Public domain image of the U.S. Constitution

The first section will talk about Lt. William McDowell, who was born in Pennsylvania in 1749 or 1750, though we were unable to pin down his exact birth date. He joined the Continental Army in 1778 and fought under General Anthony Wayne, who was commanded by General George Washington. In so doing, he was one of our patriots who fought for independence and the creation of the Constitution of the United States, which was ratified in 1787.

My father, James Maxwell Unland, fought in World War II and served to help liberate France; he fought in the Battle of the Bulge to liberate Belgium; and ultimately fought in Holland to help liberate them from Nazi occupation. His service focused on defending our Constitution for which Lt. McDowell fought to create during the Revolutionary War.

In my personal diary of my years in the White House during the days of Watergate and the resignation of President Nixon, I saw firsthand the disregard for the Constitution for which Lt. McDowell and Lt. Unland fought. So, the common thread through these three diaries and memoirs is the Constitution of the United States. One relative helped to create it, the second helped to defend it, and I, the third relative, was witness to a President who tried to subvert it.

My Unusual Political Upbringing

I come from a political family. My father, a longtime Republican, ran for congress in the 18th District of Illinois, where we were from. In 1956 he ran against a gentleman by the name of Bob Michel[2]. My dad lost by roughly 1,000 votes; a very close election. And as my father told me many times, the day after losing to Mr. Michel, my dad took out a full-page ad in the newspapers of the major cities in his district; for example, he purchased a full-page ad in the Galesburg, Illinois, newspaper, the Peoria General Star, Pekin Daily Times, and other newspapers, saying "Congratulations Bob Michel," and

signed his name, Jim Unland. That's the kind of person he was. He fought hard and he lost graciously, and Bob Michel never forgot that. The two of them were friends until my father passed away. Those were the days when there was graciousness in politics.

So, I grew up in a family of intense civic involvement. My grandfather, J. Logan Unland, and my grandmother, Rachel Unland, were deeply involved in civic affairs, not only political but social. They were the song leaders during the Great Depression out in our community park and around

---

[2] Wikipedia contributors, "Robert H. Michel," *Wikipedia, The Free Encyclopedia*, https://en.wikipedia.org/w/index.php?title=Robert_H._Michel&oldid=962811748 (accessed September 20, 2020), "Robert Henry "Bob" Michel (March 2, 1923 – February 17, 2017) was an American Republican Party politician who was a member of the United States House of Representatives for 38 years. He represented central Illinois' 18th congressional district, and was the GOP leader in Congress, serving as Minority Leader for the last 14 years (1981–1995) of a decades-long era of Democratic Party dominance of the House."

town. My grandmother would play the piano and my grandfather would lead the singing among all the audiences, churches, community activities and so forth.

My dad inherited that sense of obligation to his community and was deeply involved in many, many issues to help our community and our schools. He served on the state of Illinois Higher Board of Education, which oversaw all the universities in the state, which were significant. He was also, in addition to having run for congress, the down-state Illinois chairman for Richard Nixon's campaigns. He was just generally involved with many things.

In addition, he served in World War II under General Patton and understood the atrocities of war more than anyone I've ever known. And for me, growing up in the 1960s and 70s, politics were part of the general kitchen-table discussions. We didn't talk about much else.

My father was a very liberal Republican, deeply opposed to the Vietnam War, and I recall being of draft age at the age of 18 mentioning to him that this is something I can't imagine—being drafted and going into a war in Vietnam—a war which I truthfully did not understand.

What I remember about that war were the weekly reports by Walter Cronkite[3], or Huntley-Brinkley[4], of how many soldiers were killed at the end of every week. I remember Walter Cronkite, I believe, ending his weekly broadcasts, saying "we lost XX number of Americans this past week." I also recall footage of bombings and photos from the war being shown on TV.

Because of my father's involvement in politics and his interest in history, I was pretty dialed in to the Vietnam war era in the '60's. It was a time of great social upheaval across the country and protesting the war. It was a very turbulent time in which I grew up in a very political family.

I remember when the selective service and the draft were enacted and I was due to go down to our selective service office at the post office to register, I remember telling saying, "Dad, this just doesn't seem right." He

---

[3] Wikipedia contributors, "Walter Cronkite," *Wikipedia, The Free Encyclopedia*, https://en.wikipedia.org/w/index.php?title=Walter_Cronkite&oldid=957284882 (accessed May 20, 2020), "Walter Leland Cronkite, Jr. (November 4, 1916 – July 17, 2009) was an American broadcast journalist who served as anchorman for the CBS Evening News for 19 years (1962–1981). During the 1960s and 1970s, he was often cited as "the most trusted man in America" after being so named in an opinion poll."

[4] Wikipedia contributors, "The Huntley–Brinkley Report," *Wikipedia, The Free Encyclopedia*, https://en.wikipedia.org/w/index.php?title=The_Huntley%E2%80%93Brinkley_Report&oldid=955433103 (accessed May 20, 2020), "The Huntley–Brinkley Report" (sometimes known as The Texaco Huntley–Brinkley Report for one of its early sponsors) was an American evening news program that aired on NBC from October 29, 1956, to July 31, 1970. It was anchored by Chet Huntley in New York City, and David Brinkley in Washington, D.C."

was so opposed to this particular war that he would get into screaming matches with our good friends at dinners and social functions. I remember one of our dear friends, our doctor, by the name of Bob Rhodes being supportive of the war and my dad and Dr. Bob arguing to the point they were screaming and would get up from the table. That's how he was, though having run for congress as a Republican, he did not support the war in any way, shape, or form. So, I grew up in that type of environment. And I mention this because it will lead to my interest in politics and my path to the White House.

I can trace my interest in national politics back to 1963 when I was only 11 years old. I wrote a letter to then-President John F. Kennedy—telling him how much I sincerely admired him and his family; and I was infatuated with the glamour of Camelot and Caroline's pony, Macaroni. Not long after, I received this note from him (through his personal secretary). Funnily enough, it was addressed to my grandfather, John Logan Unland, and re-routed to his address on Bacon Street since the Post Office employees in Pekin evidently assumed my letter could not possibly have come from the 11-year-old version of him. Sadly, within 4 months of this letter, President Kennedy would be dead.

In 1972 I took a semester off from college when Richard Nixon was running again. I wanted to work on the political campaign of the governor of Illinois—Richard Ogilvy. I talked to my dad about taking the semester off and asked him if there were a way I could work on this campaign since he knew the campaign manager and others involved in this effort. I was 19 years old but I wanted to get into the grassroots of politics.

He arranged for me to interview with a campaign manager, a gentleman by the name the John Parkhurst, to see if there was anything I could do for them. Mr. Parkhurst was the greatest guy and he knew of my interest in politics and put me into a role where I drove around the state of Illinois visiting college campuses, young people, in this big International Harvester truck. And on the top of it was a big "Ogilvy for Governor" sign.

I remember driving down interstates with the wind hitting the sign, and I thought I was going to topple over. I went to many, many colleges; several campuses of the University of Illinois, Knox College, Bradley University, Northwestern University, LaSalle College, and many more all over the state. And on each visit, I tried to arrange for the senior class presidents to gather a group of students for me with whom I could speak so I could talk about the Governor and his record on issues. At this time, those of 18 years and older could vote and this was the objective: to procure their votes for the Governor.

Governor Ogilvy ran against a gentleman by the name the Dan Walker. Dan Walker was a very astute politician. And given his last name, he walked the entire state of Illinois from top to bottom, shaking hands, stopping at organizations such as Rotary Clubs, restaurants, coffee shops, etc. He did this and ultimately won the election—largely because of the media attention he received. Also, Governor Ogilvy had instituted a state income tax which, though needed, was not popular among voters.

Now, Dan Walker had a really, really nice son by the name of Dan Walker, Jr., who was a first-year law student at Northwestern University law school. The two campaigns worked together to have Dan Walker, Jr. and me appear together at these schools to "debate" one another on the issues. He, being a law student at Northwestern, was far more adept in dealing with these debate situations than I, a 19-year-old sophomore in college, but he was very, very gracious, and I don't know if either of us changed anyone's mind or moved the needle at all. We met one another on college campuses maybe 20 or 25 times. We got to know each other well, and we had a really nice relationship.

So that's my early involvement in politics. I was interested at a very young age and pursued the grassroots involvement and saw some of it firsthand.

In 1974, I was itching again to get into some type of a political position and through a friend of our family's, Steve Gamble, who was working in President Nixon's White House Domestic Council[5], I learned about the White House intern program. Steve was kind enough to put me in touch with the person who ran the program, a woman by the name of Pam Powell. I submitted an application to Pam; and I probably called her and Steve about every 50 seconds to inquire about the status of my being accepted.

In the meantime, I was attending the London School of Economics when I received a telegram from the White House in late May of 1974 telling me that I had been accepted to the program and was due to show up at the White House on June 3rd—in four or five days! (June 3rd, 1974 is where my White House diary begins)—but we will get to that section shortly.

Now, let's backtrack a little bit and talk about the town in which I was raised—Pekin, Illinois. From Pekin, which is not a very large town, came several distinguished people. It's in Central Illinois and, if you will, is comprised of very hard-working people who are farmers and work at the Caterpillar tractor plants; there's also a distillery where many people work and of course there are the usual professions such as doctors, attorneys, etc. When my dad came back from the war, he came back to Pekin and went to work at my grandfather's insurance agency.

My mom and dad bought a house literally across the block from where my grandparents lived, so I grew up with my grandparents close at hand. Many nights my grandfather would come to tuck my brother and me into bed—and these being the days before air conditioning—I could hear him whistle on his way back home with the window screens open and then the door would slam as he went into his house. It was that kind of an environment. Down the street from him, maybe four blocks, lived Everett McKinley Dirksen[6], who was the minority leader of the United States

---

[5] Wikipedia contributors, "United States Domestic Policy Council," *Wikipedia, The Free Encyclopedia*, https://en.wikipedia.org/w/index.php?title=United_States_Domestic_Policy_Council&oldid=957222477 (accessed May 20, 2020), "The Domestic Policy Council (DPC) of the United States is the principal forum used by the President of the United States for considering domestic policy matters, excluding economic matters, which are the domain of the National Economic Council."

[6] Wikipedia contributors, "Everett Dirksen," *Wikipedia, The Free Encyclopedia*, https://en.wikipedia.org/w/index.php?title=Everett_Dirksen&oldid=956208509 (accessed May 20, 2020), "Everett McKinley Dirksen (January 4, 1896 – September 7, 1969) was an American politician. A member of the Republican Party, he represented Illinois in the United States House of Representatives and the United States Senate. As Senate Minority Leader from 1959 to 1969, he played a highly visible and key role in the politics of the 1960s."

Senate for many years, especially during the years when Lyndon Johnson[7] was the majority leader. So that again added to the political foundation in which I grew up.

I remember being on the porch at my grandparent's house, with no air conditioning, playing cribbage, and often Senator Dirksen would walk up the block, unannounced, open up the screen door and say, "J. Logan Unland." He had a very deep and resonant voice. Here I was just a 12-year-old or however old, sitting and talking with Senator Dirksen (along with my parents and grandparents) too many times to count—which certainly added another element of politics to my life as well.

And as if that didn't add enough political waves to this little town, Senator Dirksen's daughter, Joy, married Senator Howard Baker[8] from Tennessee. You may recall during the Watergate era that he was a pivotal person on the Senate Watergate Committee and asked the famous question of John Dean[9]: "What did the President know and when did he know it?".

So here we have Senator Dirksen as a close personal friend; Senator Howard Baker as a personal friend of our family as well; and my father was very close to Congressman Michel who defeated him in his congressional campaign. At the time of my interest in the White House internship program, Congressman Michel was the minority leader of the United States House of Representatives. So, we have the minority leader of the Senate, Everett Dirksen, a very powerful position; the minority leader of the House of Representatives, Congressman Bob Michel; and Senator Howard Baker, Jr. in a very powerful position—all political acquaintances and family friends who lived nearby.

In addition to this, there were two other gentlemen who were very involved in the national scene. One was my father's very close friend, John

---

[7] Wikipedia contributors, "Lyndon B. Johnson," *Wikipedia, The Free Encyclopedia*, https://en.wikipedia.org/w/index.php?title=Lyndon_B._Johnson&oldid=957110695 (accessed May 20, 2020), "Lyndon Baines Johnson (August 27, 1908 – January 22, 1973), often referred to by his initials LBJ, was an American politician who served as the 36th president of the United States from 1963 to 1969. Formerly the 37th vice president from 1961 to 1963, he assumed the presidency following the assassination of President John F. Kennedy. A Democrat from Texas, Johnson also served as a United States Representative and as the Majority Leader in the United States Senate."

[8] Wikipedia contributors, "Howard Baker," *Wikipedia, The Free Encyclopedia*, https://en.wikipedia.org/w/index.php?title=Howard_Baker&oldid=977198685 (accessed September 27, 2020), "Howard Henry Baker Jr. (November 15, 1925 – June 26, 2014) was an American politician and diplomat who served as a United States Senator from Tennessee from 1967 to 1985. During his tenure, he rose to the rank of Senate Minority Leader and then Senate Majority Leader."

[9] Wikipedia contributors, "John Dean," *Wikipedia, The Free Encyclopedia*, https://en.wikipedia.org/w/index.php?title=John_Dean&oldid=956202480 (accessed May 20, 2020), "John Wesley Dean III (born October 14, 1938) is a former attorney who served as White House Counsel for United States President Richard Nixon from July 1970 until April 1973. Dean is known for his role in the cover-up of the Watergate scandal and his subsequent testimony to Congress as a witness."

T. McNaughton,[10] who served in the Pentagon under Robert McNamara,[11] and who was part of a group within the Pentagon and the Johnson administration who was opposed to the Vietnam War. He lived just blocks from our house in Pekin.

Another notable person in our small town was a gentleman by the name of Richard (Dick) Stolley,[12] who was the Editor in Chief of *LIFE Magazine* during those days, and is the gentleman who obtained the Zapruder film tapes of President Kennedy's assassination for *LIFE Magazine*. So, I grew up in this small neighborhood in a small town of influential politicians and others of national prominence—which played a large part in piquing my interest in politics and the national scene.

---

[10] Wikipedia contributors, "John McNaughton," *Wikipedia, The Free Encyclopedia*, https://en.wikipedia.org/w/index.php?title=John_McNaughton_(government_official)&oldid=976245447 (accessed September 18, 2020), "John Theodore McNaughton (November 21, 1921 – July 19, 1967) born in Bicknell, Indiana, was United States Assistant Secretary of Defense for International Security Affairs and Robert S. McNamara's closest advisor. He died in a plane crash at age 45, just before he was to become Secretary of the Navy."

[11] Wikipedia contributors, "Robert McNamara," *Wikipedia, The Free Encyclopedia*, https://en.wikipedia.org/w/index.php?title=Robert_McNamara&oldid=955184331 (accessed May 20, 2020), "Robert Strange McNamara (June 9, 1916 – July 6, 2009) was an American business executive and the eighth United States Secretary of Defense, serving from 1961 to 1968 under Presidents John F. Kennedy and Lyndon B. Johnson. He played a major role in escalating the United States' involvement in the Vietnam War."

[12] Wikipedia contributors, "Richard Stolley," *Wikipedia, The Free Encyclopedia*, https://en.wikipedia.org/w/index.php?title=Richard_Stolley&oldid=907972863 (accessed May 20, 2020), "Richard Brockway Stolley (born October 3, 1928) is an American journalist and magazine editor. He's most well-known for his work at Life magazine, which he joined in 1953."

The American Flag during the Revolutionary War from 1777-1795

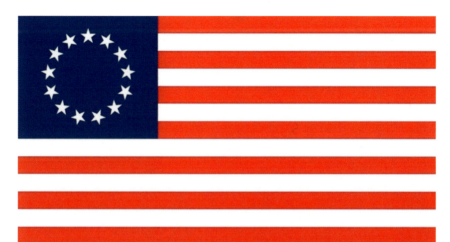

https://commons.wikimedia.org/w/index.php?title=File:Flag_of_the_United_States_(1777-1795).svg&oldid=477710500 Version of the "Betsy Ross" design of the first flag of the United States (with 13 stars in a circle)

"The Betsy Ross flag is an early design of the flag of the United States, named for early American upholsterer and flag maker Betsy Ross. The pattern of the Betsy Ross flag is 13 alternating red-and-white stripes with stars in a field of blue in the upper left corner canton. Its distinguishing feature is thirteen 5-pointed stars arranged in a circle representing the 13 colonies that fought for their independence during the American Revolutionary War."
https://en.wikipedia.org/w/index.php?title=Betsy_Ross_flag&oldid=985589504

Introduction

Due to the uniqueness of this book, here are a few important things I'd like to bring to your attention:

* The bulk of this book has been directly transcribed from original writings of the three original "authors"—therefore any views expressed by them are not necessarily the current views of "this Author."

* The information contained in the "diary" sections of this book were transcribed word-for-word from actual hand-written documents; no embellishments have been added. Only minor changes were made such as correcting obvious misspellings.

* It should be noted that some misspellings within the McDowell diary have been left that way in order to preserve the integrity of the original transcription.

* Where I felt it might be of benefit and value to the reader, images of some of Lt. McDowell's handwritten pages have been included within this book, which I hope will lend additional context to the enormous task that was undertaken in deciphering and transcribing his diary in the first place.

* Many historical references, names, and terms within this book have been footnoted in order to assist the reader with additional context and provide a more thorough understanding of the story overall.

I do hope you enjoy this semi-virtual trip back in time to the birth of our nation and the ensuing fight for its freedom from the British; as well as the battle by our brave soldiers of the U.S. Army to liberate Europe in World War II as told through the eyes of my father.

Remember that these are not fictional diaries; these men actually lived each and every minute of every day that they wrote about. When it comes to Lt. McDowell and my father, I feel it is the least I can do to make sure that their harrowing experiences—and those of countless other brave men—are never forgotten.

Now, to better prepare you for the first section of the book which takes place during the American Revolutionary War, here is a brief history lesson with a sprinkling of definitions of some of the most important terms:

Introduction

The **Declaration of Independence**[13]: "The United States Declaration of Independence (formally The unanimous Declaration of the thirteen united States of America) is the pronouncement adopted by the Second Continental Congress meeting in Philadelphia, Pennsylvania, on July 4, 1776. The Declaration explained why the Thirteen Colonies at war with the Kingdom of Great Britain regarded themselves as thirteen independent sovereign states, no longer under British rule. With the Declaration, these new states took a collective first step toward forming the United States of America. The declaration was signed by representatives from New Hampshire, Massachusetts Bay, Rhode Island, Connecticut, New York, New Jersey, Pennsylvania, Maryland, Delaware, Virginia, North Carolina, South Carolina, and Georgia.

The Lee Resolution for independence was passed by the Second Continental Congress on July 2 with no opposing votes. The Committee of Five had drafted the Declaration to be ready when Congress voted on independence. John Adams, a leader in pushing for independence, had persuaded the committee to select Thomas Jefferson to compose the original draft of the document, which Congress edited to produce the final version. The Declaration was a formal explanation of why Congress had voted to declare independence from Great Britain, more than a year after the outbreak of the American Revolutionary War. Adams wrote to his wife Abigail, 'The Second Day of July 1776, will be the most memorable Epocha, in the History of America' – although Independence Day is actually celebrated on July 4, the date that the wording of the Declaration of Independence was approved."

The **Continental Congress**[14]: The Continental Congress was initially a convention of delegates from a number of British American colonies at the height of the American Revolution, who acted collectively for the people of the Thirteen Colonies that ultimately became the United States of America. After declaring the colonies independent from the Kingdom of Great Britain in 1776, it acted as the provisional governing structure for the collective United States, while most government functions remained in the individual states. The term most specifically refers to the First Continental Congress of 1774 and the Second Continental Congress of 1775–1781. More broadly, it also refers to the Congress of the Confederation of 1781–1789,

---

[13] Wikipedia contributors, "United States Declaration of Independence," *Wikipedia, The Free Encyclopedia*, https://en.wikipedia.org/w/index.php?title=United_States_Declaration_of_Independence&oldid=981406177 (accessed October 8, 2020)

[14] Wikipedia contributors, "Continental Congress," *Wikipedia, The Free Encyclopedia*, https://en.wikipedia.org/w/index.php?title=Continental_Congress&oldid=979598148 (accessed October 8, 2020)

thus covering the three congressional bodies of the Thirteen Colonies and the United States that met between 1774 and the inauguration of a new government in 1789 under the United States Constitution.

Convened in response to the Intolerable Acts passed by the British Parliament in 1774, the First Continental Congress sought to help repair the frayed relationship between the British government and its American colonies while also asserting the rights of colonists. The Second Congress adopted the Declaration of Independence in July 1776, proclaiming that the 13 colonies were now independent sovereign states, no longer under British rule. This body functioned as the provisional government for the U.S. until the nation's first Frame of Government, the Articles of Confederation and Perpetual Union, came into force on March 1, 1781, at which time it became the Congress of the Confederation. Officially styled 'The United States in Congress Assembled,' this unicameral governing body would convene in eight sessions (a ninth would fail to achieve a quorum) prior to being disbanded in 1789, when the 1st United States Congress under the new constitution took over the role as the nation's legislative branch of government.

Much of what is known today about the daily activities of these congresses comes from the journals kept by the secretary for all three congresses, Charles Thomson. Printed contemporaneously, the Papers of the Continental Congress contain the official congressional papers, letters, treaties, reports and records. The delegates to the Continental and Confederation congresses had extensive experience in deliberative bodies, with 'a cumulative total of nearly 500 years of experience in their Colonial assemblies, and fully a dozen of them had served as speakers of the houses of their legislatures.'"

First Continental Congress[15]: *"The First Continental Congress was a meeting of delegates from 12 of the 13 British colonies that became the United States. It met from September 5 to October 26, 1774, at Carpenters' Hall in Philadelphia, Pennsylvania, after the British Navy instituted a blockade of Boston Harbor and Parliament passed the punitive Intolerable Acts in response to the December 1773 Boston Tea Party. During the opening weeks of the Congress, the delegates conducted a spirited discussion about how the colonies could collectively respond to the British government's coercive actions, and they worked to make common cause. A plan was proposed to create a Union of Great Britain and the Colonies, but the delegates rejected it. They ultimately agreed to impose an economic boycott*

---

[15] Wikipedia contributors, "First Continental Congress," *Wikipedia, The Free Encyclopedia*, https://en.wikipedia.org/w/index.php?title=First_Continental_Congress&oldid=979230417 (accessed October 8, 2020)

Introduction

on British trade, and they drew up a Petition to the King pleading for redress of their grievances and repeal of the Intolerable Acts. That appeal had no effect, so the colonies convened the Second Continental Congress the following May, shortly after the battles of Lexington and Concord, to organize the defense of the colonies at the outset of the Revolutionary War. The delegates also urged each colony to set up and train its own militia."

Second Continental Congress[16]: *"The Second Continental Congress was a meeting of delegates from the Thirteen Colonies in America which united in the American Revolutionary War. It convened on May 10, 1775 with representatives from 12 of the colonies in Philadelphia, Pennsylvania shortly after the Battles of Lexington and Concord, succeeding the First Continental Congress which met in Philadelphia from September 5 to October 26, 1774. The Second Congress functioned as a de facto national government at the outset of the Revolutionary War by raising armies, directing strategy, appointing diplomats, and writing treaties such as the Declaration of the Causes and Necessity of Taking Up Arms and the Olive Branch Petition. All thirteen colonies were represented by the time that the Congress adopted the Lee Resolution which declared independence from Britain on July 2, 1776, and the congress agreed to the Declaration of Independence two days later.*

Afterward, Congress functioned as the provisional government of the United States of America through March 1, 1781. During this period, its achievements included: Successfully managing the war effort; drafting the Articles of Confederation, the first U.S. Constitution; securing diplomatic recognition and support from foreign nations; and resolving state land claims west of the Appalachian Mountains."

The following footnote describes the evolution of the Continental Army from 1775 through 1783.

The Continental Army[17]: *"The Continental Army was formed by the Second Continental Congress after the outbreak of the American Revolutionary War by the former British colonies that later became the United States of America. Established by a resolution of the Congress on June 14, 1775, it was created to coordinate the military efforts of the Thirteen Colonies in their ultimately successful revolt against British rule. The Continental Army was supplemented by local militias and volunteer troops*

---

[16] Wikipedia contributors, "Second Continental Congress," *Wikipedia, The Free Encyclopedia*, https://en.wikipedia.org/w/index.php?title=Second_Continental_Congress&oldid=980292324 (accessed October 8, 2020)

[17] Wikipedia contributors, "Continental Army," *Wikipedia, The Free Encyclopedia*, https://en.wikipedia.org/w/index.php?title=Continental_Army&oldid=982248200 (accessed October 8, 2020)

that remained under control of the individual states or were otherwise independent. General George Washington was the commander-in-chief of the army throughout the war.

Most of the Continental Army was disbanded in 1783 after the Treaty of Paris formally ended the war. The 1st and 2nd Regiments went on to form the nucleus of the Legion of the United States in 1792 under General Anthony Wayne. This became the foundation of the United States Army in 1796.

The Continental Army consisted of soldiers from all 13 colonies and, after 1776, from all 13 states. When the American Revolutionary War began at the Battles of Lexington and Concord on April 19, 1775, the colonial revolutionaries did not have an army. Previously, each colony had relied upon the militia, made up of part-time citizen-soldiers, for local defense, or the raising of temporary 'provincial regiments' during specific crises such as the French and Indian War of 1754–63. As tensions with Great Britain increased in the years leading to the war, colonists began to reform their militias in preparation for the perceived potential conflict. Training of militiamen increased after the passage of the Intolerable Acts in 1774. Colonists such as Richard Henry Lee proposed forming a national militia force, but the First Continental Congress rejected the idea.

On April 23, 1775, the Massachusetts Provincial Congress authorized the raising of a colonial army consisting of 26 company regiments. New Hampshire, Rhode Island, and Connecticut soon raised similar but smaller forces. On June 14, 1775, the Second Continental Congress decided to proceed with the establishment of a Continental Army for purposes of common defense, adopting the forces already in place outside Boston (22,000 troops) and New York (5,000). It also raised the first ten companies of Continental troops on a one-year enlistment, riflemen from Pennsylvania, Maryland, Delaware and Virginia to be used as light infantry, who became the 1st Continental Regiment in 1776. On June 15, 1775, the Congress elected by unanimous vote George Washington as Commander-in-Chief, who accepted and served throughout the war without any compensation except for reimbursement of expenses. Supporting Washington as commander in chief were four major-generals (Artemas Ward, Charles Lee, Philip Schuyler, and Israel Putnam) and eight brigadier-generals (Seth Pomeroy, Richard Montgomery, David Wooster, William Heath, Joseph Spencer, John Thomas, John Sullivan, and Nathanael Greene) As the Continental Congress increasingly adopted the responsibilities and posture of a legislature for a sovereign state, the role of the Continental Army became the subject of considerable debate. Some Americans had a general aversion to maintaining a standing army; but on the other hand the requirements of the war against the British required the discipline and organization of a modern military. As

Introduction

a result, the army went through several distinct phases, characterized by official dissolution and reorganization of units.

Broadly speaking, Continental forces consisted of several successive armies, or establishments:

The Continental Army of 1775, comprising the initial New Enland Army, organized by Washington into three divisions, six brigades, and 38 regiments. Major General Philip Schuyler's ten regiments in New York were sent to invade Canada.

The Continental Army of 1776, reorganized after the initial enlistment period of the soldiers in the 1775 army had expired. Washington had submitted recommendations to the Continental Congress almost immediately after he had accepted the position of Commander-in-Chief, but the Congress took time to consider and implement these. Despite attempts to broaden the recruiting base beyond New England, the 1776 army remained skewed toward the Northeast both in terms of its composition and of its geographical focus. This army consisted of 36 regiments, most standardized to a single battalion of 768 men strong and formed into eight companies, with a rank-and-file strength of 640.

The Continental Army of 1777–1780 evolved out of several critical reforms and political decisions that came about when it became apparent that the British were sending massive forces to put an end to the American Revolution. The Continental Congress passed the "Eighty-eight Battalion Resolve", ordering each state to contribute one-battalion regiments in proportion to their population, and Washington subsequently received authority to raise an additional 16 battalions. Enlistment terms extended to three years or to "the length of the war" to avoid the year-end crises that depleted forces (including the notable near-collapse of the army at the end of 1776, which could have ended the war in a Continental, or American, loss by forfeit).

The Continental Army of 1781–82 saw the greatest crisis on the American side in the war. Congress was bankrupt, making it very difficult to replenish the soldiers whose three-year terms had expired. Popular support for the war reached an all-time low, and Washington had to put down mutinies both in the Pennsylvania Line and in the New Jersey Line. Congress voted to cut funding for the Army, but Washington managed nevertheless to secure important strategic victories.

The Continental Army of 1783–84 was succeeded by the United States Army, which persists to this day. As peace was restored with the British, most of the regiments were disbanded in an orderly fashion, though several had already been diminished."

First Hand

The Soldiers: [Records found by my Aunt Alice show that Lt. McDowell joined the Army on March 22, 1778 and mustered out on November 3, 1783]

"Soldiers in the Continental Army were volunteers; they agreed to serve in the army and standard enlistment periods lasted from one to three years. Early in the war the enlistment periods were short, as the Continental Congress feared the possibility of the Continental Army evolving into a permanent army. The army never numbered more than 17,000 men. Turnover proved a constant problem, particularly in the winter of 1776–77, and longer enlistments were approved.

The officers of both the Continental Army and the state militias were typically yeoman farmers with a sense of honor and status and an ideological commitment to oppose British tyranny. The enlisted men were very different. They came from the working class or minorities groups (Irish, German, African American). They were motivated to volunteer by specific contracts that promised bounty money; regular pay at good wages; food, clothing and medical care; companionship; and the promise of land ownership after the war. They were unruly and would mutiny if the contractual terms were not met. By 1780-81 threats of mutiny and actual mutinies were becoming serious. Upwards of a fourth of Washington's army was Irish. Many had recently arrived and needed jobs. A lot of Irish, mainly Roman Catholics, were hostile to British rule in Ireland.

The Continental Army was racially integrated, a condition the United States Army would not see again until the 1950s. During the Revolution African American slaves were promised freedom in exchange for military service by both the Continental and British armies. Approximately 6,600 people of color (including African American, indigenous, and multiracial men) served with the colonial forces, and made up one fifth of the Northern Continental Army.

In addition to the Continental Army regulars, state militia units were assigned for short-term service and fought in campaigns throughout the war. Sometimes the militia units operated independently of the Continental Army, but often local militias were called out to support and augment the Continental Army regulars during campaigns. The militia troops developed a reputation for being prone to premature retreats, a fact that General Daniel Morgan integrated into his strategy at the Battle of Cowpens and fooled the British in 1781.

The financial responsibility for providing pay, food, shelter, clothing, arms, and other equipment to specific units was assigned to states as part of the establishment of these units. States differed in how well they lived up to these obligations. There were constant funding issues and morale problems as the

Introduction

war continued. This led to the army offering low pay, often rotten food, hard work, cold, heat, poor clothing and shelter, harsh discipline, and a high chance of becoming a casualty.

Keeping the continentals clothed was a difficult task and to do this Washington appointed James Mease, a merchant from Philadelphia. Mease worked closely with state-appointed agents to purchase clothing and things such as cow hides to make clothing and shoes for soldiers. Mease had eventually resigned in 1777 and had compromised much of the organization of the Clothing Department. After this on many accounts the soldiers of the Continental Army often were poorly clothed and had little blankets and often did not even have shoes. The problem with clothing and having shoes for soldiers was often not the fault of not having enough but the organization and lack of transportation. To reorganize the Board of War was appointed to sort out the clothing supply chain. During this time they sought out the help of France and for the remainder of the war, clothing was coming from over-sea procurement."

Now, let's dig into the history of the "Pennsylvania troops," specifically the **1st Pennsylvania Regiment**[18], which is where Lt. McDowell spent his time in the Army.

"The 1st Pennsylvania Regiment - originally mustered as the 1st Pennsylvania Rifles; also known as the 1st Continental Line and 1st Continental Regiment, was raised under the command of Colonel William Thompson for service in the Continental Army.

The Congressional resolution of June 14, 1775, authorized ten companies of expert riflemen to be raised for one-year enlistments as Continental troops. Maryland and Virginia were to raise two companies each, and Pennsylvania six. Pennsylvania frontiersman, however were so eager to participate that on June 22 Pennsylvania's quota of two was increased to eight, organized as a regiment known as the 'Pennsylvania Rifle Regiment.' A ninth company was added to the regiment on July 11. All thirteen companies were sent to Washington's army at Boston for use as light infantry and later as special reserve forces.

Seven companies of the regiment (1st, 2nd, 3rd, 4th, 5th, 8th, and 9th) were made up of Germans, Welsh, the rare Manx, Free Quakers, even English but mostly Scots-Irish from Lancaster; the 6th and 7th companies were mostly German, from Berks and Northampton counties. Their standard weapon was the long rifle, which had greater range and accuracy than the muskets used by most of the British Army and Continental Army, but less

---

[18] Wikipedia contributors, "1st Pennsylvania Regiment," *Wikipedia, The Free Encyclopedia*, https://en.wikipedia.org/w/index.php?title=1st_Pennsylvania_Regiment&oldid=958471726 (accessed October 8, 2020)

weight of shot, slower rate of fire, and were without bayonets, making the regiment unsuitable for line-of-battle.

Doctor James Thacher, a young doctor from Barnstable who observed the regiment during many of its battles, provided this description of the riflemen:

They are remarkably stout and hardy men; many of them exceeding six feet in height. They are dressed in white frocks or rifle shirts and round hats. There men are remarkable for the accuracy of their aim; striking a mark with great certainty at two hundred yards distance. At a review, a company of them, while in a quick advance, fired their balls into objects of seven inches diameter at the distance of 250 yards . . . their shot have frequently proved fatal to British officers and soldiers who expose themselves to view at more than double the distance of common musket shot. (Source: James Thacher, 'Military Journal during the American Revolutionary War from 1775 to 1783'.)

As described under colours, the regiment in 1776 wore green hunting shirts with black caps trimmed white adorned with feather while the officers wore green coats with red facings and similar caps. By the Battle of Boston and by regulation at Valley Forge, blue coats with red facings were issued to the regiment, while most of the regiment's Riflemen continued to wear hunting shirts until wars end.

The regiment saw action during the New York Campaign, Battle of Trenton, Second Battle of Trenton, and Battle of Princeton. At the Battle of Brandywine the regiment was led by Colonel James Chambers and assigned to Colonel Thomas Hartley's 1st Pennsylvania Brigade. Under the direction of acting division commander Brigadier General Anthony Wayne, the 1st Pennsylvania Regiment fought near Chadds Ford where it held the 'post of honor', the far right flank of the division. At the Battle of Germantown the regiment was brigaded with the 2nd, 7th, and 10th Pennsylvania Regiments. The unit again fought on the extreme right flank of the division just east of Germantown Road. Afterward, the regiment's Major Henry Miller boasted to his family about how the division routed the British troops opposed to them and overran their camp. The 1st was in action at the Battle of Matson's Ford on December 11, 1777.

The unit also fought at the Battle of Monmouth in 1778 and the Battle of Springfield in 1780. Two companies, those of Captain William Hendricks and Captain Matthew Smith, accompanied Arnold's expedition to Quebec and were captured in the Battle of Quebec. The regiment was furloughed June 11, 1783, at Philadelphia, Pennsylvania and disbanded on November 15, 1783."

Now, a little information on two Generals who will be mentioned many times within Lt. McDowell's diary:

Introduction

*First, **General "Mad Anthony" Wayne**[19]: "Anthony Wayne (January 1, 1745 – December 15, 1796) was an American soldier, officer and statesman of Irish descent. He adopted a military career at the outset of the American Revolutionary War, where his military exploits and fiery personality quickly earned him promotion to brigadier general and the nickname 'Mad Anthony'. He later served as the Senior Officer of the Army on the Ohio Country frontier and led the Legion of the United States.*

Wayne was born in Chester County, Pennsylvania, and worked as a tanner and surveyor after attending the College of Philadelphia. He was elected to the Pennsylvania General Assembly and helped raise a Pennsylvania militia unit in 1775. During the Revolutionary War, he served in the Invasion of Quebec, the Philadelphia campaign, and the Yorktown campaign. His reputation suffered due to his defeat in the Battle of Paoli, but he won wide praise for his leadership in the 1779 Battle of Stony Point. He was promoted to Major General in 1783 but retired from the Continental Army soon after."

*Now, let's take a closer look at **General Nathanael Greene**[20]: "Nathanael Greene (August 7, 1742 – June 19, 1786, sometimes misspelled Nathaniel) was a major general of the Continental Army in the American Revolutionary War. He emerged from the war with a reputation as General George Washington's most gifted and dependable officer, and is known for his successful command in the southern theater of the war.*

Born into a prosperous Quaker family in Warwick, Rhode Island, Greene became active in the resistance to British revenue policies in the early 1770s and helped establish the Kentish Guards, a state militia. After the April 1775 Battles of Lexington and Concord, the legislature of Rhode Island established an army and appointed Greene to command it. Later in the year, Greene became a general in the newly-established Continental Army. Greene served under Washington in the Boston campaign, the New York and New Jersey campaign, and the Philadelphia campaign before being appointed quartermaster general of the Continental Army in 1778.

In October 1780, General Washington appointed Greene as the commander of the Continental Army in the southern theater. After taking command, Greene engaged in a successful campaign of guerrilla warfare against the numerically superior force of General Charles Cornwallis. He inflicted heavy losses on British forces at Battle of Guilford Court House, the Battle of Hobkirk's Hill, and the Battle of Eutaw Springs,

---

[19] Wikipedia contributors, "Anthony Wayne," *Wikipedia, The Free Encyclopedia*, https://en.wikipedia.org/w/index.php?title=Anthony_Wayne&oldid=978984524 (accessed October 8, 2020).

[20] Wikipedia contributors, "Nathanael Greene," *Wikipedia, The Free Encyclopedia*, https://en.wikipedia.org/w/index.php?title=Nathanael_Greene&oldid=980883276 (accessed October 8, 2020).

eroding British control of the Southern United States. Major fighting on land came to an end following the surrender of Cornwallis at the Battle of Yorktown in October 1781, but Greene continued to serve in the Continental Army until late 1783. After the war, he became a planter in the South, but failed. He died in 1786 at his Mulberry Grove Plantation in Chatham County, Georgia. Many places in the United States are named after Greene."

Other notable names you will see mentioned in this diary are Lord (Charles) Cornwallis and the Marquis de Lafayette.

First, a short introduction to **Lord Cornwallis**[21]*: "Charles Cornwallis, 1st Marquess Cornwallis, KG, PC (31 December 1738 – 5 October 1805), styled Viscount Brome between 1753 and 1762 and known as The Earl Cornwallis between 1762 and 1792, was a British Army general and official. In the United States and the United Kingdom he is best remembered as one of the leading British generals in the American War of Independence. His surrender in 1781 to a combined American and French force at the Siege of Yorktown ended significant hostilities in North America. He later served as a civil and military governor in Ireland, where he helped bring about the Act of Union; and in India, where he helped enact the Cornwallis Code and the Permanent Settlement.*

Born into an aristocratic family and educated at Eton and Cambridge, Cornwallis joined the army in 1757, seeing action in the Seven Years' War. Upon his father's death in 1762 he became Earl Cornwallis and entered the House of Lords. From 1766 until 1805 he was Colonel of the 33rd Regiment of Foot. He next saw military action in 1776 in the American War of Independence. Active in the advance forces of many campaigns, in 1780 he inflicted an embarrassing defeat on the American army at the Battle of Camden. He also commanded British forces in the March 1781 Pyrrhic victory at Guilford Court House. Cornwallis surrendered his army at Yorktown in October 1781 after an extended campaign through the Southern states, marked by disagreements between him and his superior, General Sir Henry Clinton."

Next, let's learn a little bit about the **Marquis de Lafayette**[22]*: "Marie-Joseph Paul Yves Roch Gilbert du Motier, Marquis de La Fayette (6 September 1757 – 20 May 1834), known in the United States as Lafayette, was a French aristocrat and military officer who fought in the American*

---

[21] Wikipedia contributors, "Charles Cornwallis, 1st Marquess Cornwallis," *Wikipedia, The Free Encyclopedia,* https://en.wikipedia.org/w/index.php?title=Charles_Cornwallis,_1st_Marquess_Cornwallis&oldid=979808375 (accessed October 8, 2020)

[22] Wikipedia contributors, "Gilbert du Motier, Marquis de Lafayette," *Wikipedia, The Free Encyclopedia,* https://en.wikipedia.org/w/index.php?title=Gilbert_du_Motier,_Marquis_de_Lafayette&oldid=980976197 (accessed October 8, 2020)

Introduction

Revolutionary War, commanding American troops in several battles, including the Siege of Yorktown. After returning to France, he was a key figure in the French Revolution of 1789 and the July Revolution of 1830. He has been considered a national hero in both countries.

Lafayette was born into a wealthy land-owning family in Chavaniac in the province of Auvergne in south central France. He followed the family's martial tradition and was commissioned an officer at age 13. He became convinced that the American revolutionary cause was noble, and he traveled to the New World seeking glory in it. He was made a major general at age 19, but he was initially not given American troops to command. He was wounded during the Battle of Brandywine but still managed to organize an orderly retreat, and he served with distinction in the Battle of Rhode Island. In the middle of the war, he sailed for home to lobby for an increase in French support. He returned to America in 1780 and was given senior positions in the Continental Army. In 1781, troops under his command in Virginia blocked forces led by Cornwallis until other American and French forces could position themselves for the decisive Siege of Yorktown.

He died on 20 May 1834 and is buried in Picpus Cemetery in Paris, under soil from Bunker Hill. He is sometimes known as 'The Hero of the Two Worlds' for his accomplishments in the service of both France and the United States."

History lesson concluded, so let's get to the good stuff.

Chapter One: Lt. McDowell's Role in the Battle at Stony Point

From all the information we found, and the work of Aunt Alice, it appears that Lt. McDowell was among those chosen by General Washington to serve under General Wayne in the Battle at Stony Point in 1779. The following pages precede the beginning of his actual diary, which began in May of 1781. It is apparent that McDowell joined the 1st Pennsylvania Regiment in 1778 and, we believe, shortly after completing his training, took part in this historic battle serving under General Anthony Wayne.

I have included images of the handwritten pages titled "Letters Regarding the Battle at Stony Point." I assume these were written by Lt. McDowell because it was a campaign that he was a part of and the handwriting in the letters appear to match his handwriting throughout his diary. My Aunt Alice apparently believed this as well since she wrote these thoughts in her notes.

Nonetheless, the details regarding how the battle was fought and the subsequent letters written about it are fascinating and I thought you would enjoy reading them.

To help set the stage, these are the notes I found that were written by my Aunt Alice:

"He evidently joined the Army at the beginning of the Rev. War for he served seven years and his Captain papers read 1784—so he was about 28 years old when he went into the service. I read that Washington chose his men for the battle of Stony Point, [so] he must have been one of the chosen few for he has all the orders of the Light Infantry given by Anthony Wayne, 1779—also a copy of the "thank yous" from both Washington and Wayne for the excellent job of winning the battle. Washington's headquarters was at New Windsor or "West Point." His diaries start in 1781, telling of the Southern campaign and how they marched from York, Pennsylvania, through Maryland and Virginia. He made one trip home for two weeks, then was sent to Philadelphia where he went by boat to Baltimore, then to Yorktown. From there he marched through Virginia, North Carolina and South Carolina to Charleston. He had acquired a land donation of 400 acres of land so evidently farmed, but was active in public and church affairs."

First Hand

Orders Given to the Light Infantry before the Battle at Stony Point ~ July 14, 1779

"The troops will march to-morrow at twelve o'clock, and move by the right, making a short halt at the Creek or run next, on this side of Clements's—Every office and non-commissioned officer will remain with, and be accountable for every man in their platoon—no soldier to be permitted to quit the ranks on any pretence whatever until a general halt is made, and then, to be attended by one of the officers of the platoon.

When the Van of the troops in the rear of Hill C, Col. Febiger will form his regiment into a solid column, of a half platoon in front as fast as they come up—Col. Meggs will form next in Col. Febiger's rear, and Maj. Hull in rear of Meggs, who will form the right column.

Col. Butler will form a column on the left of Febiger and Maj. Murphy in his rear. Every officer and soldier is then to fix a piece of white paper in the most conspicuous part of his hat, or cap, to distinguish him from the enemy.

At the word 'MARCH,' Lt. Col. Fleury will take charge of one hundred fifty determined and picked men and officers, with their arms unloaded, placing their whole dependence on the bayonet, will move about twenty paces in front of the right column by the route No. 1, and enter the sally port No. 6—he is to detach an officer and twenty men a little in front whose business it will be to secure the sentries and remove the abatis and other obstructions for the column to pass through. The column will follow closely in the rear with shouldered muskets under Col. Febiger with Gen. Wayne in person.

When the Works are forced and not before, the Victorious troops, will give the watchword, the Forts our own, with repeated and loud voices, and drive the enemy from their works and guns, which will favour the pass of the whole—

Should the enemy refuse to surrender or attempt to make their escape by water or otherwise, vigorous means must be used to force them to the former, and to prevent their attempting the latter—

Col. Butler will move by the route No. 2 proceeded by one hundred men with unloaded arms and fixed bayonets, under the command of Maj. Stewart, who will observe a distance of twenty yards in front of the column, which will immediately follow under the command of Col. Butler with shouldered muskets and enter the sally port. Cond.—the officer commanding the above named one hundred men will also detach a proper officer with twenty men a little in front to remove the obstructions, as soon as they gain the works they are also to give the watchword which will prevent confusion and mistakes—

Maj. Murphy will follow Col. Butler to the first figure 3 where he will divide a little to the right and left and wait the attack on the right, which will be his signal to begin, and keep up a perpetual and gauling fire and endevour to enter between and possess the works.

If any soldier presumes to take his musket from his shoulder, or attempt to fire or begin the battle till ordered by his proper officer, he shall be instantly put to death by the officer next him, for the cowardice and misconduct of one man is not to put the whole in danger or disorder with impunity—

After the troops begin to advance to the Works the strictest silence must be observed and the greatest attention paid to the command of the officers, as soon as the lines are carried the officers of the artillery with their commands will take possession of the Cannon, and to the end that the shipping may be secured and the Post at Verplanck's Point annoyed so as to facilitate the attack on that Quarter—

The General has the fullest confidence in the bravery and fortitude of the corps he has the happiness to command.

The distinguished honour conferred on every officer and soldier who has been drafted into this corps by his Excellency Gen. Washington, the credit of the state they belong to, their own reputation will be such powerful motives for each man to distinguish himself that the Gen. has not the least doubt of a glorious victory, and further he solemnly engages to reward the first man who enters the works with 500 dollars and immediate promotion- to the second, 400 dollars- to the third, 300 dollars- to the fourth, 200 dollars- and to the fifth, 100 dollars, and represent the conduct of every officer and soldier who distinguishes himself on this Action with the most favorable point of view to his Excellency who always receives the greatest pleasure in rewarding merit—

But should there be any soldier so lost to every sense of honour as to attempt to retreat one single foot or shrink from the face of danger, the officer next him is to put him to immediate death that he may no longer disgrace the name of a soldier, or the corps, or state to which he belongs—

As Gen. Wayne is determined to share the danger of the night so he wishes to participate the Glory of the Day, in common with his fellow soldiers.

Anty. Wayne B.G."

Names of the officers taken the 16th day of July in the morning at Stoney Point.

No.	Names	Rank	Regt.
1	Henry Johnston	Lt. Col	17th
2	John Darby	Capt.	17th
3	Robison, America	Lt.	17th
4	Robert Clayton	Capt.	17th
5	Wm. Tiffin P?? Artillery	Capt.	—
6	Wm. Armstrong	Lieut.	17th
7	Isaac Cary	D°	17th
8	Wm. F. Williams	D°	17th
9	Wm. Simpson	D°	17th
10	Wm. James?? Mawhood	D°	17th
11	James?? Wayman	D°	17th
12	R. Duncanon	D°	17th
13	Wm. Nairez??	D°	17th
14	John James?? Ross	D°	17th
15	John Grant	D°	17th
16	Wm. D.?? Hand??	Artillery	—

Lt. McDowell's Role in the Battle at Stony Point

No.	Names	Rank	Regt.
17	Wm. Marshall	Lieut.	C3
18	Frederick P. Robison	Ensign	17th
19	Henry Hamilton	Lieut.	17th
20	Wm. Huggiford	Lt. L.	—
21	Richard Steward	Lieut.	D°
22	Richard Auchmutry	Sergt.	—
23	Isaac Easton	Conductor	—
24	Patrick Commings,	Lieut.	17th
25	Andrew McClain	D°	17th
26	John Horn	Sergt.	17th
2	Officers Killed		

The Wounded and Surjeons sent to New York—"

[The preceding tables were transcribed from the following images of McDowell's original handwriting]

Names of the Officers taken the 16th Day of July in the Morning at Stony Point

No	Names	Rank	Regt
1	Henry Johnston	Lt. Col.	17th
2	John Darby	Capt.	17
3	— Robison, America	Lt.	17
4	Robert Clayton	Capt.	17
5	Wm Tiffin R. Artilly	Capt.	
6	Wm Armstrong	Lieut	17
7	Isaac Cary	Do	17
8	Wm T Williams	Do	17
9	Wm Simpson	Do	17
10	Wm Jno Mawhood	Do	17
11	Jno Waymor	Do	17
12	R. Duncanon	Do	17
13	Wm Naire	Do	17
14	John Ind Ross	Do	17
15	John Grant	Do	17
16	Wm Jn Tomdon		

Letters Regarding the Battle at Stony Point

No.	Names	Rank	Reg't
17	Wm Marshall	Lieut.	63
18	Fredk P. Robison	Ensign	17
19	Henry Hamilton	Lieut.	17
20	Wm Huggiford	A.L. Arriver	
21	Richard Steward	Lieut	Do
22	Richard Auchmutry	Surgt	
23	Isaac Easton	Conductor	
24	Patk Commengo, Wounded	Lieut	17
25	Andw McClain	Do	17
26	John Horn	Surgt	17
2	Officers Killed		

The Wounded and Surgeons Sent to New York

"July 16, 1779

Headquarters—Stony Point

General Wayne returns his warmest thanks to the Officers and soldiers for their coolness and intrepidity in the storm on the evening of the 15th Instant—

The perfect execution of Orders and the superior punctuality attributes on the Occation, respects the Highest Honour on the troops engaged—

The spare arms acutriments tents and military stores are immediately to be collected and deposited in a convenient place in charge of a proper guard—

The Commanding officer of Artillery will attend to the Execution of the Orders so far as they respect Millitary stores.

Ensign Bullard of Major Halls detachment to collect and secure the tents and and—

At evening gun firing the troops are to parade and lines manned—

The Commanding Officers of Regiments will point out the Disposition, 200 rank and file properly officered to compose the necessary guards for the night—

A Detail will be delivered by Major McCormick who will attend the Field Officer of the Day in forming the arrangements—

[The images that follow are photo copies made by Aunt Alice of some handwritten pages from Lt. McDowell's diary where he appears to have transcribed a letter from General Anthony Wayne to the troops after the victory at Stony Point. There is also a second letter in his handwriting that he transcribed which appears to have come from General George Washington]

Lt. McDowell's Role in the Battle at Stony Point

July 16, 1779

Head Quarters Stony Point

Genl. Wayne returns his warmest Thanks to the Officers and Soldiers for their Coolness and Intrepidity in the Storm on the Evening of the 15th Instant —

The perfect execution of Orders and the Superior punctuality Attributed on the Ocation, Reflects the Highest Honour on the Troops Engaged —

The Spare Arms Acutriments Tents and Military Stores are Immediately to be Collected and Deposited in a convenient place in charge of a proper Guard —

The Commanding Officer of Artillery will attend to the Execution of the Orders So far as they Respect Military Stores —

Ensign Bullard of Majr. Hulls Detatchment to Collect and Secure the Tents &c &c —

At Evening Gun firing the Troops are to parade and Lines Man'd —

The Commanding Officer of Reg[t] will point out the Disposition, 200 rank and file properly Officer'd to Compose the Necessary Guards for the Night —

A Detail will be Delivered by Maj[r] McCormick who will Attend the Field Officer of the Day in forming the Arrangement

---

July 16th 1779 —
Head Quarters or Yel[t] Point[?] New Windsor

The Commander in Chief is Happy to Congratulate the Army on the Success of our Arms Under the Comm[and] of Brigadier Gen[l] Wayn who last Night with Corps of Light Infantry Stormed and took the Enemys Post at Stony Point with the Whole Garrison

Cannon and Stores with Verry inconsiderable loss on our Side ——

The Gen'l has not yet Received the Particulars of the Affair but he has the Sattisfaction to learn that the Officers & Soldiers in General Gloriously Distinguished themselves in the Attact, he Requests the Brigadier, and his whole Corps, to Accept his warmest thanks for the Good Conduct and Singular Bravery Manefasted on the Occation ——

Head Quarters L. Infantry Stony Point July 17th 79

The Gen'l Desires the Officers immediately to use all possible means to get the Men Shav'd and made Clean as Circumstances will admit of and hold

Themselves in readiness to parade in a Moments Warning ——

The Plunder of the Fort, (Except the Ordinance Militetary Stores Entrench Tools Tents and Marquee's which will be paid for by the Publick) to be Collected together on the Flag Bastien at three O'Clock and there Exposed to sale for ready Money or to be paid in ten Days, for the Benefit of the Brave Soldiers who fough for it, Ensign Bullard will take an Enventary of and Keep an Account of The Whole

A Large Quantity of Amunition made into Cartriges — 100 Barrels of Powder, Arms Tents Ordinance Stores and Many other Combustables all for the Good of the Brave Soldiers the Whole Amounting to one Hundred and Eighty five Thousand Dollars

Stony Point Evacuated by the Enemy the 24th of Octr. 1779 —

July 16th, 1779

Headquarters—New Windsor—or West Point

The Commander in Chief is happy to congratulate the Army on the success of our arms under the Command of Brigadier General Wayne who last night with Corps of Light Infantry stormed and took the Enemy's post at Stony Point with the whole garrison cannon and stores with verry inconsiderable loss on our side—

The General has not yet received the particulars of the affair but he has the sattisfaction to learn that the Officers and Soldiers in general gloriously distinguished themselves in the attack, he requests the Brigadier, and his whole Corps, to accept his warmest thanks for the good conduct and singular bravery manifested on the occation.

July 17th, 1779

Headquarters L. Infantry Stony Point

The General desires the Officers immediately to use all possible means to get the men shaved and made clean as circumstances will admit of and hold themselves in readiness to parade in a moments warning—

The plunder of the Fort, (except the ordinance Millitary stores entrenching tools tents and marquee's which will be paid for by the publick) to be collected together on the Flag Bastion at three o'clock and there exposed to sale for ready money or to be paid in ten days, for the benefit of the brave soldiers who fought for it~ Ensign Bullard will take an inventory of and keep an account of the whole—

A large quantity of ammunition made into cartridges—100 barrels of powder, arms, tents, ordinance, stores and many other combustables all for the good of the brave soldiers in the whole amounting to one hundred and eighty five thousand dollars.

Stony Point evacuated by the Enemy the 21st of October 1779—

Head Quarters Moores House
August 27th 1779

The Commander in Chief has the pleasure to Anounce the Follower Resolutions which the Honourable the Congress have been pleased to pass for the Benefit of the Army —

The Disposition manifested in these Resolves is a fresh proof to the Army that their country entertains a high sence of their merits and service and are inclined to confer an Honourable and Adequate compensation —

The General flatters himself the respective States will second the Generous Views of Congress and that every proper measures to gratify the Reasonable expectations of such Off and Soldiers as are Determined to Shar share the Glory of securing their country and themselves through the War and Finishing the task they have so nobly began —— The flourishing aspect of Affairs in Europe & in the West Indies as well as in these States gives us every reason to believe that the Happy period will speedily Arrive

   In Congress Aug.t 16.th 79 —
Resolved that the Cloathier General estimate the Value of the several Articles of Soldiers Cloathing at the prices they ware respectively worth at the end of the year 78, & forthwith transmit such estimate to the Pay Masters of the several Reg.ts (who shall be furnished out of the Military Chest with Monies to pay the Soldiers for all Deficiencies of Cloathing at the estimated prices of every article as

Affixed by the Cloathier Genl., who sha[ll]
hence forward transmit the estimates
before the ~~close of~~ every year during the
War, so that the soldiers be paid by the
Regimental Pay Masters according to sue[h]
articles annually and previous to their Dis[-]
charge (when the same happens before
the end of the year) for all articles all[-]
wed them by the Resolutions of Congress
of the 6th Septr 77. which they have not
Received and which are or shall be Due
to them after the year last mentioned —

In Congress Augt. 17th 1779

Whereas the Army of the United
States of America, has by their
Patriotism Valure and perseverance
in the Defence of the rights & Liberties
of their Country become entitled to th[e]
Gratitude as well as approbation of the[ir]
fellow Citizens ———

Resolved

That it be and is hereby recommended to the several states which have not already adopted measures for that purpose to make such further provision for the Officers and Soldiers Enlisted for the war to them respectively belonging who shall continue in the Service till the Establishment of Peace as shall be Adequate compensation for the Dangers losses and hardships they have suffered & been exposed to in the Course of the present contest either by granting to the Officers half pay for Life and proper rewards for their soldiers or in such or other manner as shall appear to be most expedient to the Legislatures of the Several States —

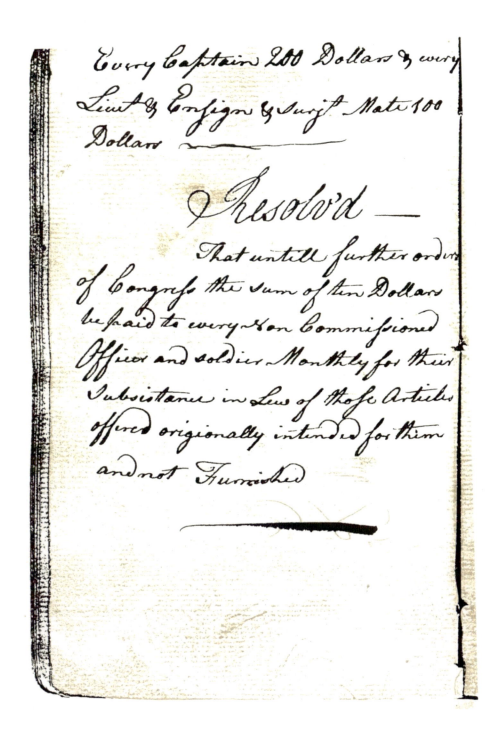

Every Captain 200 Dollars & every Lieut & Ensign & Surgt. Mate 100 Dollars

Resolv'd —

That untill further orders of Congress the sum of ten Dollars be paid to every Non Commissioned Officer and soldier Monthly for their Subsistance in Lew of those Articles offered origionally intended for them and not Furnished

"Headquarters Moores House—August 27, 1779

The Commander in Chief has the pleasure to announce the following resolutions which the Honorable Congress have been pleased to pass for the benefit of the Army—

The disposition manifested in these resolves is a fresh proof to the Army that their country entertains a high sence of their merits and service—and are inclined to confer an honorable and adequate compensation—

The General flatters himself the respective states will second the generous views of Congress and take every proper measure to gratify the reasonable expectations of such Officers and Soldiers as are determined to share the glory of serving their country and themselves through the War and finishing the task they have so nobly began—The flourishing aspect of Affairs in Europe and in the West Indies as well as in these states gives us every reason to believe that the happy period will speedily arrive.

In Congress August 16th, 1779—

Resolved that the Cloathing General estimate the value of the several Articles of soldiers clothing at the prices the ware reflectively worth at the end of the year '79 and forthwith transmit such estimate to the Paymasters of the several Regiments (who shall be furnished out of the Military Chest) with Monies to pay the soldiers for all deficiencies of cloathing at the estimated prices of every article as affixed by the Cloathing General, who shall hence forward transmit the estimates before the close of every year during the War, so that the soldiers be paid by the Regimental Pay Masters according to such articles annually and previous to their discharge (when the same happens before the end of the year) for all articles allowed them by the Resolution's of Congress of the 6th Sept. 1777 which they have not received and which are or shall be due to them after the year last mentioned—

In Congress August 17th, 1779

Whereas the Army of the United States of America, has by their Patriotism Valure and perseverance in the defense of the rights and liberties of their Country become entitled to the gratitude as well as approbation of their fellow Citizens—

Resolved

That it be and is hereby recommended to the several states which have not already adopted measures for that purpose to make such further provision for the Officers and Soldiers enlisted for the war to them respectively belonging who shall continue in the service until the establishment of peace as shall be adequate compensation for the dangers losses and hardships they have suffered and been exposed to in the course of the present contest either by granting to the Officers half pay for Life and proper rewards for their soldiers or in such or other manner as shall appear to be most important to the Legislatives of the Several States—

Resolved

That it be and is hereby recommended to the several States to make such Provision for the Widows of such of their Officers and such of their soldiers who are entitled for the War, or have Died or may die in the service as shall leave to them the sweets of that Liberty (for the attainment of which) their Husbands nobly laid down their Lives—

Resolved

August 18th, 1779

That until further Orders of Congress the Officers of the Army be entitled to receive monthly for their subsistance money the sums following: each Colonel and Chaplain 500 Dollars, every, Lt. Col. And Surjeon 400 Dollars, every Major 300 Dollars, every Captain 200 Dollars and every Lieutenant and Ensign and Surjeon's Mate 100 Dollars—

Resolved—

That untill further orders of Congress the sum of ten dollars be paid to every non-commissioned Officer and soldier monthly for their subsistance in lieu of those articles offered originally intended for them and not furnished—"

First Hand

[To follow are images of a log that was kept to track the number of killed, wounded and taken Officers and Soldiers during that assault at Stony Point on July 16, 1779. As you can see, this list was challenging to decipher the names of who was actually killed, wounded, taken, etc. and so I did not try to transcribe it]

"A Return of the Killed and Wounded and Taken in the Afsault at Stony Point the 16th Day of July in the Morning, by the Light Infantry Commanded by Brigadier General Wayne—"

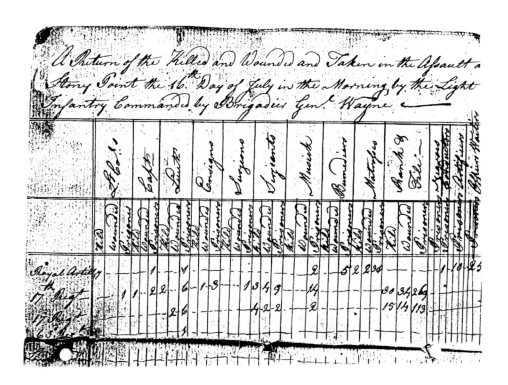

Lt. McDowell's Role in the Battle at Stony Point

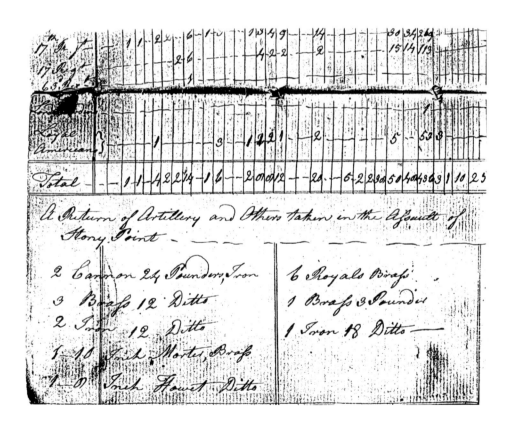

Excerpt from "Decisive Battles of the American Revolution" by Lt. Col. Joseph Mitchell[23]

This is a fascinating description of the actual battle at Stony Point, written by Lt. Colonel Joseph Mitchell, in his book, *Decisive Battles of the American Revolution*. [this page was also found typed up amongst Aunt Alice's many pages of documents]

Page 158
"On June 1, 1779 Clinton[24] occupied Stony Point on the west side of the Hudson and Verplanck's Point on the opposite shore, then began enlarging forts at these points.

From the entire army Washington had created a brigade of light infantry composed of men especially selected from every regiment for agility, alertness and daring. General Wayne, who had earned the name 'Mad Anthony' for his vigor and reckless daring in battle, was selected to command this force of about 1,360 men. In it were such steadfast officers as Colonels Christian Febiger and Return Jonathan Meigs who had served with distinction in almost every campaign of the war.

'Mad Anthony' was given the task of taking Stony Point which was practically immune to attack except by a surprise assault. He decided to advance during the night with bayonets only; not a musket was to be loaded, except in one battalion. Every precaution was taken, selected axemen and special parties led the way. Early in the morning, just after midnight of July 16, he and his brigade rushed and overwhelmed the British garrison. It was a magnificent feat of arms; the fort itself was captured in not much more than half an hour. Although Washington later inspected the fort and decided it was too large to hold, and Clinton later reoccupied it, none of this distracted from the exploit—and proved to all what this new army could do."

---

[23] Wikipedia contributors, "Joseph B. Mitchell," *Wikipedia, The Free Encyclopedia*, https://en.wikipedia.org/w/index.php?title=Joseph_B._Mitchell&oldid=913605635 (accessed November 1, 2020), "Joseph Brady Mitchell (September 25, 1915 – February 17, 1993) was an American military historian. He served for 18 years in the U.S. Army and achieved the rank of lieutenant colonel."

[24] Wikipedia contributors, "Henry Clinton (British Army officer, born 1730)," *Wikipedia, The Free Encyclopedia*, https://en.wikipedia.org/w/index.php?title=Henry_Clinton_(British_Army_officer,_born_1730)&oldid=982125883 (accessed November 1, 2020), "General Sir Henry Clinton, (possibly 16 April 1730 – 23 December 1795) was a British army officer and politician who sat in the House of Commons between 1772 and 1795. He is best known for his service as a general during the American War of Independence. First arriving in Boston in May 1775, from 1778 to 1782 he was the British Commander-in-Chief in North America."

*Revolutionary War Diary:
As Written by Lt. William McDowell
1781/1782*

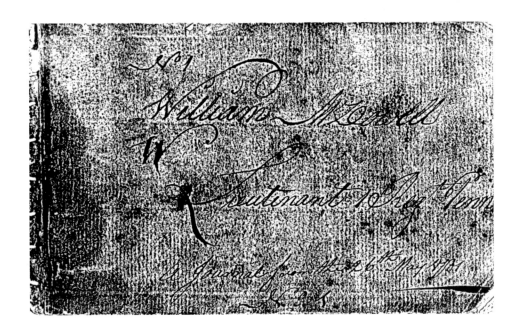

Chapter Two: The Beginning of Lt. William McDowell's Actual Diary

May 1781 ~ Pennsylvania to Virginia

York Town 26th May 1781
This day we left York (PA) at 9 o' clock in the morning with about eight hundred effective men under the command of General Wayne—and encamped 11 miles on the road to Frederick Town (MD).

27th—The General beat at sun rise and took the line of march—and halted near Peter Littles Town (Littlestown, PA) it being 14 miles—

28th—The troops took up the line of march at sun rise, marched through Tawney Town (MD) and halted near Pipe Creek being about 14 miles—

29th—The troops took up the line of march at 3 o'clock in the morning, and encamped on the S.W. side of Manochacy (Monocacy National Battlefied is on the southeast edge of Frederick, MD) 15 miles

30th—This day continued on the ground, the soldiers washed themselves and scoured up their arms and accoutrements, at 7 o'clock they were reviewed by General Wayne—

31st—Took up the line of march at sun rise, passed through Frederick Town, Maryland where there were a number of British Officers, prisoners of war, who took a view of us as we passed through the town, we made a verry respectable appearance. We crossed the Potomack at Nowland's Ferry (MD), were obliged to cross in bad boats, one unfortunately sunk loaded with artillery and a few men in which one Sergeant and three men of our Regiment were drownded—Encamped on this side of the river, a number of us dined at the Tavern, or Ordinary, as the Virginians call it, the night proved bad and we could not pitch our tents. 18 miles

June 1781 ~ Leesburg, Virginia to near Williamsburg, VA

June 1st—Continued on our ground until 4 o'clock in the afternoon, moved 5 miles towards Leesburgh (VA).

2nd—Continued on the ground untill evening it being verry wet and disagreeable—

3rd—Took up the line of march at 10 o'clock A.M. passed through Leesburgh which is but a verry small town and not built regular, we encamped at Goose Creek being 15 miles—

4th—Marched at six o'clock in the morning, had orders from General Wayne to leave our heavy baggage at this place, Mr. Koxes Mills and the sick of the line under the care of a surjeon, marched through a low country, roads being verry bad in consequence of the rains we had a few days before, and encamped at the Red House. 10 miles Prince William County (VA)—

5th—A wet morning. Cleaned up about 10 o'clock A.M.— marched at one o'clock P.M. proceeded 12 miles towards Rapahanuk where we lay out without any kind of shelter—12 miles

6th—Marched at 6 o'clock A.M. 9 miles, Farquer County (VA)—

7th—Continued on our ground in consequence of a heavy rain—

8th—Took up the line of march at sun rise, reached the north branch of Rapahanack at 10 o'clock, the troops waded the river and proceeded 25 miles—Colpepper County (VA)

9th—Took up the line of march at ten o'clock A.M. crossed the south branch of Rapahanack and proceeded 5 miles into the country—The country verry poor and buildings verry small. 14 miles

10th—Took up the line of march at 5 o'clock in the morning and joined the Marquise's Troops this day and passed a body of Militia of Virginia about 1,000 men—we had a verry severe march of 23 miles this day—Orrange County (VA)—

The Beginning of Lt. William McDowell's Actual Diary

11th—Marched at 4 o'clock and encamped at 10 A.M. 10 miles—

12th—Took up the line of march at 6 o'clock A.M., marched through thicket of pine woods, nothing but a foot path through which we got with great difficulty especially our artilery, at last we arrived on the main road leading to Fredericksbourgh (Fredericksburg, VA) which I long looked for and encamped 5 miles from where we entered the road—Louisa County (VA) 14 miles—

13th—Continued on this ground in order to refresh ourselves which we had great need of—

14th—Took up the line of march at 5 o'clock A.M. marched through poor country the water being verry scarce, this day see a number of negroes the greatest part of them being naked—12 miles—

15th **(June)**—Took up the line of march at sun rise, a great scarcity of water this day, and a verry fatiguing march—refreshed ourselves in an orchard with Col. Robinson. The Marquis and Gen. Wayne took a bite with us. 14 miles Hanover County (VA)—

16th—Took up the line of march at day brake, made a short days march of six miles being much fatigued, this day built a fine brush hutt, 6 miles—

17th—Took up the line of march at 3 o'clock in the morning, marched through the best country we have seen in this state and encamped at Dandridges[25] being 20 miles—

18th—A verry fine morning—this day the enemy advanced on us—our tents were struck, all the Continental Troops marched in order to surprise a party of Tarltons Horse[26], we continued to

---

[25] Wikipedia contributors, "Dandridge family of Virginia," *Wikipedia, The Free Encyclopedia*, https://en.wikipedia.org/w/index.php?title=Category:Dandridge_family_of_Virginia&oldid=909027338 (accessed November 1, 2020), "The Dandridge family is a prominent business and political family in the U.S. states of Virginia and West Virginia, the most notable member of which is First Lady of the United States, Martha Washington."

[26] Wikipedia contributors, "Banastre Tarleton," *Wikipedia, The Free Encyclopedia*, https://en.wikipedia.org/w/index.php?title=Banastre_Tarleton&oldid=982965424 (accessed November 1, 2020), "Sir Banastre Tarleton, 1st Baronet, (21 August 1754 – 15 January 1833) was a British soldier and politician. Tarleton was eventually ranked as a general years after his service in the colonies during the American Revolutionary War, and afterwards did not lead troops into battle. Tarleton's cavalrymen were called 'Tarleton's Raiders'. His green uniform was the standard uniform of the British Legion, a provincial unit organised in New York, in 1778."

march till day light, but on our arrival found they had gone some hours—13 miles—

19th—Lay on our arms (weapons) till 1 o'clock. Retired into the country 4 miles where we lay destitute of refreshment, bedding or covering. 4 miles—Henrico County (VA)—

20th—Marched at 6 o'clock three miles, and were received by the General, lay on our arms all night. 3 miles—

21st—Arrived at Col. Simms's Mills. Marched at 12 o'clock A.M. 8 miles and lay at Burrells Ordinary (tavern) destitute of every necessary of life. 8 miles—

22nd **(June)**—Marched at 2 o'clock through a went inhabited country, though I can give no acct of the people as I have not been on the inside of a house but one or two ordinarys.

They sometimes come to the roadside in order to take a view of us as we pass the road but a person can scarcely discern any part of their face but their nose and eyes as they have themselves muffed with linnens in order to prevent the sun from burning their fair faces. I mean the female sex. At the same time they will have a number of blacks, all naked around them nothing to cover their nakedness—

This day we passed through Richmond (VA) twenty four hours after the enemy evacuated it, a number of houses being destroyed by them, they also destroyed a quantity of tobacco which they threw into the street and set on fire, the town is built close on Jameses (James) River under a bank.

We encamped two miles on the south side of the town about 6 o'clock P.M. 20 miles—

23rd—Took up the line of march at 2 o'clock in the morning, halted at 8 for refreshment where we had an alarm, our Light Horse[27] brought intelligence the enemy was within one mile of

---

[27] Wikipedia contributors, "Henry Lee III," *Wikipedia, The Free Encyclopedia*, https://en.wikipedia.org/w/index.php?title=Henry_Lee_III&oldid=985570847 (accessed November 1, 2020), Possibly a reference to "Major-General Henry Lee III (January 29, 1756 – March 25, 1818) was an early American Patriot and politician. He served as the ninth Governor of Virginia and as the Virginia Representative to the United States Congress. Lee's service during the American Revolution as a cavalry officer in the Continental Army earned him the nickname by which he is best known, "Light-Horse Harry". He was the father of Robert E. Lee, commander of the Confederate armies in the American Civil War."

us, the Army immediately formed for action—a universal joy prevailed, that certain success was before us, we lay on our arms 10 hours, hourly waiting for action, our intelligence on the whole march was exceeding bad—but to our mortification turned out a false alarm, at 6 we moved our position for convenience of encampment, a verry heavy rain came on at 12 o'clock at night. 15 miles—

24th—Continued on this ground in order to dry our cloaths which had got wet the night before and the men to furbish their arms—etc.

This day one of our soldiers belonging to the 4th Penna. Regt. was taken diserting to the enemy, at 3 o'clock P.M. he was tried and sentenced to be shot which punnishment was inflicted on him at retreat beat. At the same time we received orders to strike our tents which we did and march at dark in order to surprise Tarltons Horse, but as he always had good intelligence, we retired. 12 miles, Citty (Charles City) County (VA)

25th—Lay by this day, at day brake took up our line of march in order to overtake Col. Jones's Horse who had the rear guard with a great number of cattle. Plundering as he was making his way to James Town, left one negro man with the small pox laying on the road side in order to prevent the Virginia Militia from pursuing them which the enemy frequently did, left numbers in that condition starving and helpless. 12 miles—

26th **(June)**—At six o'clock in the morning we were informed that a covering party of horse were but a small distance before us—Gen. Wayne immediately ordered the front Platoons of each Battalion to turn out immediately which orders being complied with, being four Platoons and Major McPherson's party of leginary Horse, we persued them for 5 or 6 miles in full speed, at last we came within a short distance of them—

Major Hamilton had the command of a party of infantry from our line, about forty in Capt. Ogdan's Company of Jersey Troops were ordered to mount behind the same number of Dragoons[28] and persued them and soon overtook them, we had a skirmish[29] with their Horse and Infantry in which we took a number of their Horse and cattle and killed 40 of their Infantry, our loss was verry inconsiderable—

Major McPherson's horse threw him in the field of action but fortunately made his escape, I expected they would attack our small party of Infantry which was posted on a small eminence to cover our light Dragoons—

27th—This day we lay at Birds Ordinary—

[Byrd Tavern, as shown on the following map]

---

[28] Wikipedia contributors, "Dragoon," *Wikipedia, The Free Encyclopedia*, https://en.wikipedia.org/w/index.php?title=Dragoon&oldid=986089670 (accessed November 1, 2020), "Dragoons originally were a class of mounted infantry, who used horses for mobility, but dismounted to fight on foot. From the early 17th century onward, dragoons were increasingly also employed as conventional cavalry, trained for combat with swords from horseback. Dragoon regiments were established in most European armies during the late 17th and early 18th centuries."

[29] Wikipedia contributors, "Battle of Spencer's Ordinary," *Wikipedia, The Free Encyclopedia*, https://en.wikipedia.org/w/index.php?title=Battle_of_Spencer%27s_Ordinary&oldid=984114016 (accessed November 1, 2020), "The Battle of Spencer's Ordinary was an inconclusive skirmish that took place on 26 June 1781, late in the American Revolutionary War. British forces under Lieutenant Colonel John Graves Simcoe and American forces under Colonel Richard Butler, light detachments from the armies of General Lord Cornwallis and the Marquis de Lafayette respectively, clashed near a tavern (the "ordinary") at a road intersection not far from Williamsburg, Virginia."

The Beginning of Lt. William McDowell's Actual Diary

Detail from a 1781 French map prepared for Lafayette depicting his and Cornwallis's movements. The clash at Spencer's is marked by "le 26 Juin". ("Byrd Tavern" was drawn in near the top.) By Michel du Chesnoy (1746-1804) - https://upload.wikimedia.org/wikipedia/commons/2/29/Virginia1781_SpencersAndGreenSpring.jpg

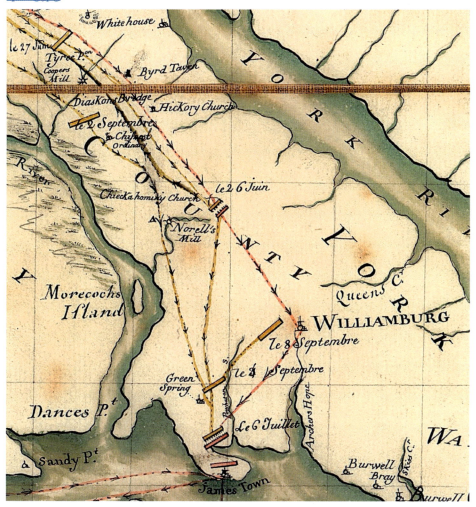

28th—Made some movements for advantage of ground—

29th—Maneuvered considerable in consequence of bad intelligence—

30th—Greatly fatigued, lay by the greatest part of this day, our tents came to us this evening—

July 1781 ~ Near Williamsburg, VA to Jamestown and the Battle of Green Spring

1st July—Marched at day brake 8 miles to York River for the troops to wash and refresh themselves where Doctor Downing of the 6th Regt. Penna. was unfortunately drownded, that evening we struck tents at dark and marched to our former ground—8 miles—

2nd—Marched down to Birds Ordinary, returned again that night to our old ground—8 miles

3rd—Marched at sun rise to Mr. Old Fields, manouvers retrogate and many, the troops almost worn out in verry hot weather—

4th—A wet morning, cleared up at 10 o'clock—this day we had a Fude of Joy[30] in celebration of our Independence, after that General Wayne performed some new manouvers, in which we fired, had the thanks of the Marquis, the Fude of Joy was with a running fire from right to left of the Army—

5th—Took up the line of march at one o'clock on our way to Williams Burgh[31] which I longed much to see, proceeded as far as Chickahominy Church where we lay on our arms till sun rise—6 miles—

---

[30] Wikipedia contributors, "Feu de joie," *Wikipedia, The Free Encyclopedia*, https://en.wikipedia.org/w/index.php?title=Feu_de_joie&oldid=955378140 (accessed November 1, 2020), "A feu de joie (French: "fire of joy") is a form of formal celebratory gunfire consisting of a celebratory rifle salute, described as a "running fire of guns." As soldiers fire into the air sequentially in rapid succession, the cascade of blank rounds produces a characteristic "rat-tat-tat" effect. It is used on rare landmark occasions of national rejoicing. During the 18th and 19th centuries, a feu de joie has celebrated a military victory or birthday."

[31] Wikipedia contributors, "Williamsburg, Virginia," *Wikipedia, The Free Encyclopedia*, https://en.wikipedia.org/w/index.php?title=Williamsburg,_Virginia&oldid=982112572 (accessed November 1, 2020), "Williamsburg was founded in 1632 as Middle Plantation, a fortified settlement on high ground between the James and York rivers. The city served as the capital of the Colony and Commonwealth of Virginia from 1699 to 1780 and was the center of political events in Virginia leading to the American Revolution."

The Beginning of Lt. William McDowell's Actual Diary

6th July—At sun rise we took up the line of march for James Town[32] at which place the enemy lay encamped—

The first Battalion of our line were detached with a small party of riflemen, which brought on a scattering fire in front, and on the flanks of our Battalion, that continued for two or three hours, with the Yagers[33]—our Battalion was then ordered to form collums and advance when we had intelligence of the 2nd and 3rd Battalions, with one of the Infantry in sight of us we then displayed to right and left, the third Battalion on our right and the 2nd on our left, being then formed brought on a general action, our advance was regular, and at a charge till we came within 80 yards of the whole Army, they being regularly formed standing at one yards distance from each other, their light Infantry being in front of our Battalion we advanced under a verry heavy fire of grape shot[34] at which distance we opened our musquetry, but being overpowered were obliged to retreat with precipitation and in bad order for at least one mile, where we formed and retired in good order—Happy for us the enemy did not press us at this critical moment or our troops would have unevitably been cut off—We retired to Chickahominy Church about 8 miles where a number of the officers wounds were dressed, and all the Privates who were wounded,—it being at this time about 10 o'clock at night—

---

[32] Wikipedia contributors, "Jamestown, Virginia," *Wikipedia, The Free Encyclopedia*, https://en.wikipedia.org/w/index.php?title=Jamestown,_Virginia&oldid=986579908 (accessed November 1, 2020), "The Jamestown settlement in the Colony of Virginia was the first permanent English settlement in the Americas. It was located on the northeast bank of the James (Powhatan) River about 2.5 mi (4 km) southwest of the center of modern Williamsburg. It was established by the Virginia Company of London as "James Fort" on May 14, 1607 and was considered permanent after a brief abandonment in 1610. It followed several failed attempts, including the Lost Colony of Roanoke, established in 1585 on Roanoke Island. Jamestown served as the colonial capital from 1616 until 1699."

[33] Wikipedia contributors, "Jäger (infantry)," *Wikipedia, The Free Encyclopedia*, https://en.wikipedia.org/w/index.php?title=J%C3%A4ger_(infantry)&oldid=983660369 (accessed November 1, 2020), "Jäger is a German military term that originally referred to light infantry, but has come to have wider usage. While it may be literally translated as "hunter", in German-speaking states during the early modern era, the term Jäger was used to describe skirmishers, scouts, sharpshooters and runners. Jäger came to denote light infantrymen whose civilian occupations made them well-suited to patrolling and skirmishing, on an individual and independent basis, rather than as part of military unit."

[34] Wikipedia contributors, "Grapeshot," *Wikipedia, The Free Encyclopedia*, https://en.wikipedia.org/w/index.php?title=Grapeshot&oldid=986456607 (accessed November 1, 2020), "In artillery, grapeshot is a projectile that is not one solid element, but a geometric arrangement of round shot packed tightly into a canvas bag and separated from the gunpowder charge by a metal disk of full bore diameter."

A list of the wounded Officers of our Line[35]—
　　Capt. Crossby, Artilery—
　　Officers of Infantry—
　　Capt. Doyle, 6th Penna. Regt.
　　Capt. Van Lear, 9th Penna. Regt.
　　Capt. Finney, 6th Penna. Regt.
　　Capt. Stake, 1st Penna. Regt.
　　Capt. McClellan, 1st Penna. Regt.
　　Capt. Montgomery, 7th Penna. Regt.
　　Lieut. Herbert, 6th D° taken prisoner
　　Lieut. Piercy, 2nd Penna. Regt.
　　Lieut. Feltman, 1st Penna. Regt.
　　Lieut. White, 1st Penna. Regt.

The number of killed, wounded and taken prisoners—Sergts, rank and file being 97 *[an image of this handwritten page out of McDowell's diary follows]*

---

[35] Wikipedia contributors, "Battle of Green Spring," *Wikipedia, The Free Encyclopedia*, https://en.wikipedia.org/w/index.php?title=Battle_of_Green_Spring&oldid=984116964 (accessed November 1, 2020), "The Battle of Green Spring took place near Green Spring Plantation in James City County, Virginia during the American Revolutionary War. On July 6, 1781 United States Brigadier General "Mad" Anthony Wayne, leading the advance forces of the Marquis de Lafayette, was ambushed near the plantation by the British army of Earl Charles Cornwallis in the last major land battle of the Virginia campaign prior to the Siege of Yorktown."

The Beginning of Lt. William McDowell's Actual Diary

about 10 O'clock at Night —

A List of the Wounded Officers of our Line — Capt Crossley — Artillery —
— Officers of Infantry

Capt Doyle 6th Penn'a Reg't
Capt VanLear 9th Penn'a Reg't
Capt Finney 6th Penn'a Reg't
Capt Steake 1st Penn'a Reg't
Capt McLellan 1st Penn'a Reg't
Capt Montgomery 9th Penn'a Reg't
Lieut Herbert 6th D'o taken Prisoner
Lieut Peircy 2d Penn'a Reg't
Lieut Fettman 1st Penn'a Reg't
Lieut White 1st Penn'a Reg't

The Number of Killed wounded and taken Prisoners — Serj'ts Rank and File being 97

7th

We Remained on our Ground at Montgomery Church until the

7th **(July)**—We remained on our ground at Chickahominy Church until the wounded were dressed and sent off to the hospitable—

8th—The enemy came out about four miles, we lay on our arms ready for their approach, but they retired—

9th—Continued on the same ground for refreshment—

10th—Marched at 2 o'clock P.M. to Holt's Iron Works—4 miles—

11th—I received orders from Gen. Wayne to proceed to Hanover Courthouse with a party of men, and four waggons to press spirits for the Army, I went about twenty miles that evening to a gentlemen's house who was exceeding kind and treated me well. 20 miles—

12th—The next day proceeded on my journey, and arrived at the Court House about 10 o'clock at night, but to my mortification there was no spirits there, remained that night there—20 miles—

13th—The next day the Gentleman of the House set out with me in quest of the spirits, went 9 miles where we got one waggon load, left the waggon and a guard with orders to meet me at the Court House, and proceeded on with the other three, went about 9 miles further where we remained all night. 18 miles—

14th—I collected enough to load the three and proceeded towards camp, when I came to the Court House the General had sent an express informing me the Army had marched and would meet me at Richmond, night coming on I remained with a poor man who was exceeding kind—30 miles

15th **(July)**—I proceeded to meet the Army with all expedition possible, came to Richmond about 12 o'clock, while I was refreshing myself, Lieut. Campbell came to town and informed me that the Army was about 14 miles from there, that an Incorporation had taken place and that himself and me with some more was to go home[36], this gave me fresh spirits, and we

---

[36] Believed to be his family home in Mercersburg, (Franklin County) Pennsylvania

took the other bottle of wine on the news of leaving the ancient Dominican ("Old Dominion" or Virginia), which few of us were fond of—Proceeded on to the Army, waited on General Wayne who thanked me for my vigilence, and ordered me to deliver the spirits to the Commissary and take his receipt for the same, which was 708 gallons. 28 miles—

16th—This day was employed in crossing the Jameses River, and taking leave of our Brother Officers who were to remain with the Army. I then steered for Penna. once more, and arrived in little York the first of Aug. during which time I took no acct. of the occurrences which happened, altho many worth notice, however when we arrived here a report was that Cornwallis intended to visit Baltimore, General Irvine would not let any of us go home untill the certainty was known, after this ordered a Court Martial to sit in Carlisle, Col. Wm. Butler to preside. The Court met agreeable to orders and tryd thirteen prisoners in thirteen hours. The whole of the members of the Court dined with the General that day the Court adjourned. The next day with Col. Butler, then Maj. Moore and I set out for Conocacheague where we spent two weeks verry agreeable. Then went to little York where we were a week, then received orders from General St. Clair to repair to Philadelphia, where we lay some time at the 100 acres—

Chapter Three: Rejoining My Brothers in Arms

October 1781 ~ Philadelphia to Baltimore to Yorktown

October 4th, 1781—Philadelphia—We were ordered on board of vessels to carry us to Cristeen Bridge, went on board and dropt down the river a small distance and dropt ancre, then went on shore and spent the evening verry agreeably in town then went on board—

5th—Then hoisted sail, this night was something stormy, waves ran high, our small vessel tossed about and I took sick—

6th—This morning we have sight of the mouth of Cristeen Creek, the wind falling, with difficulty got within 2 miles of the bridge—

7th—Landed and marched to the Bridge where our waggons were ready to carry our baggage to the head of Elk. Marched to the head of Elk that day—12 miles—

8th—Remained this day for craft to carry us to Baltimore—

9th—Being disappointed, remained this day—

10th—Our disappointment continued—

11th—About 2 o'clock went on board and dropt down the creek—

12th—Hoisted sail, the winds contrary and the channel difficult, were obliged to cast ancre at dark—

13th—This morning the wind appeared to favour us for some time, but a storm arose which separated our small fleet, we were obliged to put into harbour, and had near been lost, some were drove almost on shore and some no acct. of for three weeks. After this storm we had a fair wind and arrived at Baltimore—

14th—Remained in Baltimore this day—

15th—Hoisted sail about 4 o'clock in the afternoon, a storm arose when opposite Black Point, were obliged to cast ancre—

16th—A fair and pleasant breeze and made great way—

17th—The wind not so fair, this day one of our soldiers died which we cast overboard, at night came to ancre least we should go foul of the French Fleet—

18th—Came in sight of some of the fleet run up to York—

19th—We landed at 12 o'clock—At one o'clock this day Maj. Hamilton with a detachment marched into town and took possession of the Batteries, and hoisted the American Flag—The British Army marched out and grounded their arms in front of our Line—Our whole army drew up for them to march through—the French Army on their right and the Americans on their left. The British prisoners all appeared to be much in liquor—After they grounded their arms they returned to town again—

20th—This day the prisoners remained in town—I took a walk to see the town and works which were something strong. Their officers appeared a good deal cast down on the occation—

[A communication received by the troops from General Washington]

> Head Quarters near York—October 20th 1781
>
> The General congratulates the Army uppon the glorious event of yesterday. The generous proofs which his most Christian Majesty has given of his attachment to the cause of America, must force conviction in the minds of the most deceived among the enemy. Relatively to the desision good consequences of the Alliance, and inspire every citizen of these States with sentiments of the most unalterable gratitude—His Fleet the most numerous and powerful that ever appeared in these seas, commanded by an Admirall whose fortune and talents ensure great events.—
>
> An Army of the most admirable composition both in Officers and men are the pledge of his Friendship to the United States, and their cooperation has secured us the present signal success—
>
> The General uppon this occation intreats his Excellency, Count de Rochambeau[37] to accept his

---

[37] Wikipedia contributors, "Jean-Baptiste Donatien de Vimeur, comte de Rochambeau," *Wikipedia, The Free Encyclopedia*, https://en.wikipedia.org/w/index.php?title=Jean-Baptiste_Donatien_de_Vimeur,_comte_de_Rochambeau&oldid=985970143 (accessed November 1, 2020), "Marshal Jean-Baptiste Donatien de Vimeur, comte de Rochambeau (1 July 1725 – 10 May 1807) was a French nobleman and general whose army played the decisive role in helping the United States defeat the British army at Yorktown in 1781 during the American Revolution. He was commander-in-chief of the French Expeditionary Force sent by France in order to help the American Continental Army fight against British forces."

acknowledgements for his council and assistance at all times, He presents his warmest thanks to the Generals, Barron De Viominel, Chavilier Chartelux, Marquis De St. Simons and Count De Viominal and to Brigadier Gen. De Choisey who had a separate command; for the illustrious manner in which they have advanced the intrist of the common cause—He requests the Count de Rochambeau will be pleased to communicate to the Army under his immediate command the high sense he entertains of the distinguished merits of the officers and soldiers of every corps and that he will present in his name to the Regiments of Agenois[38] and Deux Ponts the pieces of brass ordinance captured by them as a testimony for their gallantry in storming the enemys redoubts the night of the 14th instant where Officers and men so universally vied each other in the exercise of every soldierly virtue—

The General's thanks to each individual of merit would comprehend the whole Army, but he thinks himself bound however by affection, duty, and gratitude to express his obligation to Maj. Gen. Lincoln, [Marquis de] La Fayette and [Baron Von] Steuben[39] for their disposition in the trenches—

To General Duportail and Col. Carney for the vigour and knowledge which were conspicuous in their conduct of the attacks, and to Gen. Knox and Col. Abervalle for their great care, attention and fattigue in

---

[38] Wikipedia contributors, "Régiment d'Agénois," *Wikipedia, The Free Encyclopedia*, https://en.wikipedia.org/w/index.php?title=R%C3%A9giment_d%27Ag%C3%A9nois&oldid=970386646 (accessed November 1, 2020), "The Régiment d'Agenois was a French infantry regiment created under the Ancien Régime in 1595. It participated in the American War of Independence."

[39] Wikipedia contributors, "Friedrich Wilhelm von Steuben," *Wikipedia, The Free Encyclopedia*, https://en.wikipedia.org/w/index.php?title=Friedrich_Wilhelm_von_Steuben&oldid=985729274 (accessed November 1, 2020), "Friedrich Wilhelm August Heinrich Ferdinand Freiherr von Steuben (born Friedrich Wilhelm Ludolf Gerhard Augustin Freiherr von Steuben; September 17, 1730 – November 28, 1794), also referred to as Baron von Steuben, was a Prussian and later an American military officer. He served as Inspector General and a Major General of the Continental Army during the American Revolutionary War. He was one of the fathers of the Continental Army in teaching them the essentials of military drills, tactics, and discipline. He wrote Regulations for the Order and Discipline of the Troops of the United States, the book that served as the Army's drill manual for decades. He served as General George Washington's chief of staff in the final years of the war."

bringing forward the artilery and stores and for their judicious and spirited management of them in the Paralells[40], he requests to the gentlemen above mentioned to communicate his thanks to the Officers and soldiers of their respective commands—

Ingratitude which the General hopes never to be guilty off, would be conspicuous in him was he to omit thanking in warmest terms His Excellency Governor Nelson[41] for the aid he has derived from him and from the Militia under his command to whose activity, emulation and courage such applause is due. The greatness of the acquisition would be an ample compensation for the hardships and hazards which they encountered with so much patriotism and firmness.

In order to diffuse the great joy in every brest, the General orders those men belonging to the Army who may now [be] in confinement shall be pardoned, released and join their respective corps—

Devine Service is to be performed in the several Brigades or Divisions—The Commander in Chief earnestly recommends it that the troops not on duty should universally attend with that seriousness of deportment and gratitude of heart which the recognition of such reiterated and astonishing interposition of providence to us—

21st **(October)**—This afternoon the prisoners marched out of town, under the care of three divisions of Militia—We had

---

[40] According to https://en.wikipedia.org/wiki/Siege_of_Yorktown and https://en.wikipedia.org/wiki/Siege#Age_of_gunpowder "After surrounding a town, if they did not surrender, the attackers would next build a length of trenches parallel to the defences (these are known as the "First parallel") and just out of range of the defending artillery."

[41] Wikipedia contributors, "Thomas Nelson Jr.," *Wikipedia, The Free Encyclopedia*, https://en.wikipedia.org/w/index.php?title=Thomas_Nelson_Jr.&oldid=985285096 (accessed November 1, 2020), "Thomas Nelson Jr. (December 26, 1738 – January 4, 1789) was an American planter, soldier, and statesman from Yorktown, Virginia. In addition to serving in the Virginia General Assembly for many terms, he twice represented Virginia in the Continental Congress and fellow Virginia legislators elected him to serve as the Commonwealth's Governor in 1781. He is one of the U.S. Founding Fathers. He signed the Declaration of Independence as a member of the Virginia delegation, as well as fought in the militia during the Siege of Yorktown."

orders to hold ourselves in readiness to march at the shortest notice—

22nd—This day His Excellency ordered that every Officer in the American Army which was here, to receive £20 worth of cloathing out of the stores, the dollar at 6 shillings—

23rd—Remained here 24th, 25th, 26th, 27th, 28th, 29th, & 30th, 31st, Nov. 1st, 2nd—

3 Nov.—My boy diserted with one of the soldiers and stole 2 jackets and two pair of britches from me—

4th **(November)**—This day I had partys searching for them but could not find them—

5th—This day our line marched and the Maryland Regt. past Cheese Cake Church and Burrels Mills and encamped within half a mile of said Mill. 10 miles—

6th—This day the troops took up the line of march at sun rise, and encamped near Birds Ordinary 19 miles—

7th—Marched this morning at day light and encamped at Kent Court House 14 miles—

8th—Took up the line of march at sun rise and passed Savages farms and encamped within half a mile of Bottoms Bridge 16 miles—

9th—Took up the line of march at day light and encamped on the heights at Richmond 14 miles—

10th—This day the Maryland Regt. crossed Jameses River—

11th—This day the artilery crossed, it being verry rainy and disagreeable—

12th—This day the Q. M. General of Military Stores crossed—

13th—This morning one of the Penna. Battalions crossed with their baggage.

14th—This day the last of the troops and baggage crossed, and encamped one mile on this side of the river—

15th—This day the troops took up the line of march at 10 o'clock and encamped near Ozburns Ware Houses 15 miles—

16th—Marched at day light, passed Ware Church and encamped near Appamatuck River 10 miles—

17th—This morning Capt. Marshall and I crossed the Appamatuck to Petres Burgh before the troops to provide stores for the Mess which we did, viz—

    60 lb. shugar

    2 lb. tea

    30 lb. coffee

    2 lb. pepper

    6 lb. chocolate etc., etc.

and sundry other articles before the troops were all over—a wet day 1 mile—

18th **(November)**—This day we remained on our ground for the troops to wash—

19th—Took up the line of march at sun rise, and were joined by Col. White with about 200 Horse one half in front, the other in rear of the troops. Passed Dunwiddy Court House and Stony Creek, encamped half a mile over the bridge. 19 miles—

20th—Took up the line of march at sun rise,—(a verry heavy frost) crossed Notaway River, Luis Joans Bridge and encamped on Sir Joanses Farm—Brunswick County (VA) 14 miles—

21st—Marched this morning at sun rise and crossed two small bridges encamped on Erl Edmison's farm being 15 miles—

Yesterday morning Ensign Beaty and Capt. Mintzer of the Maryland line fought a duel, the latter was shot through the head and died immediately and was buried on the ground they fought on—

22nd—The troops took up the line of march at sun rise. Crossed Mayherrin Creek on a bad bridge, and encamped near Mitchels Ordinary, Macklingburgh County. 16 miles—

23rd—Took up the line of march at sun rise passed through a verry bad country, encamped at Henry Millers on Sir Payton Skipper's farms 12 miles—

24th—Took up the line of march at sun rise, by the left crossed Allen Creek which was within half a mile of the ground we left this morning at about 11 o'clock A. M. arrived at the

Rowenoak River, our troops immediately crossed with their baggage. N.B[42]. this was at Taylors Ferry 10 miles—

25th—A verry rainy and disagreeable day—this place abounds with deer and wild turkey etc—

26th—A verry clear sun shiny day, we employed it in drying our cloaths which had got wet the day before—

27th—This morning I went out to hunt, but killed nothing but one squirrel—

28th—Last night and this morning it rained verry hard which prevented us from marching this day—

29th—Took up the line of march at sun rise, passed through a fine level country, roads verry sloppy, marched ten miles into N. Carolina and encamped near Wms Borrough, this town is composed with a church, one tavern, one smith shop and six small log houses—10 miles—

30th Nov.—This morning Lieut. Reeves was left on command with the sick—The Troops took up the line of march at the usual time and encamped at Harrisburgh, which is two elligant buildings and some ware houses—Granwell County 12 miles—

1st **December**—Took up the line of march it being exceeding bad marching in consequence of the last nights rain, passed through a fine country and encamped at Gen. Persons, a verry large farm, he holds eighty-five thousand acres of land in one tract, and with all this possession he has not the comforts of life, lives verry poor and it is reported that his mother while alive was obliged to lay on a bed of straw on acct. of his contracted hart—13 miles—

2nd—The troops took up the line of march this morning at sun rise passed through a fine wood country. Roads verry bad in consequence of last the nights rain, encamped near Pains Ordinary—Kaswell County 16 miles—

---

[42] Wikipedia contributors, "Nota bene," *Wikipedia, The Free Encyclopedia*, https://en.wikipedia.org/w/index.php?title=Nota_bene&oldid=985753461 (accessed November 1, 2020), "Nota bene is a Latin phrase which first appeared in English writing c. 1711. Often abbreviated as NB, n.b., or with the ligature NB, the phrase is Latin for "note well." In Modern English, it is used, particularly in legal papers, to draw the attention of the reader to a certain (side) aspect or detail of the subject being addressed. While NB is also often used in academic writing, note is a common substitute."

3rd—Marched this morning at sun rise, passed Kaswell Court House, verry hilly and sloppy. This evening I went on guard 10 miles—

4th—This morning marched at sun rise the country verry hilly, crossed Hico and County line creek, this day there came on a heavy snow which lasted during the day—

Capt. Bartholomew of the 5th Regt. Penna. unfortunately got his leg broke by a fall of his horse—18 miles

5th—This day we lay still to give our soldiers rest, and wait for the waggons which fell behind on acct. of the bad roads which the snow had made—

6th—We remained on the same ground as some of the waggons were still behind. The snow still continued to cover the face of the Earth—

7th—Took up the line of march at sun rise. This morning we left our heavy baggage under command of Maj. Moore who was to come on as he could; we were obliged to ford the Haw River the cold and the snow laying on the ground—Encamped on the bank of said river—16 miles—

The number of miles which I traveled whilst I kept this book is 1384—

Carried to No. 2

Brought from 1848
No. of miles 1884

Gilford County Decm 18th 1781

...morning at daylight the...
...the line of march...
...a very fine country...
...and Encamped at...
...House, 20 miles

...It was on this Ground that the
...battle was fought between Genl Green
and Lord Cornwallis... there was a
...of Musquets laying on
...the Enemy had broke...

...day we remained on this Ground
...Expectation of getting cloathing
...but the weather turned out to
be very wet and disagreeable
...

Chapter Four: "Brought from Journal #1"

Number of miles 1384—

Gilford County (NC) **Dec. 8th**, **1781**
This morning at day light the troops took up the line of march—passed through a verry fine country for land (no pine) and encamped at Gilford Court House 20 miles—

N.B. This was the ground that the action was fought between Gen. Greene and Lord Cornwallis, there was a number of buts of musquets[43] laying the ground which the enemy had broke—

9th—This day we remained on the ground in expectation of getting cloaths washed but the weather turned out to be verry wet and disagreeable—This place is called the Irish Settlement—

10th Dec.—We received orders to remain this morning to wash our cloaths. This day verry windy and disagreeably cold—

11th—This morning at sun rise the troops took up the line of march—Passed through a verry fine country settled by Quakers who have tolerable good plantations and crossed two branches of Deep Creek and encamped near Barney Idles. 15 miles

12th—The troops took up the line of march this morning at the usual time, passed through a country settled by Germins who have verry good plantations and a small quantity of meadow, which is seldom to be seen in this part of the country—some pines this day—left Maravin Town eight miles on our right—Encamped on a hill near Mr. McCrays. Roan County 16 miles—

13th—This morning at sun rise the troops took up the line of march, passed through a fine country, crossed the Yadkin River in boats—the baggage forded the river, and encamped a mile on this side. 13 miles—

---

[43]Wikipedia contributors, "List of infantry weapons in the American Revolution," *Wikipedia, The Free Encyclopedia*, https://en.wikipedia.org/w/index.php?title=List_of_infantry_weapons_in_the_American_Revolution&oldid=986292636 (accessed November 1, 2020), "The Brown Bess musket was the gun used by the British military from 1722 until about 1838. It was used throughout the Revolutionary War and the Napoleonic Wars. It was capable of firing approximately three to four shots per minute. The Brown Bess Musket was a flint-lock musket, meaning it would use flint in order to spark the gunpowder loaded into the gun to cause the gun to fire."

14th—The troops took up the line of march at sun rise, passed through Salsbury, which is a fine little town, two or three eligant houses, and encamped within half a mile of the town. Here I met with Christian Stake who was going to Penn'a. I employed this evening in writing letters by fire light for fear of missing the opportunity. 7 miles—

15th—The troops took up the line of march at sun rise, passed through a verry fine country for land—Encamped at Mr. Taylor's—Roan County 12 miles—

16th—Marched at the usual time, crossed Caddle Creek, and Mr. Fifers Ordinary, passed through a fine country and encamped at Rocky Run. Macklenburgh County 14 miles—

N.B. Within half a mile of our encampment there was an Indian town of about eighty in number, their principal town is some distance, these are Cutapis and they hold fifteen miles square of a verry fine country, no pines here.

17th **(December)**—This day remained on the ground in consequence of a heavy rain—

18th—This morning a great frost—The troops took up the line of march at the usual time—Crossed Mullet Creek, marched through Charlotte Town and encamped within half a mile of the town. There are but three tolerable houses in this town and about a dozen of small ordinary buildings. 13 miles—

19th—The troops took up the line of march at the usual hour and crossed McCoppens Creek and several other small runs and encamped this side of Clems Branch, we see verry few houses this day. 15 miles—

20th—The troops took up the line of march at the usual time, passed through a fine level country and encamped at Twelve Mile creek,—Indian land—Now in South Carolina Cambden District—This creek being verry high occationed by a remarkable heavy rain which fell yesterday, we were obliged to fall trees for the troops to cross on. 10 miles—

21st—The troops took up the line of march at 12 o'clock A.M. Crossed the Twelve Mile creek and passed through a fine

"Brought from Journal #1"

country and encamped at Waxaw Creek. At this place were seventeen British Officers on parole. A warm day—7 miles—

22nd—This morning at day light the troops took up the line of march, crossed Waxaw Creek, Cane Creek, Camp Creek, Gills Creek and Bear Creek and encamped on the south side of South Creek, Maj. Barkley's farm—Cambden District 10 miles—

23rd—This morning took up the line of march at sun rise, passed through a piney, and what they call black jack country—a fine level road. See a number of waggons destroyed and a number of buts of musquets and encamped one mile on the south side of the Flat Rock—this is the ground where a number of our soldiers were cut to pieces by Tarlton[44] on the retreat of Gen. Gates. Marched through a great part of the long leaf't pine—

N.B. This place called the flat rock is about three acres of a rock—flat and solid—Cambdon District 20 miles—

24th—The troops took up the line of march at the usual time—this day verry disagreeable marching, rainy and very sloppy—Encamped within two miles of Cambdon on the ground where Gen. Greene had almost experienced a surprize. 16 miles—

25th—A verry dull Christmas indeed, had nothing to make us comfortable, we remained on this ground being much fatigued and cloaths all dirty—a warm day~

26th—The troops took up the line of march at sun rise, marched through Cambdon, a small town and destroyed by the enemy—they had it fortified and was one of their capital posts—crossed the Waterree a midling large river about two miles on

---

[44]Wikipedia contributors, "Battle of Waxhaws," *Wikipedia, The Free Encyclopedia*, https://en.wikipedia.org/w/index.php?title=Battle_of_Waxhaws&oldid=984114712 (accessed November 1, 2020), "The Battle of Waxhaws (also known as the Waxhaws, Waxhaw massacre, and Buford's massacre) took place during the American Revolutionary War on May 29, 1780, near Lancaster, South Carolina, between a Continental Army force led by Abraham Buford and a mainly Loyalist force led by British officer Banastre Tarleton. Buford refused an initial demand to surrender, but when his men were attacked by Tarleton's cavalry, many threw down their arms to surrender. Buford apparently attempted to surrender. However, the British commanding officer Tarleton was shot at during the truce, causing his horse to fall and trap him. Loyalists and British troops were outraged at the breaking of the truce in this manner and proceeded to fall on the rebels. While Tarleton was trapped under his dead horse, men continued killing the Continental soldiers, including men who were not resisting. Little quarter was given to the patriots/rebels. Of the 400 or so Continentals, 113 were killed with sabers, 150 so badly injured they could not be moved and 53 prisoners were taken by the British and Loyalists. "Tarleton's quarter", thereafter became a common expression for refusing to take prisoners."

First Hand

the south side of Cambdon, and encamped in a pine woods and some black jack—5 miles—

27th—This morning took up the line of march at sun rise, passed through a verry disagreeable pine swamp about two miles long and half leg deep with water and mud. Encamped near one Mr. Reynold's lately from Penn'a—a tennant of Col. Carshaws—10 miles—

28th—Took up the line of march at sun rise, very level road—all long leaf't pine—this day had a verry fatiguing march being verry warm—see three or four good houses—Encamped within half a mile of Congaree River—23 miles—

29th—This morning at sun rise we crossed the Congaree River and encamped on the south side of Col. Thompson's, a gentleman who lives in great affluance 5 miles—

30th—This morning at sun rise the troops took up the line of march and encamped in a Germine settlement, these like the great part of this country—all Torys—a verry warm day—Orrange Burgh District 13 miles—

31st—The troops marched at the usual time, passed through a Germine settlement, crossed a number of swamps—passed Orrangeburgh Town, this place the enemy burnt except one house and the Goal—there are a number of Horse and foot doing duty in this place to keep the Torys in order 13 miles—

First January 1782

The troops took up the line of march this morning at sun rise. We were obliged to cross a number of verry disagreeable swamps, no bridges could be made and we were obliged to wade them knee deep—any quantity of pine this day, our encampment surrounded with swamps—20 miles—

2nd January 82—Took up the line of march at the usual time, passed through a low swampy piny country for about seventeen miles. Encamped within three miles of the Edisto River 15 miles—

3rd—Took up the line of march at nine o'clock, crossed the Edistow River on two elligant saw mills, each of them had four saws and as they saw the boards they raft them down the river to

"Brought from Journal #1"

Charles Town, the river runs verry rapid—This whole days march was exceeding disagreeable on account of swamps, our artilery and waggons could scarcely go along—This day we met the Virginia returning home whose times were expired—10 miles—

4th—A verry heavy dew and fogg. The troops took up the line of march at the usual time—nothing but one continual swamp—Joined Gen. Greene's army this morning at eleven o'clock. Encamped in the woods at Round O. 5 miles—

5th—An exceeding heavy dew, then cleared away and was verry warm, so warm that I could not have my coat—

6th—The water here is verry bad, no springs—nothing but pons and swamps—this obliged us to sink wells—

7th—Captain Kirkwood informed me he was going to Penn'a—I employed this day in writing home to my friends—

8th—The weather still continued warm, I remained close in camp—now our living was entirely on poor beef and rice—

9th—This morning our Brigade took up the line of march at eight o'clock, the roads exceeding good and straight—see a number of eligant houses a small distance from the road and fine avinews leading to them, and large rice plantations. Marched through Jacksonsbourgh a small town two or three tolerable good houses—Encamped within a quarter of a mile of said place. 13 miles—

10th **(January)**—This morning I mounted the Governors Guard—being an entire stranger, and no person to introduce me to him or family—I was neglected by him at dinner time, but Mr. Foshaw, an inhabitant of the place invited me to dine with him, which I did—in the evening about sun set Governor Rutledge[45] sent for me and appologised for the neglect—I spent the afternoon verry agreeably drinking wine and smoking segars—

---

[45] Wikipedia contributors, "John Rutledge," *Wikipedia, The Free Encyclopedia*, https://en.wikipedia.org/w/index.php?title=John_Rutledge&oldid=983716703 (accessed November 1, 2020), "John Rutledge (September 17, 1739 – July 23, 1800) was an Associate Justice of the Supreme Court of the United States and its second Chief Justice. Additionally, he served as the first President of South Carolina and later as its first governor after the Declaration of Independence."

11th—This day I employed, after I was relieved, in fixing my tent and digging a well—This morning at the Governor's table I eat bread made of rice which was the first I ever eat, it was made thin like buckwheat cakes, some in round balls and fry'd in a pan with some fat—

12th—This morning received orders to hold ourselves in readiness to march at the shortest notice—in the evening we struck our tents and loaded our baggage, crossed the Ponpon River[46], marched all night, and in the morning one hour before day light we arrived within half a mile of Stone Ferry—Col. Laurences infantry in front of us who were to surprize a party of the enemy on John's Island about four hundred foot and sixty Horse, our plan fell through. Day light appearing and a number of the infantry could not get over the marsh—this was verry hard to cross as it was middle deep of mud, and the tide making fast, some of them stuck fast untill they were assisted, those who got over were up to their sholders in water on their return—Our Brigade was to support the infantry. 22 miles—

13th **January 1782**—As soon as day light appeared the infantry and our Brigade retired about one mile and a half from Stone Ferry and lay uppon our arms all day, the weather now cold and disagreeable, and no tents or baggage—in the evening the other part of the Army joined us—

14th—This day we built a brush hutt to shelter us from the cold—about eleven o'clock two of our six pounders were ordered to the publick landing about one mile from Stone to drive a Row Galley[47] of the enemys away which lay in a narrow

---

[46]Wikipedia contributors, "Edisto River," *Wikipedia, The Free Encyclopedia*, https://en.wikipedia.org/w/index.php?title=Edisto_River&oldid=955873369 (accessed November 1, 2020), "The Edisto River is one of the longest free-flowing blackwater rivers in North America, flowing over 250 meandering miles from its sources in Saluda and Edgefield counties, to its Atlantic Ocean mouth at Edisto Beach, South Carolina. It rises in two main tributaries (North Fork & South Fork) from springs under the Sandhills region of West Central South Carolina, just to the south of the Piedmont Fall Line. It is the longest and largest river system completely contained by the borders of South Carolina. Its name comes from the Edisto subtribe of the Cusabo Indians. Near the coast, part of the river was once known as the Ponpon River."

[47]Wikipedia contributors, "Row galley," *Wikipedia, The Free Encyclopedia*, https://en.wikipedia.org/w/index.php?title=Row_galley&oldid=886961133 (accessed November 1, 2020), "A row galley was a term used by the early United States Navy for an armed watercraft that used oars rather than sails as a means of propulsion. During the American Revolution, row galleys, such as *Spitfire* and *Washington*, with crews of up to 60 oarsmen, were employed successfully in battle against larger warships."

pass to prevent our Troops to go on the Island, they fired a dozen of shots, three of which struck her, but the mistle was two light to do her much harm—They evacuated the Island—a party of our Troops at low water went on it and got some small articles which they in their hurry could not take off—

15th—This day orders no Officer or Soldier to leave camp on any account. We were informed the enemy were out in force this day—in consequence of which we marched two miles towards Charlestown and returned a little of the way towards the Borrough 8 miles—

16th—This morning the whole Army took up the line of march at sun rise and encamped in the woods near Mr. Frazer's farm, about four miles from the Borrough. Continued cold. 10 miles—

17th **(January)**—This day I got a horse and went to the baggage to get a clean shirt—Dined with Col. Craig who was there lame—and returned to our camp in the pine woods—

18th—I took a walk out of camp with a gun to kill some wild ducks which are verry plenty—but rain came on. I returned to camp without any—

19th—General Greene was down reconnoitering the enemy, went within one mile of Charlestown with a small party of Horse, the enemy fired cannon exceeding hard for some time but to no purpose—

20th—This day Governor Burk[48] of North Carolina arrived to headquarters who made his escape from Jameses Island, was paroled there—the Field Officers of the Army were called together to inquire into his conduct wheather he was justifiable or no—what they did was kept a secret—

21st—This morning verry cool, remained still in this situation without our baggage—

---

[48]Wikipedia contributors, "Thomas Burke (North Carolina politician)," *Wikipedia, The Free Encyclopedia*, https://en.wikipedia.org/w/index.php?title=Thomas_Burke_(North_Carolina_politician)&oldid=960157933 (accessed November 1, 2020), "Thomas Burke (ca. 1747 – December 2, 1783) was an Irish physician, lawyer, and statesman who lived in Hillsborough, North Carolina. He represented North Carolina as a delegate to the Continental Congress and was the third Governor of the state."

22nd—This morning a large white frost, took a walk about four miles into the country and see negroes working in a rice mill—

23rd—Remained close in camp smoking over a pine fire, our baggage came to us this evening—

24th—This morning we took up the line of march, and encamped about one mile from our former ground—Just when we had our tents pitcht orders came for our Battalion to march immediately for Jacksonsburgh to guard the Governor and [General] Assembly which was sitting there—we got there about dark and pitcht our tents.

Here our Battalion remained on this duty until the seventh day of March when we were ordered to join the main Army as the Assembly was done sitting—Whilst we were here a difference happened between (Governor Matthews who was appointed while we remained on this duty)—and the Officers of our Battalion, the difference was this, after the Assembly was done sitting they made a dinner in the house they sat in, and this was the house the Officer of the Guard remained in—the dinner was ready, all the Assembly and the Governor sat down, and no attention paid to the Officer who was in the house with them, altho on duty,—the Officer could take it in no other light than an insult, and as such we all resented it. After this we had invitations from the Governor to come to eat with him, but none would go near him. I was so unfortunate as to be left on this guard when the Battalion marched, was sent for to make the matter up, I refused and would not go—two days after I had to wait on the Governor to know how the Guard was to be supply'd with provisions, the matter was then talked over and all sattisfaction necessary, I then went to his table as formerly, the Officer was Lt. Thornberry—

This is all remarkable that happened from the 24th of January '82 until the 8th of March 1782~

Chapter Five: March 1782

After Special Duty

9th March, 1782—Whilst at dinner with the Governor the relief came to me, I was relieved and joined the main army—5 miles—

10th—Remained on the ground this day and visited the Officers of my acquaintance—

11th—Busy about settling the Incorporation[49] which was to take place—

12th—The Incorporation took place. I wrote home by Capt. Wilkins. The Officers who went home was Col. Craige, Maj. Alexander, Capt. Wilkins, Doctor Magaw, Capt. Claypoole, Capt. Seely, Lt. Ball, Lt. Stricker, Lt. Thornberry, Lt. Gilgrece, Lt. Dickson.

13th—Employed in coppying a journal.

14th—D°—D°—(Ditto)

15th—About 3 o'clock I was warned for guard, the Troops were to manouver this afternoon, I was on the parade. Whilst I was there a detachment was ordered out, I was the first for command. Maj. Moore commanded the detachment, we marched at sun set through mud and water twelve miles, to Mr. McQueen's 12 miles—

16th—I joined Col. Laurence about one mile from Barons Bridge at 8 o'clock at night—marched back to said bridge—8 miles

17th—At half past four in the morning took up the line of march, the Legionary Infantry in front—the two companies of Delaware next and our detachment the cavalry composed of Col. Washington's and Lee's in our rear passed through Dorchester, a small town irregularly built, consisting of one church and about a dozen houses, the church and other houses destroyed by the enemy whilst they kept garrison there, passed over two bridges,

---

[49] While no references to this can be found after much research, it is believed an "Incorporation" during the Revolutionary War would be similar to a "Change of Command" ceremony within the ranks of today's American military.

between these was an old British fort on a commanding hight, went down within six miles of the Centre House where the main army of the British lay, took post at a meeting house, lay there for some time, then returned back as far as the widow Ozards, a lady of the first fortune and taste in these parts, this lady for the honour of St. Patrick gave the soldiers a jill of spirits, we then returned to Baron Bridge. 12 miles

18th—Remained on new ground and built an eligant hutt, my feet hurt so much with my boots that I could not walk.

19th—Remained here this day—I borrowed a pair of slippers from Maj. Moore to walk about in as I was destitute of baggage save what I had on me.

20th **(March)**—Still continued on this ground.

21st—This day expected the enemy—Maj. Moore and three or four of us paid a visit to Mr. Ozard, one of the delegates of Congress from this state, and slept there this night—

22nd—Still continued on this ground without anything to eat but rice, on this we have lived for three days, except last night's supper—

23rd—Remained in this situation until eight o'clock in the evening, when Maj. Moore, Capt. Patterson, Capt. Marshall, Lt. Moore and myself were sitting down to our usual dish, a large plate of rice and a little salt, when Col. Laurence and Mr. Ozard came to us, we invited them to partake in our repast, they expressed sorrow for our situation, they went home, Mr. Ozard sent us a quarter of vennison and a fletch of bacon which afforded all the officers of our detachment a supper, we then went to bed.

24th—The remains of Mr. Ozard's present afforded us all a breakfast, an no expectation of any more—

25th—We were ordered to march altho hungry—and to add to our misfortune came on a verry heavy rain which we us sufficiently, we marched to Dorchester and got into the empty houses—we all dined with Col. Laurence, and got plenty of wine and grogg—3 miles

26th—We quartered in an eligant house but our landlady was in Charlestown and no appearance of anything to eat—

27th—Continued in this situation—

28th—We got a little beef and rice and a little grogg this day—

29th—A remarkable change of weather, snowed verry fast for some time, then cleared up. Cold.

30th—Still continued cold—received orders to march to join the army at headquarters—these orders were countermanded, we marched a quite different rout at three o'clock in the afternoon, continued our march until eleven o'clock, when we halted and made fires to warm our supplies and dry our feet, and give the cavalry time to cross the river, we then took up the line of march and crossed the Strawberry River, by this time day light appeared—a remarkable frost. St. John's Parish 20 miles

31st—Remained here until one o'clock to draw and cook provisions, whilst we remained here Doctor Botton, an inhabitant, invited all the officers of the detachment to dine with him, we chearfully accepted of the invitation. Dined uppon an excellent wild turkey and had plenty of wine and grogg. The doctor begged that if we ever came this road again we would let him know a few hours before, and he would provide for us, we then marched to Goose Creek Bridge and lay in the woods. 9 miles

April 1st, 1782—The weather still continued verry cold, marched at eight o'clock to Mr. Thomas farm, an eligant situation where Maj. Moore had some dinner provided we all took a bit and a drink of grogg. 8 miles

2nd—Marched at eight o'clock in the morning and crossed Gairings Bridge and Wapatoo Bridge where grows a large quantity of cabbige trees, made a short halt, then took up the line of march to Hadrils Point on the northeast side of Charlestown, there is was supposed the enemy were out. After dark intelligence came to us the enemy were returned, we then faced to the right about and crossed Wapatoo Bridge where we lay under an old tree. 24 miles

3rd—Took up the line of march at eight o'clock, crossed Gairings Bridge, took the lower road to Charlestown it being somewhat nearer, made a short halt, then an express came from Gen. Greene for us to return immediately lest we should be cut off before assistance could be given, we then made a D march to a branch of Cooper River, crossed at Bonneau's Ferry, then took up the line of march and came to Strawberry River where our old friend the Doctor had a supper provided for us, we supt with him and then crossed the river, after we crossed, some of the soldiers began to plunder the negroes, one of Legion Infantry fired and shot one of the soldiers of our regiment. 20 miles

4th—Marched at eight o'clock and made a halt, we were ordered not to let the soldiers cook, we were to march immediately, here we lay in the woods without anything to eat or drink, and would not be allowed to cook in this situation. We remained until four o'clock, when Col. Laurence had dined and filled himself with wine, we then took up the line of march and came to Bacons Bridge where we lay all night without anything to shelter us from the dew and it was so late we could not provide anything for our comfort, so much for Col. Laurence's wild goose chase. N. B. Ever since the 15th of March I never slept a night with my cloaths off. 22 miles

5th—Buried the soldier who was wounded on the night of the third instant, remained there this day.

6th—Received orders for Maj. Moore's detachment to join the army at Headquarters, joined about three o'clock, dined with Maj. Moore. 4 miles

7th **(April)**—Employed in coppying my journal—

Whilst I was on this detachment a difference happened between Gen. Greene and some of our officers about a Capt. Detachment which was ordered out, in which the Captain was allowed to choose the subbatrons[50] (subalterns) who was to go

---

[50] Wikipedia contributors, "Subaltern (military)," *Wikipedia, The Free Encyclopedia*, https://en.wikipedia.org/w/index.php?title=Subaltern_(military)&oldid=970425508 (accessed November 1, 2020), "A subaltern is a primarily British military term for a junior officer. Literally meaning "subordinate", subaltern is used to describe commissioned officers below the rank of captain and generally comprises the various grades of lieutenant."

with him on this duty. Lieut. Marshall was the officer whose tower it was for command, and was warned, after he went to the grand parade, Capt. Wilmot made choice another, this appeared to be a reflection on the officer who was warned, he would not have the parade until he see an order from the Gen. for this irregular manner of proceeding, which was presented to him, he then came home his feelings injured much, whereupon the majority of the officers of our line wrote him the following letter—

Dated
Camp, March 28th, 1782
Sir:

When the subjects of a state conceive their rights infringed on they readily suppose it arrives from some mistake in the executive part of the Government—or that the Governor means to adopt a mode of governoring altogether new and what the subjects have hitherto been unacquainted with, to determine which it is natural for the good subjects as men who have a sense of subordination knowing it to be the basis on which these priviledges and happenings of the people so much depend and more particularly in an army to inquire and modes they ask an explanation.

In the situation of injured subjects do the captains and subattrons of the Pennsylvania Line review themselves when they reflect on the circumstances attending the formation of Capt. Wilmot's detachment.

We do therefore beg the General will inform us wheather it was his intention that Capt. Wilmot's command should be formed on the principals it was, or wheather by mistake—should it prove the latter we shall be happy and have not a doubt but that Gen. Greene's sense of equity and honour will lead him to do the justice to the feelings of the body of inquired officers.

For the purpose of better explaining the points where in we conceive ourselves agreived, we enclose a copy of the order—

We have the honour to with respect your obedient and verry humble servants.

[General Greene's answer]

Headquarters-29th March 1782
Gentlemen:
The Constitution of the Army and that of civil Government are uppon different principals, the object of one so different from the other, that what might be essential to millitary operations in the formation of an army would be found too simple for the various interests and differrent claims under Civil Government. The business of an army is to cover the country and anoy the enemy, that of civil government is to protect and insure the rights of individuals,—therefore to argue from analogy to the rights of men under those different Governments confounding things that have no relation, and resoning upon principals that never can be admitted in an army, It is necessary both to the s.... of an army, that the movements should be simple and secret, If the Constitution of an Army is not uppon the principal it can answer the designs of government, and to form an Army uppon any plan which must defeat the great object of it will burden the community with a great expense without utillity.

I am always in tender of the feelings of Officers as possible, but if they go into refinements and urge injuries, which have no foundation but from improper modes of reasoning, I cannot sacrifice the publicks good and the reputation of the army at large, to accomodate millitary opperations to their way of thinking.

You are to consider yourselves as officers of the Continental Army bound by its laws and governed by

March 1782

millitary maxims, as ours are under Millitary not civil governors.

If you feel any injury it must be as Officers of the line of the Army and not those of any particular state— But if you will give yourselves the trouble to read "Millitary Authors" and consider the practice of other Armies and reflect without prejudice uppon the nature and design of detachments you cannot but be convinced your greavances immaginary.

When detachments are made it is for some particular purpose to make it therefore in a manner, not perfectly calculated to answer the design, would both sacrifice the publick good and by degrees the reputation of the Army. There are more things to be taken into consideration in making a detachment than merely the millitary abillities of the officer commanding or his rank in the line of the army.

There is a knowledge of the country, the people and other local circumstances which are verry material considerations to be attended to, to give success to an enterprise.

A man of an inferior capacity with a knowledge of those things would be able to execute a command much better with these than a man of superior capacity without them—I have ever made it a rule and I find it well warranted by the best millitary writers as well as from the reason and nature of the thing, to detach such men and officers as I may think requisite for the service to be performed.

Nothing short of this can give success to an Enterprise, I hope therefore you will consider this explanation satisfactory, you may be assured I have the strongest disposition to oblige and do justice to the merit and service of every officer but must confine myself to such maxims of millitary government as are necessary to do justice to the publick and the Army at large.

I am Gentlemen your most obedient humble servant
Nathan Greene

[Answer to General Greene's letter]

Camp 3rd April 1782
Sir:
That Civil and Millitary governments differ we grant—but that they are both constituted on principles of justice is a circumstance in itself too evident to admit of a doubt—

Therefore to quote civil government and deduce from thence that a subject tho not of the state we had a right to ask redress of grievances and not deemed unreasonable—for that millitary subjects have not a claim to justice altho the government is supposed to hold it in its verry principals is a matter that we have never yet been acquainted with.

From what circumstances the General judges when he supposes us to have taken up the matter as Officers of the Army and not of the Continental Army, we are at a loss to know—and can only answer that it is not in our power to account for the feelings of and ideas of any body but ourselves—

But offer to explain why it should affect us particularly as there was an Officer of our line sent by regular detail with the detachment to the Grand Parade and was dismissed from thence by Captain Wilmot who produced an order visiting him (Capt. Wilmot) with power to approve of or reject such officer as he might think proper. If the General will reflect a moment on the circumstances he must naturally unless he supposes us void of every delicate sensation, that we have cause of complaint.—We conclude with observing that altho the answer to our address was not so satisfactory as we could have expected we are induced from the peculiar situation of the army and our zeal for the publick good to decline any further steps on the occasion.

9th April 1782—This day a scarcity of provisions in camp—This is a field day with the enemy, a regular discharge of cannon and small arms about ten o'clock which continued untill twelve—

10th—Cloudy and windy and threatens rain—in the evening a verry heavy rain which almost drowned us in our tent—

11th—Still continued wet and disagreeably cold for the season—

12th—This morning cleared up—cold.

13th—A verry heavy dew, and cold—This morning at nine o'clock the army fired blank cartridges the first was a discharge of our pieces of artilery, then the small arms by platoons from right to left. Then four pieces of artilery, and the next fire was by divisions from right to left—the North Carolinans and Marylanders made verry bad fire, it resembled a running fire more than anything I can compare it to—our troops fired exceeding well—it was all like one gun—

14th **(April)**—This day a small party of Enemy's Cavalry came to Dorchester and took Lieutenant Carrington prisoner, one of Col. Lee's officers, who was reconnoitering—this night the soldiers slept with their cloaths on and lay on their arms—

15th—Employed in maneuvering the troops—This day Gen. St. Clair, Capt. Keen, Capt. Jackson went from camp for Pennsylvania—

16th—This morning Capt. Orndorff of the Maryland Line solicited a command to go on the British lines and obtained it—Gen. Greene moved his quarters to the house where General St. Clair had quartered—verry fine weather.

17th—The weather still continues pleasant and warm—

18th—This day we drew up a premonstrance to send it to the Assembly of Pennsylvania in behalf of the Officers and Soldiers of that Line, setting forth the fraudulent manner in which we were settled with, and one third of our deprication paid in bills scarce worth one sixth of their nominal value, and in many instances not one eighth—this was signed by all the Field and other Officers of the Line and sent to Philadelphia.

19th—This morning four of the soldiers of our battalion deserted with their arms, and took a quantity of amunition and two from a detachment which was on the lines and some from the Maryland Line and North Carolinans—in all nine, and went to the enemy.

20th—A great uneasiness with the Maryland Line in regard of certificates which their state wanted to give them for the depriciation of their pay, they would by no means take them—

This morning a party of the enemies Calvary came to our Advance Puquet Guard, the guard fired on them, they went back again, on of their men deserted with his horse and accoutrements—This afternoon an officer and 24 men deserted from Jameses Island with their arms and accoutrements and came to our camp, these were Refugees, what the people in this part of the country call Scofes, a number of Sergts. Confined on suspicion of raising a mutony—

21st **April**—This day a party of the enemys Black Cavalry came to Dorchester, a party of our Horse fell in with them ours made a charge and killed their black Captain and wounded some of their men, one of ours was killed and one wounded and some amissing—This day I was on Guard in a swamp amongst owles and musquitoes—

22nd—This afternoon at 3 o'clock Sergt. Goynel was executed for encouraging and offering to head the mutaneirs—and six other sergents of our Line were sent to Penna. as they were suspected to be in the plot, but no proof could be made against them—Yesterday Lieut. Feltman of our Regt. and Lt. Cunningham of the 3rd resigned—

23rd—This morning Lt. Feltman and Lt. Cunningham went from camp for Pennsylvania. I wrote a letter to my Father by Capt. Campbell. This day the court marshall sat to try the rest of the mutaniers—

24th—This morning Gen. Greene came verry early to camp and informed us the enemy was out, we made the men fall in, examined their arms and amunition then stacked arms on the parade, after some time we had orders to strike tents and load baggage, in this situation we remained until 3 o'clock when we had orders to pitch them again—

25th **April 1782**—This morning I went on the right flank Pisquet Guard which there was no shelter for me in case of rain, which it threatened much. I built a good shade and covered it with bark—This day we got a milk cow, with a calf, for our mess which was better than the poor rice and beef—

26th—This day still threatens rain—

27th—This morning I went fishing in the Ashley River but caught nothing.

28th—This day continued warm and cloudy. In the evening came a heavy thunder shower and continued raining the greater part of the night.

29th—This morning somewhat wet, I mounted guard, it cleared up about 10 o'clock, and about 2 there came on a heavy thunder shower which wet me sufficiently, then cleared up and had a pleasant night.

1st **May 1782**—This evening something extraordinary for this army, the Officers drew a quart of rum and the soldiers a gill, to celebrate the American 4th, maypoles were errected—

2nd—This day we were reinforced by a party of militia from this state. Horse and Infantry, consisting of about six hundred and encamped on our right flank—

3rd—This morning one of Capt. Boude's men deserted. This afternoon four Hesseon's deserters came to us—

4th—This morning one of Captain Steels company deserted, one of the eighteen month's men which was drafted to our regiment—This morning I went on guard—

5th—This morning six of the second battalion deserted, a lamentable circumstance indeed that disertion is likely to continue in our army—but what can we expect in their sittuation, whithout cloaths and pay for two years, every person must allow there is still virtue in the Army when we have any left—This evening two of the British deserted to our Army—and confirmed the report of eight hundred troops sailing for some of the islands—

6th—This day I dined with Col. Mentges, where Gen. Gist and all the Field Officers were there—

7th—This morning I went on general fatiegue to build a house for the Provost, after all the prisoners had run away. This afternoon the North Carolina Brigade manouvered with blank cartridges and fired amazingly bad—

8th—This morning we moved our tents a little in front to change our ground and make the camp clean—

9th—This day one of our soldiers which diserted some time ago diserted back again, with a new suit of cloaths—

10th—A verry heavy rain with thunder and wind which began at one o'clock at night and continued until 12 o'clock this day. In the most of this rain I mounted the Governor's Guard which was five miles from camp, and was verry wet when I got there, I lived exceeding well—

11th—This afternoon there was orders for a command to be in readiness to march the next morning at sun rise, the Command consisted of one Major, three Captains and 100 men—

12th—The Command marched at sun rise and joined Col. Laurence and his detachment.—This evening at 10 o'clock the whole returned to camp with 5 prisoners which they took near the Quarter House—

13th—This morning employed in making a bowery to keep the scorching heat of the sun from my tent—

14th—This morning five British diserters came to us—

15th **(May)**—This morning I went on Gen. Greene's Guard, whilst on this Guard I received two letters, one from Mr. King dated January 28th 1782. The other from my brother, Alexander dated 24th January 1782—

16th—This afternoon I employed in writing to Mr. King and brother Alexander—but was disappointed, the person who was to carry them went two days before his trist with me.

17th—This evening a small party of the enemy came to our Advance Piquet and fired on the Sentry—

March 1782

18th—This morning so cool that it was disagreeable to us, numbers of Officers wore their great coats.

19th—This day continued cool and cloudy—

20th—This morning I mounted the Advance Guard of the Army which was at Bacon Bridge, in the morning two flags went down to the enemies lines—about 2 o'clock Captain Sckelly, aid to Gen. Lestly came to my Guard with a flag, was desirus to see Gen. Greene. I had to send the field officer of the day and from that to the General as he informed me his business was of consequence to both Armys, while he remained with me we had a good deal of conversation, he hoped that matters were on a fare footing for peace, he hoped that we would soon have the pleasure of drinking a glass of wine and taking each other by the hand in peacable terms—he then asked me to take a drink of porter with him, after this I indulged him to go to Mr. Ozard's to refresh himself until the General would come, immediately after there came a second flag, a young lady and her brother to see some of their friends, I detained this one also, about sun set the General came and remained at my out sentinal with Captain Skelly until 8 o'clock at night then dismissed the flag—

21st—Fine agreeable weather, I had to go to manouver this afternoon not withstanding I came of Guard—

22nd—This morning I had to sit on a court marshall to try a soldier which denied his enlistment—

23rd—Captain Davis and I received a note from Gen. Greene to dine with him this day which we answered—

24th—This day I mounted the Advance Guard and received one flag—

25th—I employed this day in writing letters one to Mr. King, one to brother John and one to brother Alexander and enclosed them in a few lines to Mr. Fettis Allison. This afternoon in opening a company book—

This ends the year since I began to keep a Journal—I now sum up the number of miles which I traveled during this time, which is—1891 miles exclusive of marching about camp, on guard and from them—

26th **May 1782**—This evening came orders for a Lieut, Sergt, Corporal and fourteen men to parade on the Grand Parade the next morning at sun rise.

27th—This morning I was ordered for this command and had not fifteen minutes to prepare for it, the command was to go to the Congaree River to guard cloathing to the army for the Torys was verry troublesome, I went to Mr. Summers and dined with him—8 miles—then went on and remained with a poor widow that night in midst of the Tory settlement. 25 miles

28th—Went on the next morning taken with sickness and distracted with the toothache, and halted at Mr. Dunkland's where the Lady made me a good dish of tea. I got some better of the sickness but the toothache was more violent, I went on my journey and on the road I killed a alligator seven foot long, came to the Widow Thompson's. 25 miles

29th—This morning my face was swelled very much and the pain still worse to have, I went on through this desolate country no a house for twenty miles, I came to Col. Thompson's whilst they were at Tea. I drank two dishes and then went on to Gen. Hugars where the cloathing was—27 miles

30th—I got the waggons loaded and after breakfast I returned to Col. Where I had to remain until I sent four miles for provisions and forage. I took dinner and evening tea there, proceeded on—7 miles

31st—Still distracted with the toothache went 24 miles

1st June 1782—This day Col. Thompson and Col. Dart with seven waggons came to me and took protection of my good through the Tory country, I was now almost dead with pain, want of sleep and could take no nourishment but a little milk or tea without eating anything—20 miles

2nd—Left Mr. Dunkland's who was verry kind to me and came to old Summerses—25 miles

3rd—This morning the swelling broke but still painfull, I came to camp—8 miles

4th—This morning sick and my face painfull—

5th—The pain now abated a little—

March 1782

6th—This morning I took a vomit which almost killed me—

7th—This day came in a number of diserters, I continued sick—

8th—This day cloudy and threatened rain, I now get somewhat better—

9th—A verry wet day and still threatening more—

10th—Still wet and worse—

11th—Wet wet and wet

13th—A verry wet spell indeed—

14th—This day cleared up, I mounted Gen. Greene's Guard, where I had the pleasure of seeing a coppy of the Treaty between General Merian and the Tory's.

15th—This day a detachment was ordered out to consist of 100 men fit for Light Infantry properly officered to join the Horse and Infantry on the lines, the whole to be commanded by Gen. Gist—

16th—Last night a small party of the enemy came out and fired on the sentries of our Advance Guard which alarmed the camp, we rose out of our beds and paraded our men, we were two hours under arms before we dismissed the men—which was half after twelve o'clock—this day the infantry left—

17th **(June)**—This day I mounted guard—I received a note from Gen. Greene to dine with him tomorrow—

18th—A wet morning, this disappointed me of waiting on the General—This day we had the report of Iaver as being evacuated on the 15th of this instant—

19th—This day wet and showery—

20th—This day I mounted the guard, a fine day but verry warm—

21st—An exceeding hot day—

22nd—This day we drew shoes for every man, some shirts, overalls, and some hats and some shirts for the men. This day the Officers drew some articles of cloathing, amounting to five pounds of sterling each, the articles which I got was 1 piece of black silk patrons for britches, 7 yards coarse linnen, 1 pair shoes, 1 pen knife, 1 spoon, 2 / 1 oz. thread, 1 handkerchief. This is the way we pay for things delivered to us, if they would give us our pay we could purchase one third cheaper—

23rd—This day I mounted guard—

24th—This day worried is Lieut. Lazion verry dissatisfied about an order which Gen. Greene issued some time ago allowing Col. Laurence to have the command of the Legion Infantry, in consequence of this Maj. Trudolf and all the captains of the core gave their resignations to Gen. Greene which he accepted of—

25th—Still warm and showery—

26th—This evening a soldier of our Line had to run the gauntlet for breaking a store at Georgetown and another received 100 lashes—

27th—This day I mounted guard—

28th—This day I went fishing in the Ashley River at Bacon Bridge but caught nothing, a hot day—

29th—This day I went to the Light Infantry to try to procure some articles from Charlestown—

30th—A warm spell of weather—

July 1st, 1782—An exceeding warm day indeed—

2nd—This day I mounted guard and was almost eat up with mesquitoes—

3rd—A most extraordinary storm of wind and rain, this day I dined with Lt. Col. Mentges and Maj. Moore—

This day there was orders for a Fude of Joy to be fired tomorrow at five o'clock the whole army to be drawn up in one line and to salute the Gen. then thirteen cannon to be fired from the park of artilery in celebration of our Independence, and twenty one for the forged Doffin of France[51], then a running fire of small arms from right to left of the Army, this is to be repeated three rounds—then march past the General and salute

---

[51]Wikipedia contributors, "Louis XVI," Wikipedia, *The Free Encyclopedia*, https://en.wikipedia.org/w/index.php?title=Louis_XVI&oldid=985509601 (accessed November 1, 2020), "Louis XVI (23 August 1754 – 21 January 1793) was the last king of France before the fall of the monarchy during the French Revolution. He was referred to as Citizen Louis Capet during the four months just before he was executed by guillotine. In 1765, upon the death of his father, Louis, Dauphin of France, he became the new Dauphin. From 1776, Louis XVI actively supported the North American colonists, who were seeking their independence from Great Britain, which was realised in the 1783 Treaty of Paris."

him—The whole of the Captains and subattrons to dine at headquarters. The Field Officers and General dined with the Governor—

4th **(July)**—The orders of yesterday were complied with. The fore part of the day in firing the afternoon in dining and drinking wine—

5th—This day we made a Brigade Dinner and all the officers of our line dined together in camp and invited the field officers and a number of acquaintances to dine with us, we had 52 dishes and drank thirteen toasts, spent the evening verry happy—

6th—This morning I mounted guard, about eight o'clock in the evening came up a thunder shower which continued for six hours as severe as I ever experienced in my life for thunder and rain, and I without any shelter.

7th—This morning the troops took up the line of march at sun rise and marched 7 miles—this is the first march for the army since the 22nd of March and now encamped at Ashley Hill within 8 miles of the Quarter House.

8th—This day employed in building hutts to shelter ourselves from the weather—

9th **(July)**—This day I received three letters from Penna., one from Lieut. Crawford dated at Christmas, one from brother Nathan dated 31st December 1781, and one from Col. Irvine dated January 3rd 1782. This day twelve pounds of tobacco was issued to each company—

10th—This day I mounted guard in a fine and shady grove on the plantation of Mr. Middleton a member of Congress and one of the finest I have seen—

11th—This day verry warm—This day the enemy evacuated Savannah in Georgia—

12th—This day the 2nd Battalion of our Line was mustered and inspected, for the months of April, May and June—

13th—This day our Battalion was inspected—

14th—This day I mounted guard—

15th—This morning at five o'clock Lieut. McCollough of the 5th Penna. Regt. died at the flying hospital—

First Hand

16th—This evening at 7 o'clock he was buried with the Honours of War and I commanded the party consisting of one Sergt., one Corp. and 24 Privates.

17th—This day I mounted guard near Mrs. Middleton and she was kind enough to send me a bottle of Port wine which I divided among the sick of the company I commanded— N.B. This is the fifth day without rice—

18th—This day somewhat cool after a severe rain last evening. This day we buried a soldier of our Battalion. This day the officers each drew a quart of rum and the soldiers a jill—

19th—This day remarkably cold for the season and clowdy—

20th—This day I mounted guard—somewhat warm—

21st **(July)**—This day warm, a report from a line of the enemy, having their heavy cannon on board—

22nd—This day verry warm—at 5 o'clock a shower—

23rd—This day warm indeed—

24th—This day nothing to eat but rice without salt or beef—

25th—This day I mounted guard at Headquarters, this afternoon a little beef—

26th—Warm and showery—

27th—Warm warm and and—

28th—This afternoon the whole army ordered to march at 7 o'clock—Marched agreeable to the orders, I was ordered on command to forward the boats to Ashley Ferry within 3 miles of the Quarter House, I arrived at the Ferry at one o'clock in the morning. 6 miles from this place, I put four of the boats on waggons, the other three remained in the river, here we remained to refresh and draw provisions.

29th—Remained on this ground until 6 o'clock in the afternoon and had nothing to live on but corn and water mellons, then marched to camp, arrived here at 8 o'clock, I then mounted guard with a hungry belly—12 miles

30th—This morning nothing to eat until we had to kill one of our cows which we bought in Virginia. Now we are paying for ten thousand guineas which the state has given to General Greene—

31st—This day a small supply of beef, but no salt yet—

August 1, 1782—This day without beef until 1 o'clock, but no salt, verry warm—

2nd—This day I mounted guard—This day 9 Scofis came from Jameses Island, and two Hessions[52] from the Quarter House which says they are verry sickly in town —

3rd—This day verry warm, our men verry sickly and some dying—

4th—This afternoon came on a hurricane and verry sharp thunder, the house at Head Quarters was struck and three of the servants a little hurt with the lightning—

5th—This day showery and warm—

6th—This day the enemy evacuated the Quarter House—

7th—This day the troops drew a gill of rum, each officer a quart—

8th—Twelve diserters came to 6 of them was militia and the rest British—I mounted guard, excessive warm—One of the soldiers of our battalion was shot by the (Waggon Masters Clerk) who died in half an hour—one sergt. and one man died this day with sickness—

9th—This day ninety two degrees by the thermometer, By reports an evacuation of Charles Town will soon take place, (Agreeable news indeed to think of going to the north)—

10th—Refugees, Scofis of all ranks and denominations are coming out of Charles Town to make their peace with the State, and Hissions and British diserters—

11th **(August)**—This day we have acct. by a flag that they are to evacuate New York and all the posts in America—

12th—Monday—This day cool and agreeable—The officers drew each a quart of rum and the soldiers a gill—

---

[52]Wikipedia contributors, "Hessian (soldier)," *Wikipedia, The Free Encyclopedia*, https://en.wikipedia.org/w/index.php?title=Hessian_(soldier)&oldid=984915084 (accessed November 1, 2020), "Hessians were German soldiers who served as auxiliaries to the British Army during the American Revolutionary War. The term is an American synecdoche for all Germans who fought on the British side, since 65% came from the German states of Hesse-Kassel and Hesse-Hanau. Known for their discipline and martial prowess, around 30,000 Germans fought for the British during war, comprising a quarter of British forces."

13th—Tuesday—Fine cool day as I ever felt for this time of the year—

14th—Wednesday—Still continues cool, this day I mounted guard and was much troubled with Scofis coming from town to lay hold of the Gov. proclamation, hear three hundred came to the Gov. and a great many sent to Georgetown—

15th—Thursday—This day cool, Gov. proclamation over this day, Gen. Wayne and Col. Posey with the Virginia Regiment which was at Georgia came to camp this day—the d....t quantity of Scofis I ever see in my life—

16th—Friday—Somewhat warm this day, Gen. Wayne arrested Capt. Dier who was Forrage Master—

17th—Satterday—This day the Court Martial sat—Major Hambleton was President—Gen. Wayne took his Quarters at Drayton Hall (about five miles in front) took the Virginia Regiment to guard him—

18th **(August)**—Sunday—This day I mounted guard—

19th—Monday—This day pleasant and not verry warm—

20th—Tuesday—Pleasant but somewhat warm—

21st—Wednesday—This day I got a regimental coat cut out—a fine shower—

22nd—Thursday—This day I took a vomit to prevent sickness, as it is a sickly time—

23rd—Friday—I mounted guard this afternoon—Capt. Bird of the Maryland Line was buried with the Honours of War—

24th—Satterday—Dutton of Capt. Davis's Company died—a warm day—Capt. Baude and I went and drank punch with Col. Posey—

25th—Sunday—This day I dined with General Greene by invitation. This day Mrs. Greene went to Tuller Island for her health. Received a letter from Lieut. Crawford.

26th—Monday—Warm and disagreeable—

27th—Tuesday—This day I wrote a letter to brother John, for Maryland—

28th—Wednesday—This day I wrote two letters, one to my Father and the other to Lt. Crawford—

29th—Thursday—This day we have an acct. of a skirmish which Col. Laurence had with some of the enemy at Cumber, wherein Col. Laurence was killed and Capt. Smith of the artilery wounded and a Howister taken from them—I mounted guard this day—

30th—Friday—We are under some little apprehension of the enemy's coming from Charles Town to pay us a visit since the arrival of the Fleet—a cool fine day—We are dayly experiencing instances of mortality among us, soldiers dying fast—

31st—Satterday—Cool and pleasant for the season—

1st **Sept.**—Sunday—The officers drew a quarter and the soldiers a gill of rum. Two Dragoons diserted and brought four horses and one Hession with his arms—who says the enemy will leave town the fifteenth of the month—

2nd—Monday—Wet and cool, twelve diserters came out together this day—

3rd—Tuesday—This day came to us a Sergt. which informs us all the heavy cannon is a board and that they are only waiting for their forraging party to come in—

4th—Wednesday—I mounted guard this day—

5th—Thursday—This day I dined with Major Moore—

6th—Friday—Two buryings from our battalion this day—warm day and cool nights—

7th—Satterday—Two more died in our battalion this day—Two commands went out this morning, one to George Town, the other under command of Lt. Adams, all saylors to man a progally which Gen. Gist took at Cumber with two 6 pounders. Beef and rice on board.

8th—Sunday—Diserters come in dayly, three hundred and twenty sick in general hospital out of this small army, and better than half of the men sick in camp, we are scarcely able to relieve our guards—

9th—Monday—This day I mounted guard, we got some suggar and coffy—

10th—Tuesday—Warm and showery—

11th—Wednesday—A Court Marshall to try Capt. Farwell of the Maryland Line—

12th—Thursday—Cool and wet, I had to relieve Lt. Butler who took sick on guard—

13th—Friday—Cool—four diserters came in this day with their horses and accoutrements—

14th—Satterday—Still cool—Three diserters came in this day without their arms—

15th—Sunday—Six diserters this day and one woman from the enemy—

16th **(September)**—Monday—This day I mounted guard—

17th—Tuesday—This day we drew cloathing for our men—

18th—Wednesday—This day warm—

19th—Thursday—This day two men and three women and four horses with their bedding and furnature from John's Island—

20th—Friday—This day I mounted guard—The officers drew a quart of rum and the soldiers a gill—

21st—Satterday—Gen. Greene exceeding sick—Gen. Wayne getting better. Warm

22nd—Sunday—Warm, no news amongst us this day. I wrote a letter to Capt. McNutt.

23rd—Monday—Warm, sickly—

24th—Tuesday—Warm, this day I dined with the Adgt. Gen. Doctor McDowell took sick—

25th—Wednesday—I wrote a letter to Uncle ?? Maxwell—

26th—Thursday—This day I mounted guard—This day died the emiable Mrs. Ozard, the most hospitable and the most generous this county could afford—

27th—Friday—This day a diserter came in with his horse and accoutrements, Major Moore bought them for fifteen guines—

28th—Satterday—This morning came in seven diserters with their horses and accoutrements, they say that the Loyalists have imbarked and all the valuable Horse, and the officers baggage. Capt. Ziglar went on command at two o'clock—a Major command went out at 10 o'clock at night—

29th—Sunday—Two deserters came in this day and informed us that Gen. Lestly had gave Garrison Orders for the loyalists to go on board for St. Augustine—This evening I took the fever—

30th—Monday—This day I took a vomit and was verry sick—

1st October—Tuesday—I had the fever all this day—

2nd—Wednesday—I took the bark all this day—

3rd—Thursday—I had the fever this day and was verry sick all night—

4th—Friday—I again take the bark—This day Lt. Story of the 4th Regt. of Artilery died—

5th—Satterday—Sergt. Welch of our company died and Lieut. Story and him were both buried this afternoon—This day the officers drew a quart and the soldiers a gill of rum—

6th—Sunday—This day I got some better, still continue at the bark—Gen. Wayne relapses again—

7th—Monday—This day 5 deserters came to us—a wet cool day—I still continue to get better—

8th—Tuesday—A wet day and disagreeable—The officers drew a quart and the soldiers a gill of rum this day—

9th—Wednesday—Cool and agreeable—

10th—This morning a small frost—I received a letter from brother John dated 20th May 1782

11th—Friday—I rode out to see Lieut. Butler who was sick in the country—

12th—Satterday—A remarkable circumstance for this part of the country—no news—

13th—Sunday—Two deserters this day which say the refugees are all on board, and file down to the five fathoms hole they are bound for St. Augusteen—

14th—Monday—The officers drew a quart and the soldiers a gill of rum—I received a letter from brother Andrew dated Carlyle, July 21, 1782

15th **(October)**—Tuesday—Cool and pleasant—This day came to camp 44 of the North Carolina troops enlisted for 18 months and brought with them 150 British prisoners for exchange—I receive a letter from brother Andrew dated Carlyle, 6 September—

16th—Wednesday—Cool pleasant weather with frost—

17th—Thursday—I wrote a letter to brother Andrew—

18th—Friday—A verry severe frost—

19th—Satterday—Two diserters came in this morning—very cold, a severe white frost—I had a spell of the ague (chills) and fever—Two Hession diserters and a woman came to us this afternoon—

20th—Sunday—I mounted guard and unfortunately took verry sick, and was obliged to send to camp for relief. Mrs Middleton hearing of my illness sent me half a glass of wine and a little soop, I sent it back to her with my compliments that I could not take it. I received a letter from St. John Holliday—I was relieved at sun set and came home—

21st **(October)**—Monday—I took a vomit, after this I was something better—this is the tenth day without rice—I want potatoes and beans in place of it—

Total number of miles in No. 2—2071 miles   carried to No. 3

No. of Miles brought from last No. 2
2071 —

Tuesday 22 October 1782 —
This Day I had a Violent fever and pain
in my head & Bones — — —

Wednesday
23 I take Bark while the fever is off

Thursday
24 Four Deserters came in this Day —
I had no fever this Day, but weak —

Friday
25 four Hessian Deserters this morning —
no fever — a verry warm Day —
not one single mouthfull of meat in Camp

Saturday
26 a little Beef this Day — verry warm
Two Deserters which say the Hallifax
Fleet has arrived — — —

Sunday
27th a Corporal & six Deserters with
their Horses & Accutriments came in
this morning; one of them Deserted
from our line in May last —
Cloudy morning and threatens rain

Chapter Six: "Brought from Journal #2"

Number of miles brought from No. 2—2071

Tuesday 22 **October 1782**—This day I had a violent fever and pain in my head and bones—

23rd—Wednesday—I take bark while the fever is off—

24th—Thursday—Four deserters came in this day—I had no fever this day, but weak—

25th—Friday—Four Hession diserters this morning—no fever—a verry warm day—not one single mouthful of meat in camp—

26th—Satterday—A little beef this day—verry warm—Two diserters which say the Hallifax Fleet has arrived—

27th—Sunday—A corporal and six diserters with their horses and accoutrements came in this morning, one of them diserted from our line in May last—Cloudy morning and threatens rain which is much wanted at this time. Not a single mouthful of beef in camp this day—

28th—Monday—Fine cool morning—The officers got a little beef but the soldiers not a mouthful—poor times indeed—

29th—Tuesday—Cool and cloudy—No beef this day—Gen. Greene ordered an officer and sixteen men from each Brigade to impress provisions where they could find it—

30th—Wednesday—No beef yet nor any expectation of it. This day another incorporation of Regiments is on foot—I have some expectation of being one of the Retiring Officers which pleases me verry well—

31st—Thursday—Beef came into camp this afternoon at 5 o'clock—a wet night—

Friday 1st November 1782—This day I got a horse saddle from Doctor McDowell to carry me home.

2nd Nov—Satterday—This day I collected the number of deaths from our Line since the first of July untill this day which amounts to 106 soldiers. This day all the officers of our Brigade got a pair of boots each pair six dollars. The orders about the incorporation came out—

3rd—Sunday—This day the Field Officers were busy about settling the arrangements.

4th—Monday—This day the Officers and Noncommissioned Officers were fixed to Camp 7. A command of ours killed 3 negroes and took two prisoners—

5th—Tuesday—This day wet—the officers drew a quart of rum and a soldiers a gill—Gen. Greene still obstinate about letting us Retiring Officers go home before the 18 months men—

6th—Wednesday—This day every thing in confusion until the men were fixed to companys.

7th—Thursday—This day the Companys were formed, except the Light Infantry formed this afternoon. I dined at the Hospital on wild turkey—

8th **November**——This day Gen. Greene has granted us a waggon to carry our baggage, and forrage for our horses until we leave camp and promised to do everything in his power to make us comfortable.

9th—This day we got a waggon to carry our baggage—

10th—This day we settled our accounts with the clothier and the trifling articles which we received amounted to £7"15"3 sterling—

11th—This day each Retiring Officer waited on Gen. Greene and received three half IOUs—

12th—This day we left camp, crossed Bacon Bridge and lay at Captain Stevenson's, a violent fever this afternoon. 20 miles

13th—I was verry bad with the fever all this day, we went to Martins Tavern—18 miles

14th—Tolerable well this morning, halted at Eutaw Spring, a remarkable place in this part of the country, two capital actions have been fought here—the last was Gen. Greene and drove the British—We went to Laurences Ferry—27 miles

15th—Friday—Crossed the Ferry, here we met with a misfortune broke the tongue of our waggon, went from that to Dority Ritchisons, a damned?? cross woman—15 miles

16th—Went to Captain Shingleton's on the high hills of Santee. 14 miles—

"Brought from Journal #2"

17th—Went to Wheelers Tavern. 16 miles—
18th—A wet day went to Camdon. 16 miles—
19th—Went to Col. Rugely's—13 miles
20th—Went through wild wilderness and came to Daniel Usher's. 30 miles—
21st—Went to Mr. Stewards 25 miles—
22nd—Went to Captain Fifers 22 miles—
23rd—Went from Fifers to Salsbury 20 miles—
24th—Remained in Salsbury this day to refresh—
25th—Monday—Went from Salsbury, crossed the Yadkin River, went to Leathermans—25 miles—
26th—From the Leathermans to Salim, a Maravin Town in North Carolina—12 miles—
27th—From Salim to Carmichal's ford—24 miles—
28th—Crossed the Dan River came to Mr. Lemmons—22 miles—
29th—Crossed Mattrimony Creek and Smiths River, Caskade Creek and Sandy River,—now in Virginia Potsilvania County and remained at Mr. Ashtons—24 miles—
30th—From Mr. Ashtons to Mr. Corbins—21 miles—
Sunday **December 1**, **1782**—From Corbins to Patonsburgh here I had to take a vomit which almost killed me—8 miles—
2nd—Remained here this day and was verry sick and weak—
3rd—Now in Hallyfax County went to Bannisters Bridge 9 miles—
4th—Went from Bannisters Bridge and forded the Stanton River at Coles or Farques Ferry—18 miles—
5th—Charlott County, from Coles Ferry to little Roenoak Bridge, a small creek—22 miles—
6th—Friday—Prince Edward County, from Roenoak to Rights Ordinary 25 miles—
7th—Cumberland County, from Rights to Mr. Gentries—20 miles—
8th—Portann County, from Mr. Gentries to Cumberland Old Court House 8 miles—

9th—Monday—Went from the Court House to Col. Jameses where we were well treated—8 miles—

10th—Crossed the Jameses River at Carters Ferry—now in Lowes County went to Hunters Ordinary 18 miles—

11th—A wet day—went to Col. Bogesells Ordinary—22 miles—

12th—Orrange County, went to James Taylors where the doors were shut against us. Capt. Davis forced them open and a pretty piece of work ensued, went to his brothers and was well treated—18 miles—

13th—Crossed the Rapadan River and came to the place called Dutch Coopers—20 miles—

14th—Fauquere County, went from the Dutch Coopers, crossed the Rappahannock at Normans ford went to Morgans Ordinary 16 miles—

15th—From Morgans Ordinary to the Red House—24 miles—

16th—Prince William County, a verry snowy day, went to Moores Ordinary—12 miles—

17th—From Moores to Leesburgh where I remained with Mr. Beard all night—12 miles—

18th—Lowden County, went from Leesburgh to Nowlins Ferry on the Potoemack River, here we had to cut the ice half across the river and ford it, now in Maryland—16 miles—

19th—Frederick County, went to Frederick Town, here I took verry sick—I took out my baggage and remained this day—10 miles—

20th—Friday—From Frederick Town to Hagers Town—26 miles—

21st (December, 1782)—From Hagers Town Home—22 miles—

The number of miles which I have traveled since the 26 of May 1781 is—**2755 miles**—

Chapter Seven: History of the McDowell Family

According to my Aunt Alice's notes, she discovered some interesting information regarding the McDowell family (which also reaches back into my own family) history. Here are some of her most important findings:

"Pioneer—William McDowell

Among the first settlers was William McDowell, born in 1680. From what information we have, he was born in Scotland and went to Ireland during the uprising in Scotland. He married in Ireland to "Mary" —her family name is unknown.

William McDowell emigrated to Pennsylvania between 1714 and 1717 and settled in Chester County (at that time this included the present Chester, Lancaster, Cumberland, and Franklin Counties). About 1735 he moved to Conococheague Valley where he obtained a warrant for a plantation at the foot of Parnell's Knob, in what is now Peters Township, Franklin County. He lived in peace and comfort with his family until the beginning of the French and Indian War. After Braddock's defeat in 1735, and because of the Indian forays of 1755, he and his wife, Mary, fled to the Susquehanna where he died in 1759 and is buried in the graveyard by the Donegal Church. (It is a beautiful spot and we have pictures we took of the church and the large flat tombstone with the following inscription:

In Memory of
William McDowell
Late of Conococheague
Who was a Tender Parent
Careful Inftructor (f instead of s)
And an Example of Piety to a
Numerous Progeny
When the Settlement was obliged to fly
By the barberous Indian War
He deceased in these Parts
So was interred here
September 12, 1759
Age 77 Years

His wife died here in 1760 but we have not found where she was buried. As his sons reached manhood, they settled on farms in the neighborhood—some of which were occupied by decendents when we were there in 1955.

Their children were:

First Hand

*1. **John** (This is the ancestor of Arleen Wyche in New Iberia, Louisiana)*
He obtained a warrant for the land on which he built the mill—famous in frontier history—known as McDowell's Mill. It was built on the east side of the west branch of the Conococheague where is sitting the village of Bridgeport, now called Markes. It was built on a "Military Road" that was to furnish General Braddock with supplies. (There are some interesting stories about the raids and wars in this locality before the Revolution and how the Mill and the McDowell's were a part of it all. There is a stone bridge over the Conococheague near where the Mill was built)

2. **William** *(our Ancestor on separate page)*
3. Nathan

NATHAN MCDOWELL (born in 1722—died June 2, 1801), son of William and Mary McDowell, was a farmer and extensive land owner. He married Catherine Maxwell, daughter of William and Susanna Maxwell; they had issue:

1. MARY (born April 16, 1754—died January, 1828), married Jan. 31, 1775, John Holliday (born in 1740—died in 1818), son of James and Elizabeth (McDowell) Holliday (XI). He was the first Chief Burgess of the borough of Chambersburg; they had no issue.

2. WILLIAM, born May 9, 1756, died Jan. 30, 1782.

3. JAMES, born Aug. 14, 1759, died April 9, 1789.

4. JOHN, born Aug. 5, 1761, died Jan. 25, 1785.

5. SUSAN, born Feb. 12, 1764, died March 29, 1790.

6. NATHAN (XVIII).

7. MAXWELL (born Feb. 8, 1771—died in 1848) was a physician; he practiced at York, Pa., and

> was afterward at Baltimore, Md., where he died. He married Ruth Bayley (born in 1773), daughter of John and Hannah (Clark) Bayley. They had issue: John, Mary and Susanna.

4. James

> JAMES MCDOWELL (born in Chester county, in 1728—died Feb. 5, 1811), son of William and Mary McDowell, was a farmer near Mt. Parnell in Peters township. He was an accomplished surveyor. In 1769 he was arrested by Sheriff Homes, of Cumberland county, on suspicion of being concerned with his brother-in-law, Capt. James Smith, in the capture of Fort Bedford. He was an Associate Judge of Franklin county, 1791-1811. Judge McDowell married June, 1761, Jane Smith, a sister of Col. James Smith, the hero of "Border Life," and captain of the "Black Boys." They had issue: 9 children

There are seven more children in this family, I have some information on each one. All of the sons were elders in the Upper West Conococheague Presbyterian Church.
Captain[53] William McDowell, Wrote Revolutionary War Diaries
Son of William and Mary Maxwell McDowell"

---

[53] Promoted to rank of Captain on March 20, 1784. A copy of the certificate of promotion is included with these writings.

First Hand

First Lieut. William McDowell 1st Penn. Cont. Line, 2nd Infantry, Mar 22 1778; mustered out Nov. 3, 1783; died at St. Thomas, Franklin Co., June 19, 1835, aged 86. He was an original member of the Society of the Cincinnati. His membership in the Society was not continued. His tombstone states: "He was 7 years in Service of his County in the Struggle for Independence under Washington." He left a Journal of his Southern Campaign, an interesting document. He left 3 daus. Mary and Margaret unmar., and Jean Van Lear Davison; sons Wm; John; Thomas. He was entitled to 400 acres Donation land and in his will he divides his land between the sons and dau Jean. Land in Dist. 1, Butler Co., on Muddy Creek; a tract in the 3rd Dist., Mercer Co., No. 446, also a tract in Ohio as well as the Home place. To the daus he gave shares in the Bank of Columbia, Farmers

> *Bank of Md., and in the Bank of Alexandria, furniture, etc. A division between sons of "my wedding apparel, all my silver buttons, My Diploma, etc." The above Wm. McDowell was a son of Wm. McDowell and wife Mary Maxwell and a grandson of pioneer Wm. McDowell. He was mar. by Dr. John King to Elizabeth Van Lear, Feb. 8, 1786. Penna. Arch. 5th Ser. Vol. 2, p. 630*

In 1786 he married Elizabeth Van Lear and they had six children:
1. Mary—b. 1786
2. Jean Van Lear—b. 1790 Married Patrick Davidson (she is buried at Delavan, Il.)
3. William E. —b. 1792 Married Sallie Work [This is our ancestor and they had a son William that had a son John, grandfather of Alice Brants and James Maxwell Unland (my father)]
4. Margaret—b. 1793
5. John
6. Thomas

> *2. JOHN (born Feb. 11, 1751— died Dec. 22, 1820) was graduated at the College of Philadelphia (University of Pennsylvania) in 1771. He spoke the English oration at Commencement. He was a tutor in the college, 1769-82. Under the call of July 28, 1777, he served as a private in Capt. Samuel Patton's marching company. After leaving the university he went to Cambridge in Dorchester county, on the Eastern shore of Maryland, where he engaged in*

teaching and studied law. Among his pupils was Charles Goldsborough, afterward a representative in Congress and Government of Maryland. The teacher inspired his pupil with sentiments of esteem and affection so marked and so lasting that a life-long friendship resulted, and found expression in an interchange of letters covering a period of thirty-five years. Many of the Goldsborough letters were preserved by the recipient and are still in existence. The first of the series was written from Philadelphia Jan. 19, 1784, and it shows that Mr. McDowell had just come to the Bar of Dorchester county, Md., but was uncertain whether he would engage in practice at Cambridge. He does not seem to have fully made up his mind at the close of the year, for he was admitted to practice in the Franklin county courts at the first trial term in December, 1784. He finally returned to Cambridge and entered upon the practice there. Legal memoranda that that were preserved with The Goldsborough letters prove that he was in full practice in Dorchester in 1780. Among his clients were his friends, Charles Goldsborough and John Henry, the latter one of the first Senators in Congress from Maryland. In 1790 he was elected principal of St. John's College at Annapolis by a unanimous vote. He had previously filled the professorship of Mathematics in the college for a short time. He filled this office until 1806, when he resigned to become professor of Natural Philosophy in the University of Pennsylvania. McDowell Hall, in which the centennial anniversary of the college was celebrated in 1890, is the monument to his service in behalf of the institution. He was in Philadelphia only a few months when he was elected provost of the university. He resigned in 1810, because of ill health, but again performed the duties of the office for his successor, Dr. Andrews, to 1812. He subsequently returned to Annapolis and was again elected principal of St. John's, in 1815, but declined. His last years were spent at the home of his sister, Mrs. Maris, in Peters township, where he died. In his will he bequeathed his Latin, ???, Mathematical and Philosophical books to the University of Pennsylvania. He never married, but the Goldsborough letters show that he was on terms of the ??? intimacy with that distinguished Maryland family from his early manhood. He received the degree of LL. D. from his Alma Mater.

3. SUSAN (born in 1752—died May 1839) married Feb. 5, 1778, John Mar??, a physician of Talbot county, Maryland they had issue: James, who married Elizabeth Talbot, daughter of Major Jeremiah Talbot, a Revolutionary soldier, and had William, Jeremiah T. and Matilda Crawford; and William, Mary, Nancy, Janes and Margaret.

4. JAMES, born in 1754, died young.

5. MARY (born in 1756—died May 9, ???) married October, 1790, Dr. William Magaw (born in 1740—died May 1, 1829), son of William and Elizabeth Magaw. He was a distinguished surgeon of the Revolution. She was his second wife; they had no issue.

6. NATHAN (XIII).

7. ALEXANDER (XIV).

8. ANDREW (XV).

9. MARGARET (born in 1765—died ??? 17, 1853) married May 6, 1806, Mat?? Maris (born in German township, Philadelphia, May 19, 1747—died Oct. 9, 1811), a wealthy Baltimore shipping

merchant, who came to Peters township to live after his marriage; they had no issue.

10. AGNES, born August, 1767, died June 2, 1801?)

11. PATRICK (XVII??).

12. THOMAS (XV???).

First Hand

Information from a Page out of "American Revolutionary Soldiers" Book

PATRICK MAXWELL: Served as pvt., under Capt. Walter McKinnie, 1780-81-82. He was a brother of James Maxwell, Esq. He was married Oct. 19, 1769 to Hannah Whitehill, at Lancaster. Patrick died Sept. 14, 1786, his wife, May 18, 1805. They had 4 sons: Wm.: James; Patrick; John; 3 daus.: Rachael; Susanna; Elizabeth. John Davison mar. Rachel Maxwell, Apr. 16, 1793. Susanna Maxwell mar. James McClelland Dec. 29. 1802. Elizabeth Maxwell died prior to her mother. The will of Hannah Maxwell, widow of Patrick, dated and prob. 1805, bequeaths to dau. Rachel Davidson "my Silver cream pot; son Wm., my clock; son James large looking glass, Son Patrick silver table spoons; Son John a chest of drawers." Penna. Arch. 5th Ser. Vol. 6, p. 266, 298, 300, 305.

MAJOR WILLIAM MAXWELL: Provincial Service, appears with Col. Benjamin Chambers under "Officers of the Associated Regt., of Lancaster County, over the River Sasquehanna" 1747-48. Wm. Maxwell an early settler in the present Montgomery Twp., applied for land Nov. 12, 1745.

History of the McDowell Family

A Patent was granted by the Penns., Feb. 12, 1749, for land on Conococheague Creek; in Rath Mullen Twp. Lancaster Co., Penna. His neighbors were the widow Davis, Aaron Alexander's heirs, Thomas David, the Welsh Settlement and Philip David. The will of Major Wm. Maxwell was dated Oct. 10, 1772, and Church records show the death of Wm. Maxwell as Sept. 27, 1777. The death of Susanna as Dec. 30, 1781. He left to wife Susanna, 10 lbs., yearly household goods, riding horse and saddle, a cow "My Negro wench called Nell to my wife, after her death to son James. To son James that part of my Original Dwelling Plantation whereon I now live. To son Patrick that part whereon he now lives. Also to Patrick and James a small tract in the Barrens adj., Archbd., Irwin xx a tract in Virginia called Swanpons xx a tract in the Great Cove. To son Patrick the negro girl Chloe. TO son-in-law Wm. And Nathan McDowell my right and title to a tract of land at Augwick for which I have Warrants in their names. To sons-in-law George Brown and Wm. Reynolds that tract of land in Virginia near Sleepy Creek. To Wm. McDowell, aforesaid, I bequeath my coat and silver buttons, upon which buttons he is to get engraved my name, and also his own. To his wife Mary, I bequeath the negro girl Dina and to his son John (this is the father of Mary Maxwell McDowell) 10 lbs., out of my personal estate. To dau. Catherine McDowell, the negro child Fanny and to her son John 10 lbs. To dau. Ruth Reynolds the negro child Phillis and 10 lbs. To 2 grandaus., Susanna and Sarah Brown 1/3 part of the price of the tract of land their father sold for me to Phillip McGuire; residue to sons James and Patrick. Signed: Will Maxwell. It is probably that the Maxwells were buried in the John McClelland Graveyard. At least two stones were standing, in recent years, to the Maxwell, of a later generation. Penna. Arch. 2nd Ser. Vol. 2, p. 438, 439.

ALEXANDER MAXWELL: Sept. ye 23, 1777, Alexander Maxwell took the Oath of Fidelity before Hugh Martin, Esq., in Westmoreland Co., Penna. A list of 94 persons who subscribed is given by James Kinkead, Recorder. Alexander Maxwell served first in Cumb. Co., Militia, in the Cont. Line, later serving from Westmoreland Co., Penna. He appears first in 1772, as a communing member of the Presby. Church of Mercersburg. Thomas Maxwell in 1771. A Jean Maxwell, and John, compose a family in 1769. Penna. Arch. 2nd Ser. Vol. 3, p. 31. Penna. Arch. 5th Ser. Vol. 4, p. 298.

JAMES MAXWELL, CAPTAIN: Son of Major Wm. Maxwell, appears as an Ensign in the Provincial service. He was in Braddock's Expedition against Fort Duquesne; a Justice of the Peace for Cumb. County; a member of the Committee to erect the Court House and Jail; Govnr. Mifflin Appointed him Associate Judge of the Courts; in addition to above he gave service during 1780-81-82, with Captain Walter McKinnie. He died Dec. 10, 1807. He was an Attorney, wrote many of the early wills in his vicinity. To his nephew James Maxwell Reynolds; to his nephew Wm. M. Brown his riding horse, saddle and bridle; to nephew Wm. Maxwell his sword and pistols; to niece Eliza Maxwell a negroe girl; Pompey, Joe, black Grace and Mulato Grace to be set free. Penna Arch. 2nd Ser. Vol. 2, p. 484. Penna. Arch. 3rd Ser. Vol. 1, p. 178. Penna Arch. 5th Ser. Vol. 6, p. 266, 298, 300, 305.

First Hand

Certificate of Promotion to Captain

In Pursuance
Of an Act of
Congress
Of the Thirtieth Day of SEPTEMBER,
A.D. 1783,
William McDowell Esquire—
Is to Rank as a Captain — by Brevet,
In the ARMY of the UNITED STATES
of AMERICA.
GIVEN under my Hand
At Annapolis—the 20th
Day of March —1784
(Signed) Thomas Mifflin[54]
Recorded in the War Offices
(Unreadable Signature)

---

[54] Wikipedia contributors, "Thomas Mifflin," *Wikipedia, The Free Encyclopedia*, https://en.wikipedia.org/w/index.php?title=Thomas_Mifflin&oldid=987441428 (accessed November 9, 2020), "Thomas Mifflin (January 10, 1744 – January 20, 1800) was an American merchant, soldier, and politician from Philadelphia, Pennsylvania. He served in a variety of roles during and after the American Revolution, several of which qualify him to be counted among the Founding Fathers. He was the first Governor of Pennsylvania, serving from 1790 to 1799; he was also the last President of Pennsylvania, succeeding Benjamin Franklin and serving from 1788 until 1790." He was also "elected President of the Continental Congress in 1783."

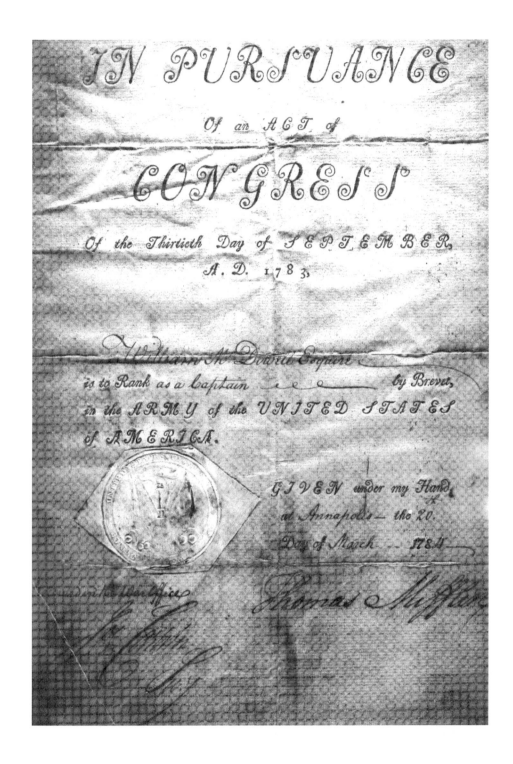

World War II Memoir:
As Written by James Maxwell Unland
1987/1988

The flag of America while fighting to defend freedom

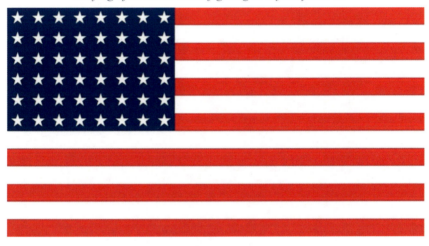

https://commons.wikimedia.org/w/index.php?title=File:Flag_of_the_United_States_(1912-1959).svg&oldid=429636918 *U.S. Flag with 48 stars. In use for 47 years from July 4, 1912 to July 3, 1959.*

Lt. James Maxwell Unland (circa 1944)

Chapter Eight: World War II Memoir of James M. Unland

This is the beginning of the memoirs of James Maxwell Unland from the period August, 1939 through World War II. I am doing this at the request of my son, John Logan Unland, and especially hope that my grandsons, Logan Smith Unland and Tyler Crawford Unland (and any other grandchildren who may be forthcoming), will read and hopefully appreciate those trying days when our country joined with other allies to rid the world of Nazi-ism and the scourge of the Imperial Japanese.

My story begins in late August, 1939 when my mother, Rachel McDowell Unland, and my father, J. Logan Unland, and I were returning to Pekin, Illinois from California. We had taken about a month's trip in our Chevrolet prompted by a convention of the Aetna Life Insurance Co., which was held at The Broadmoor in Colorado Springs. Following the convention, we motored to California visiting relatives in Pasadena and the McNaughtons in San Diego. We also visited the World's Fair in San Francisco and were returning through the desert the night of August 31st when we heard the ominous news that Hitler had invaded Poland, which signaled the beginning of WW II. I was 17 and just entering the University of Illinois as a freshman.

Although we were amazed and later apprehensive that this meant trouble for our country, none of us that night in August felt any immediate danger for America or us personally.

And so, off to college I went. It was mandatory that each entering freshman enroll in what was called the Reserved Officers Training Corp (ROTC). I enrolled in the Cavalry as I thought it would be a good way to learn how to ride a horse. Little did I know that the so-called horses were four-legged creatures which had been ridden incessantly until they had no feeling in their mouths…just like leather. And, they were ornery…real ornery. Nevertheless, that was the way it was and so I struggled along and began to enjoy the experience in my sophomore year and worked for good grades and reports so that I would be eligible for Advanced ROTC my junior year. Two years of military training was all that was required, but if you really felt so inclined you could continue during the junior and senior years and graduate as a 2nd Lieutenant in the Reserves.

And so, in the fall of 1941, I entered my junior year and was admitted into the Advanced class in the Cavalry. My, we did look sharp in our cavalry twill breeches, full-length leather boots, spurs, olive green jackets and officers cap. The training became increasingly difficult, complete with long rides in the country, jumping, refined movements of the entire platoons, retreat on Friday afternoons.

One day I was on a particularly stubborn mount and we were jumping, but this nag decided to stop abruptly before the jump and over I went into a pile of mud. Fortunately, the mud cushioned the shock and all I got was plenty muddy. I had a "coke date" with Judy (my future wife) and she was hilarious. I should say that a "coke date" meant Coca-Cola…not cocaine; which was unheard of in those days.

And so, in the fall of 1941 it became obvious to all of us that somewhere, somehow, war was inevitable and that sometime in the future there would be trouble. Some of my fraternity brothers were already enlisting in either the Navy or the Air Corp (later to be known as the Air Force). But most of us just plugged along and hoped for the best…anxious to complete our college education and get on with our lives, all the while hoping that some miracle would prevent our entering the service under wartime conditions.

Then came December 7th, 1941. 'Twas a Sunday. I was in the Alpha Tau Omega fraternity house in the afternoon when word came through that Pearl Harbor had been bombed. Please remember we had no television but depended solely on the radio for our quick news, and it was beginning to hit the air waves fast and furiously.

Within a few minutes all the brothers were gathered in the front room listening and speculating on what was going on in that faraway place in Hawaii, which was just a blip on the map.

Then, later in the evening, the rumor spread over the airwaves that San Francisco had been bombed and we all (in semi panic) stood on the front porch of 1101 W. Pennsylvania Avenue scanning the sky to see if we could pick up the enemy bombers. The entire populace of the country was horrified and scared. I remember one of the brothers by the name of Jefferson Davis Giller (later to become a law partner in a prestigious law firm in Houston) came out on the front porch in full military regalia and somewhere he'd filched a sword and was waving it around like a Wildman. A hilarious sight and it took the seriousness of the situation away for a spell at least.

From this "infamous" day (as described by President Franklin Roosevelt[55]), we all again reorganized our lives and took up where we'd left off on December 7th. This act of war prompted more enlistments and the draft was beginning to also take its toll on the members of the fraternity. Since I had opted to take Advanced ROTC, it appeared that I'd be able to finish my education and get my degree in the spring of 1943. And, as it turned out, that's what happened.

While so many young men (and women) became actively involved in the war, my life went blithely along like nothing was changed. I began dating Judy Johnston at the Chi Omega sorority in the spring of 1942, and the summer of '42 was great because I had been chosen Rushing Chairman, presented with a check for $250 (a huge sum then) to cover my expenses and told to go out and interview possible candidates as pledges for the fall of 1942. What a summer!

My close friend, Warren Thal (now deceased) from Elmhurst had been given a new black Ford convertible for graduation and

---

[55] Wikipedia contributors, "Franklin D. Roosevelt," *Wikipedia, The Free Encyclopedia*, https://en.wikipedia.org/w/index.php?title=Franklin_D._Roosevelt&oldid=975960079 (accessed September 1, 2020). "Franklin Delano Roosevelt (January 30, 1882 – April 12, 1945), often referred to by his initials FDR, was an American politician who served as the 32nd President of the United States from 1933 until his death in 1945. A member of the Democratic Party, he won a record four presidential elections and became a central figure in world events during the first half of the 20th century. Roosevelt directed the federal government during most of the Great Depression, implementing his New Deal domestic agenda in response to the worst economic crisis in U.S. history. As a dominant leader of his party, he built the New Deal Coalition, which realigned American politics into the Fifth Party System and defined modern liberalism in the United States throughout the middle third of the 20th century. His third and fourth terms were dominated by World War II, which ended shortly after he died in office."

he had enlisted in the Navy so was unable to use it and loaned it to me while I was recruiting in the Chicago area. What a deal! I became most adept at driving up the Outer Drive which was brand new and all through the suburbs of Wilmette, Glencoe, Winnetka…you name it…I was there.

I remember, one night, listening to Billie Holiday in the Sherman Hotel until dawn as she warbled to the accompaniment of Red Allen. Man…those were great times and I was just 20 years old.

Then back to school for my senior year and it seemed like every night was "party night" as some fraternity brother or close friend was either leaving for the military or had just returned with his wings or bars or whatever…having completed his initial training. So, in addition to attending classes and riding in the cavalry classes twice a week, it was partying to the hilt.

To further add "fuel to the fire," I was taking 22 hours in my final semester! Seems some dizzy advisor got me in an untenable situation. I thought I'd be carrying about 12 hours and could "coast in," but instead needed 22 to graduate; which meant going to class from 8 to 4 every day.

Then along comes Friday afternoon and Retreat is compulsory. It means getting into uniform, charging over to the Armory for the weekly ceremony…charging back to the ATO house, quickly changing into civilian clothes and rushing to the train for Chicago and a weekend with Judy, who had graduated in January and was all settled in at 1420 Lincoln Park West in an apartment with two sorority sisters. I'd leave Chicago on the late train Sunday night arriving back in Champaign about 1 AM, plop into bed and begin the week all over again. It was indeed a fast track.

Suddenly, it's time to graduate. I was engaged to Judy and we had set June 3rd as our wedding date…The year is now 1943. The wedding day was typically hot and muggy, the fraternity brothers were on their good behavior and the Chi Omega sisters sang their Sweetheart Song at the wedding, which was held in the living room of Chi Omega sorority on Green Street. Both sets of parents thought we were crazy getting married knowing that I'd soon be on active duty, but we did anyway. Judy's mother was 7 months pregnant with Sue Ellen, who came into the world on August 5th.

Following the wedding came commencement, then back to Pekin, Illinois (our hometown) awaiting orders to report to active duty. During the interim, George Stolley put me to work making cardboard boxes at Standard Brands, but it didn't last long as orders came for me to report to Camp Grant (near Rockford, Illinois).

First Hand

His "Orders to Active Duty" were effective as of July 21, 1943 and he had to report on that date to Camp Grant, Illinois for "physical examination and processing."

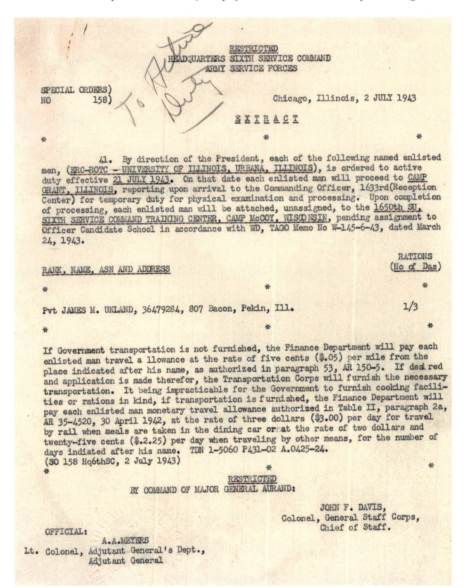

World War II Memoir of James M. Unland

After he graduated from Officer Candidate School on January 21, 1944, my father received this official appointment letter from the "War Department" promoting him to 2nd Lieutenant.

MAL 4341

S—7752

WAR DEPARTMENT
THE ADJUTANT GENERAL'S OFFICE
WASHINGTON

IN REPLY REFER TO: AG 201 Unland, James Maxwell
(25 Mar 43)PR-A

SUBJECT: Appointment under Section 37, National Defense Act, as amended.

Graduation Date: 21 January 1944

Through: The Commandant,
The Infantry School,
Fort Benning, Georgia.

A O-540236
R.O.T.C.

To: Mr. James Maxwell Unland,
807 Bacon Street,
Pekin, Illinois.

(Appointed 2nd Lt. Inf-Res)

1. By direction of the President, you are appointed and commissioned in the Army of the United States, effective this date, in the grade and section shown in address above. Your serial number is shown after A above.

2. You will not perform the duties of an officer under this appointment until specifically called to active duty by competent orders.

3. There is inclosed herewith a form for oath of office, which you are requested to execute and return promptly to the agency from which it was received by you. The execution and return of the required oath of office constitute an acceptance of your appointment. No other evidence of acceptance is required.

4. This letter should be retained by you as evidence of your appointment as no commissions will be issued during the war.

5. Waiver is granted for underweight, height 72 inches, weight 138 pounds, on physical examination report dated 19 October 1943, made at Dispensary, 3rd Stud. Tng. Regt., Fort Benning, Georgia.

Inclosure:
Form for oath of office.

By order of the Secretary of War:

Copy for: C.G., Army Ground Forces.
C.G., Fourth Service Command.
C.G., Sixth Service Command.
P.M.S.& T., University of Illinois,
Champaign, Illinois.

Major General,
The Adjutant General.

First Hand

So, I did, and was sent to Camp McCoy, Wisconsin, where I joined my other Illinois ROTC comrades for some pre-OCS (Officers Candidate School) training.

It was nice and cool in Wisconsin and the ardors of training weren't too severe, but the honeymoon was soon over as we boarded a troop train for Fort Benning, Georgia. We went from ideal climate to the extreme opposite in 48 hours and were thrown into some dinky huts called barracks.

My father kept this photo because it was given to him by a buddy of his at OCS.

We're now in late July, 1943. Judy is home living with my parents in Pekin trying to figure out how to get to Columbus, Georgia (nearest town to Ft. Benning), and I'm down in the hot hell hole trying to figure out how to stay alive in the unbearable Georgia summer heat. Temperatures ranged around 100 degrees daily and not much cooler at night.

We were stacked into temporary barracks like sardines and it was almost too hot to sleep at night, even though we were physically exhausted. The principal activity was the 20-mile hike with full gear (weight about 50 lbs). These marches would begin before daylight in order to take advantage of the cooler (?) air and we'd be back in our area about noon, drenched from sweat. Frequently I'd just walk in the shower with all clothes on as they were soaked anyway in an attempt to cool off.

To say that the training was arduous is an understatement. My old friend Sam Young and I would meander over to the officers' mess and my fraternity brother Charlie Caudle would sneak us a steak dinner out the back door and some cold beer. Those were life-saving gestures on his part.

After several weeks of this inhumane treatment (at least we thought so), we finally got into an Officers Candidate School (OCS) class…#316, and we would be in this training for 16 weeks. Half of the class would "wash out" before graduation. Luckily, I was not one of them. OCS was really a breeze after the preliminary training and we had a company commander who was rather lenient, so life was bearable. And Judy decided she was coming to be with me and fortunately found a bedroom in a private home and a job teaching school.

Most weekends I was able to join her at least for Saturday afternoon until Sunday evening. We had some great Saturday night parties with our buddies. A big evening were drinks and dinner (huge steaks and all the trimmings) and the tab for the two of us would be less than $10.00. Of course, my monthly pay was $32.00 and Judy was probably making $150.00. We had a delightful Thanksgiving and Christmas dinner at the base, so all in all OCS was indeed tolerable.

And finally, graduation day came and I was now a 2nd Lieutenant in the Infantry, sometimes referred to as a "shavetail" and/or "cannon fodder." (And in June of 1944, I got a raise to $140.00 per month)

First Hand

This document states that my father's monthly pay in the amount of $140.00 is to be deposited to the credit of my mother (Judith Unland) beginning June 1, 1944, for an indefinite number of months, until discontinued.

[Authorization for Allotment of Pay form]

It is now the middle of January, 1944 and we're on the train returning to Illinois for a ten-day furlough. The trains were overcrowded. Sam Young generously gave us his berth (I couldn't get one) so we could get some sleep, so we both climbed in the lower berth and pretty soon the conductor came by raising hell because I had a woman in bed with me, so I had to pay him again for the berth…naturally he pocketed the money.

'Twas good to see home again and we basked in the luxury of Rachel Unland's cooking and all the friends we could muster to spend a moment with. I remember that Jim Welch and Jean Jacobs were with us one night and I gave them a big sales pitch on getting married, which they subsequently did, and within a year had twins.

Back on the train to Columbia, South Carolina, and report to the 87th Infantry Division. I drew a rifle company with a real mean character as the company commander and Sam Young (we're still together!) drew Cannon Company. Best part of his duty is the abundance of jeeps for the officers. Not many in a rifle company. Sam spent most of his time riding around while I was walking.

Life in Columbia, S.C. was pleasant. Our good friends Claude and Jane Spilman shared a large ranch house with us and while we had our normal differences, most of the time was compatible. Two freshly married women in the kitchen together can be somewhat "sticky," but all in all it worked out well.

Warren and Jane Malik came down for a weekend from Ft. Bragg. Dixie Howell popped in one night. My folks drove a car down for us, which was indeed a fantastic gesture. Spring was in the air and South Carolina can be beautiful that time of year. Training was not bad and life was good.

May 9th came along and I traipsed downtown to buy Judy a birthday present, and I remember it was a white purse…cost $6.00 and headed home for our birthday party, shared by the Spilman's. Claude (more commonly known as Baldy) wasn't home yet, so Jane, Judy, and I sat down with a little libation awaiting his entry and pretty soon in he came with a long face. Seems just as he was leaving both his and my orders came in to report to Ft. Meade, Maryland for overseas duty in a week. Well, there was one birthday party that flopped fast. I don't think a bite was eaten by anyone that night.

Chapter Nine: Off to Join the War

And so, off to Baltimore we went in our Ford. 'Twas a sad week but we made the most of it and even attended the Preakness. Abe Goodman was with us a day or two, but eventually it was time for the tearful good-bye as Baldy and I reported to Ft. Meade. Judy and Jane headed for Indianapolis and Pekin. Took them a week to drive home!

After a few days picking up equipment and transferring to the Boston area, we boarded ship. Seems to me it was in the Boston area that I took a train to New Haven and had a big bash with Woody and Bob Piggott. But these days were numbered and now we're on a fast ship ready to pull out of Boston Harbor. The morning of June 6, 1944, as we were heading out of the harbor, the church bells were ringing all over town. It was D-Day in Europe and the Allies were storming the beaches of Normandy. 'Twas indeed eerie, looking back from the stern of the ship at the city of Boston, hearing the church bells tolling and knowing we were indeed headed for something other than a "Sunday School picnic."

First Hand

Every soldier was required to execute a Last Will and Testament before leaving the United States to go overseas for any type of deployment and my father was no different. This is a copy of his will that I found amongst many other items of memorabilia. (transcription following)

LAST WILL AND TESTAMENT

I, James M. Unland, a legal resident of Perkin, Illinois, United States of America, now in the active military service as a Lieutenant, (Army serial No. 0540836), in the Army of the United States, do hereby make, publish and declare this instrument as my last WILL and TESTAMENT, in manner following, that is to say:

1. I hereby cancel, annul, and revoke all wills and codicils by me at any time heretofore made;

2. I hereby give, devise, and bequeath to Judith Johnston Unland, now residing in Morton, Illinois, United States of America, all my estate and all of the property of which I may die seized and possessed, and to which I may be entitled at the time of my decease, of whatsoever kind and nature, and wheresoever it may be situated, be it real, personal, or mixed, absolutely;

3. I hereby nominate, constitute, and appoint Judith Johnston Unland, of Morton, Illinois United States of America, as my executrix and request that she be permitted to serve without bond or whithout surety thereon;

4. I hereby authorize and empower my executrix in her absolute discretion to sell, exchange, convey, transfer, assign, mortgage, pledge, invest or reinvest the whole or any part of my real or personal estate.

IN WITNESS WHEREOF, I have hereunto set my hand and seal to this my last WILL and TESTAMENT, at Fort George G. Meade, Maryland, this 25th day of May 1944.

James M. Unland (SEAL)
JAMES M. UNLAND
2ND LT. INFANTRY,

Signed, sealed, published, and declared by the above-named testator, James M. Unland, to be his last WILL and TESTAMENT in the presence of all of us at one time, and at the same time we, at his request and in his presence and in the presence of each other, have hereunto subscribed our names as witnesses, and do hereby attest to the sound and disposing mind of said testator and to the performance of the aforesaid acts of execution at Fort George G. Meade, Maryland, this 25th Day of May, 1944.

WITNESSES   PERMANENT ADDRESSES

_____   _____
(Signature)   (Street, town, State)

_____
(Name printed or typed)

Off to Join the War

"LAST WILL AND TESTAMENT

I, James M. Unland, a legal resident of Perkin, (sic) Illinois, United States of America, now in the active military service as a Lieutenant, (Army serial No. 0540236), in the Army of the United States, do hereby make, publish and declare this instrument as my last WILL and TESTAMENT, in manner following, that is to say:

1. I hereby cancel, annul, and revoke all wills and codicils by me at any time heretofore made;

2. I hereby give, devise, and bequeath to Judith Johnston Unland, now residing in Morton, Illinois, United States of America, all my estate and all of the property of which I may die seized and possessed, and to which I may be entitled at the time of my decease, of whatsoever kind and nature, and wheresoever it may be situated, be it real, personal, or mixed, absolutely;

3. I hereby nominate, constitute, and appoint Judith Johnston Unland, of Morton, Illinois United States of America, as my executrix and request that she be permitted to serve without bond or whithout (sic) surety thereon;

4. I hereby authorize and empower my executrix in her absolute discretion to sell, exchange, convey, transfer, assign, mortgage, pledge, invest or reinvest the whole or any part of my real or personal estate.

IN WITNESS WHEREOF, I have hereunto set my hand and seal to this my last WILL and TESTAMENT, at Fort George G. Meade, Maryland, this 25th Day of May 1944.

Signature of James M. Unland (SEAL) 2ND LT. INFANTRY"

My buddy, O.T. Willrich, and I were in charge of 200 enlisted men on board and that took plenty of our time…just making sure they didn't jump overboard or pull some dumb stunt. As it worked out, they were a good bunch and caused us precious little trouble.

One of my fond memories concerned Baldy. Whiskey was at a premium in England and so we bought several fifths each and packed them in our duffle bags to sell at a profit upon landing. I can see Baldy now, meticulously wrapping each fifth so that it would not break. These duffle bags were heavy and we had to lug them up the gangplank and down those narrow steep stairways until finally we'd reach our berth. As Baldy slung his to the floor from his shoulder there came a loud "clink." Sure enough, one of his fifths had broken and completely saturated most of his clothing contained therein. I don't think I've ever laughed so hard. The area smelled of bourbon for days.

When I think of what we took overseas to fight a war, I become hilarious. Do you know each officer, in addition to a huge duffle bag filled with every conceivable piece of equipment, also had a foot locker? Unbelievable. I think my foot locker finally caught up with me about 4 months after entering combat…all filled with dress pink trousers, officers dress coat, shirts, hat…you name it. Incidentally, the locker is still in the house at 622 Washington Street, Pekin, above the garage. It's seen a lot of miles.

Off to Join the War

As in the previous diary where Lt. McDowell lists the provisions provided to him during the Revolutionary War, here is my father's list of "Clothing & Personal Equipment" that the Army provided to him prior to his deployment overseas.

HEADQUARTERS 87TH INFANTRY DIVISION
Fort Jackson, South Carolina

16 April 1944

MEMORANDUM)
:
TO   ) CO, _____

1. The infantry officers designated for shipment to AGF Replacement Depot No. 1, Ft George G. Meade, Md., will be equipped as follows:

Clothing & Personal Equipment

a. The following list of items of clothing and equipment indicates the minimum required and those items which are optional for officers to procure prior to arrival at Army Ground Force depots for overseas shipment.

Item	Required	Purchase Optional
Belt, cloth, O's, ea	1	
Belt, web waist, ea	1	
Book, memorandum, pocket, w/pencil, ea	1	
Brush, clothes, ea		1
Brush, hair, ea		1
Brush, shaving, ea		1
Brush, shoe, ea		1
Brush, tooth, ea		1
Cap, garrison, O's, o. d., ea	1	
Cap, garrison, cotton, khaki, ea	1	
Coat, tropical worsted, ea		1
Coat, wool, service, ea	1	
Comb, ea	1	
Drawers, cotton, shorts, ea	3	
Drawers, wool, ea	2	
Gloves, chamois colored leather, pr	1	
Handkerchiefs, cotton, ea	6	
Insignia, cap, O's ea	1	
Insignia, collar, O's (Arm or service) pr	2	
Insignia, collar, O's, "US", pr	2	
Insignia, grade, ea	4	
Jacket, field, ea	1	
Knife, pocket, ea		1
Laces, shoes, extra, pr	1	
Leggings, canvas, dismounted o.d., pr	1	
Mirror, ea		1
Necktie, cotton, mohair, o.d., ea	1	1
Overcoat, o.d., O's, ea	1	
or		
Overcoat, short, O's, ea	1	
or		
Overcoat, field, long, ea	1	
(Fabric-cotton, cloth, wind resistant and water repellent peplin or twill, 5-oz. Color - olive drab shade No. 2).		
Pajamas, pr		2
Pen, fountain, ea		1
Raincoat, ea	1	
Razor, ea	1	
Shirt, cotton, khaki, ea	3	
Shirt, wool, o. d., ea	2	
Shoes, Army, russet, pr	2	
Slippers, or gymnasium shoes, pr		1
Soap, hand, ea	1	
Socks, cotton, tan, pr	3	
Socks, wool light or wool heavy, pr	3	
Towel, bath, ea	2	
Towel, face, ea	2	2
Gloves, wool, o. d., pr	1	

- 1 -

First Hand

Our ship was named the SS LeJune, and because of its speed, did not go with a convoy but sailed solo to Liverpool via the North Atlantic; which even in June is cold. Food was good and we amused ourselves with card games, listening to the progress of the invasion, writing letters and spending time on deck. Of course, no smoking allowed on deck after dark. Reason for travel far north of England was to escape the U-boats which stalked the Atlantic like a pack of wolves. I think we arrived in Liverpool about 7 days after leaving Boston; which wasn't bad (took twice as long coming home in a convoy).

So, there is Liverpool, and even from aboard ship you can see the damage resulting from the pounding of the Luftwaffe as they attempted to destroy that lovely city in the summer of 1940…four years prior. Off the ship into 2 1/2 ton trucks and off to a "staging area"…a tent city serving as temporary quarters prior to shipping off to France.

It's now about June 18th and again we train with lots of marches to keep in shape. I remember one requirement was wearing our gas masks wherever we went. Everyone was paranoid about the Germans dropping poison gas bombs (which they did not do) and if you were caught without your gas mask you were in deep trouble.

I found Chuck Power (fraternity brother), who was flying C-43 (cargo plane) and managed to get over to his unit a couple of times. One time he took me up in one of those old twin engine planes and scared me to death as he flew at tree top height around the countryside. He hadn't changed a bit…was always the wildest one in the fraternity.

On weekends we'd head for London, although prohibited legally by the Commanding Officer so we were Absent Without Leave (AWOL). It meant that if we got killed by a "buzz bomb," Judy would not collect any government insurance…worth $10,000. We went anyway and had some great parties, particularly with the Air Force officers who were usually glad to share their booze with the Infantry.

Off to Join the War

We'd stay at the Red Cross who had top floors of bunks for guys like us. John O'Brien and I were on the top floor one night and the next morning looked out and saw a large hole up the street where a bomb had dropped that night. That was our last night in London. The town was constantly partying…everybody who had not yet gone to France was in a celebrating mood and it was New Year's Eve every night.

I was with Chuck Power one night when Baldy called and told me we were shipping out and to get back fast…which I did. Another hair-raising ride with Power in a jeep…but I made it, got my gear together and in the middle of night we headed for the southern coast of England aboard a train and within a few hours were on board an LST on our way across the channel. Pitch dark and rough…man it was rough, but somehow, I did not get seasick.

An LST is not a big ship. Not much on it except the necessary equipment including machine guns, but no heavy guns. Obviously their main mission was to transport troops…Landing Ship Troops; and so it wasn't like cruising on the Queen Elizabeth…we were cramped in like sardines and tossed around the Channel like a tin can, but eventually daylight appeared and soon we were approaching Utah Beach, one of the two landing areas

Bailey Bridge Photo Credit: https://commons.wikimedia.org/w/index.php?title=File:PontBailey.jpg&oldid=208659456

during the invasion on June 6th. Since it is now some six weeks after the invasion, most of the litter on the beach had been cleared but there was still plenty of evidence that more than a

"Sunday School picnic" had transpired. Bailey bridges[56] and temporary docks had been erected by the engineers so foot soldiers plus the artillery and tanks could be brought ashore.

It's impossible even today for me to have any conception as to the amount of equipment and material which was unloaded and brought ashore in Europe during those eleven months from June, 1944 to V-E Day[57], May 8, 1945.

The time finally came for us to debark and head for the hill to the trucks which would take us to our units. O'Brien, Willrich, and I were assigned to the 35th Infantry Division under the command of General Baade. This was the old Kansan-Nebraska National Guard division who's claim to fame was that Harry Truman had been a Captain in the Field Artillery with this unit in World War I.

They had landed about two weeks after D-Day and had experienced nothing but this hedgerow fighting since that time. Their casualties had been high (as had all divisions), so obviously they needed plenty of replacements.

The trucks took us first to division headquarters where we were greeted by one of the

Hedgerow photo by John & Linda Unland

---

[56] Wikipedia contributors, "Bailey bridge," *Wikipedia, The Free Encyclopedia*, https://en.wikipedia.org/w/index.php?title=Bailey_bridge&oldid=960325349 (accessed June 18, 2020), "...a portable, pre-fabricated, truss bridge...developed in 1940-1941 by the British for military use during the Second World War...has the advantages of requiring no special tools or heavy equipment to assemble. The wood and steel bridge elements were small and light enough to be carried in trucks and lifted into place by hand, without the use of a crane. The bridges were strong enough to carry tanks."

[57] Wikipedia contributors, "Victory in Europe Day," *Wikipedia, The Free Encyclopedia*, https://en.wikipedia.org/w/index.php?title=Victory_in_Europe_Day&oldid=979761274 (accessed October 30, 2020), "Victory in Europe Day is the day celebrating the formal acceptance by the Allies of World War II of Germany's unconditional surrender of its armed forces on Tuesday, 8 May 1945, marking the end of World War II in Europe. Several countries observe public holidays on the day each year, also called Victory Over Fascism Day, Liberation Day or Victory Day. In the UK it is often abbreviated to VE Day, or V-E Day in the US, a term which existed as early as September 1944, in anticipation of victory."

staff and given a description of the fighting which they had encountered. It wasn't a pleasant description. Following that we were assigned to a regiment. Each division had three regiments and the three of us were assigned to the 320th Infantry under command of Col. Byrne. He personally greeted us and gave us his version of the dilemma the army found itself in, namely that nobody was going anywhere due to the terrain and the fact that the Germans had every square foot of hedgerows zeroed in with their deadly 88's and life was not very funny. He wished us luck and sent us on our way to our battalion.

The three of us were assigned to the 2nd battalion…Willrich to G company (a rifle company), O'Brien to H company (heavy weapons…they supported the other three rifle companies in the battalion with 50 caliber machine guns and 80 millimeter mortars), and I was assigned to F company, also a rifle company.

Each infantry battalion consisted of 3 rifle companies. Each rifle company had 4 platoons. Each platoon had 3 squads consisting of 12 men in a squad, so each company had 144 men—a platoon commanded by either a 2nd or 1st Lieutenant. Company commanded by a Captain. Battalion commanded by a Lt. Colonel. Each battalion

U.S. ARMY FIELD STRUCTURE:

TEAM: Four soldiers led by a Sergeant or Corporal

SQUAD/SECTION: Two Teams of soldiers led by a Staff Sergeant

PLATOON: Two to three Squads (up to 36 soldiers) led by a 1st or 2nd Lieutenant

COMPANY/BATTERY/TROOP: Three to four Platoons (up to 200 soldiers) commanded by a Captain

BATTALION/SQUADRON: Four to six Companies (up to 1,000 soldiers) commanded by a Lt. Colonel

BRIGADE/REGIMENT/GROUP: Two to three Battalions (3,000 to 5,000 soldiers) commanded by a Colonel

DIVISION: Three to four Brigades (10,000 to 15,000 soldiers) commanded by a Major General

CORPS: Two to five Divisions (20,000 to 45,000 soldiers) commanded by a Lieutenant General

FIELD ARMY: Two or more Corps or more than four Divisions (up to 90,000 soldiers) commanded by a General Lieutenant General

Source: https://en.wikipedia.org/w/index.php?title=United_States_Armed_Forces&oldid=985933253

also had a staff who followed the commanding officer—supported the battalion with intelligence, supplies, etc.

It certainly became apparent that everybody was in a sour mood and scared. Frustration was rampant because this was not the kind of war the Infantry had been trained for. Our mission was to attack, take over, clean up and advance again. We were to be supported by artillery and tanks. But nobody in the Infantry had geared up for this kind of terrain which consisted of 6 to 8 feet dirt hedgerows, dating back to the invasion of the Normans…this is how they divided their land. And the narrow dirt roads were used by oxen then horses then jitney trucks to haul the produce from the farm to market and the market consisted of small towns and villages scattered throughout Normandy.

One such town which became famous (or infamous, depending on our point of view) was a focal point because of its strategic road network leading out of town from several directions known as St. Lo. The Germans held all the high ground surrounding the town and they controlled the road networks which eventually led to flat ground and they were determined not to give up St. Lo. So, the entire 1st Army consisting of several divisions was bogged down until, somehow, we could break out of this area.

So, as I reported to my company commander at F company, it was obvious that nobody was having any fun. It was a dour bunch of officers and enlisted men who were present. And of course, they had all lost some of their buddies, not the least of which was a very popular platoon leader, who I was to replace. I was introduced to the platoon sergeant, a cocky Irishman from Chicago by the name of Sweeney and I could sense that he was less than impressed with this skinny kid who had been sent to replace his former platoon leader.

He took me around and introduced me to the squad leaders and the platoon guide. Each rifle platoon had three squads of 12 men each and their immediate boss was a sergeant known as a squad leader. Actually, the squad leader's job was among the toughest in the Infantry because he had 12 men directly under his command, which is more than anybody else had…for example, the Division commander had 3 regimental commanders, the regimental commander had 3 battalion commanders, the battalion commander had 4 company commanders, the company commander had 4 platoon leaders, and the platoon leader (me) had 3 squad leaders; but that poor ole squad leader had 12 guys he had to corral around and be responsible for…one tough task.

Well, by now it's 10:00 PM and almost dark. I'm to bunk with the platoon guide who's a great kid from Anderson, Indiana. He takes me "under his wing" and briefs me on the hazards of life in the infantry as applied to the hedgerow country. Nothing I hear makes me feel any better as it's all rather gory with lots of examples of how you can get your leg blown off by a land mine, how the '88's come in with a vengeance and it's usually too late to duck after hearing them, and all sorts of cheerful items including how my predecessor got killed. With that we curl down in the foxhole for a lovely night's sleep, interrupted from time to time by artillery fire, mortar fire and other dandy sounds. However, I was so tired I don't think it really bothered me. One great thing about cumulative fatigue…it does finally take over and out you go.

Next morning, Sunday, July 16th, was bright and clear and warm. We were in woolens and believe me those shirts and pants get hot when the temperature rises in the summertime in sunny France. No need for a field jacket, so I just left it on top of our foxhole. Orders came down that all platoon leaders were to meet with the Company Commander at 1400 (2:00 PM for you non-military readers). This meant snaking my way over a couple of hedgerows, trying not to bring attention to the German artillery observers. Guess I didn't do a very good job 'cause within seconds in came the '88's. Fortunately, nobody got hurt except my jacket which I had left on top of the foxhole. It was in shreds. So much for that piece of equipment.

But, back to the meeting of the platoon leaders. Being the "new boy" I was introduced to the other Lt's and you could immediately sense the feeling that I was indeed a greenhorn. They all looked like they'd been through plenty, especially the C.O. He was irritable and edgy and gave us the orders which were to get ready for a night march to a new position. So, we packed our gear and when it was pitch black, about midnight, headed up one of those sunken roads which had already been cleared of land mines and booby traps. The Germans were pros at laying mines…of course they had plenty of time to prepare for this invasion and they did their job well.

    I remember that we finally got to our new position, which was just another hedgerow, and were digging in when we heard this big explosion on the road we had just vacated. A jeep had hit a mine (which the sappers had missed, apparently) and parts of that jeep landed all around us. There wasn't enough left of the driver or passenger to identify them. Well, by now I'd come to realize this was a serious business and no tellin' how one could get killed.

Off to Join the War

Undated letter from "Jeem" (my father's family nickname) to his Dad: "Dear Dad—Thought perhaps you might like one of these—Some of them you may not appreciate, but laugh at the ones you do—Save the book as imagine 20 years from now I'll get a big bang out [of] it—

Love,

Jeem

P.S. Take good care of Jude and keep her happy—big kiss to Rachel & Jude for me—Thumbs up!

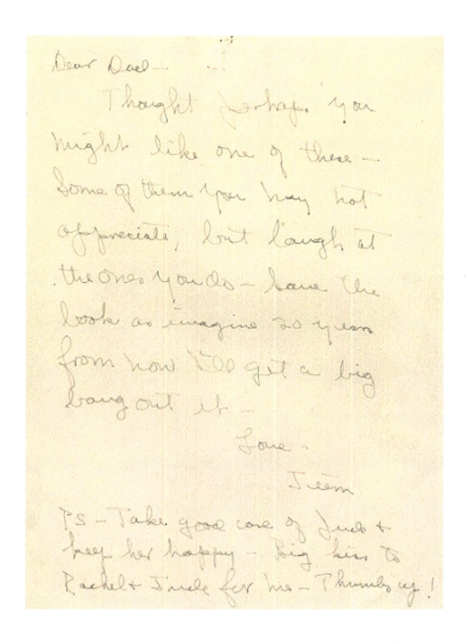

Chapter Ten: July, 1944

As I have indicated, the 35th division was one of several divisions attempting to take the town of St. Lo; which was a medium-sized town—I'd guess about 2,000 to 5,000 population—sitting at the very strategic road network position and was sort of situated in a bottom of a bowl, the town surrounded by hills, and it was really difficult for the allies to make any headway because the Germans had all of the key positions and their artillery was placed in such a strategic position that we were just not moving. So, we were sent up to relieve the 29th infantry division which had been in a line constantly since D day and these guys were beat. I mean they were beat!

My platoon was designated as the forward platoon of the entire division and we were sent into a hedgerow area where fox holes were deep and the Germans knew exactly where we were. Every night they would lob in their small mortars and they were terribly accurate. Virtually every night we would have one or two casualties as they could lob those small mortars right into our fox holes.

On July 24th, they lobbed one into the small entryway where we slid in and out like a snake and the shell lit into the entry way and caused a tremendous explosion and blew my helmet off. I reached up to wipe my head and my hand came down red so I knew I had been hit. Every infantry man is given a first aid kit which consisted of a large bandage and a small capsule of sulfa pills. The procedure was to bandage the wound and take the sulfa pills with a canteen of water. I took the bandage and put it on top of my head and tied it under my chin, which I'm sure was a grotesque looking sight but didn't even bother to open the canteen. I just shoved those sulfa pills down without even taking any water and bid my foxhole mate good-bye and was able to navigate on my own two feet, so I crawled out of the foxhole and managed to crawl and walk back to the company command post battalion first aid station.

Naturally, I was scared and my prime concern was that I would lose my eyesight, but fortunately the wound was not that deep. Finally, I was driven by jeep back to an evacuation hospital which I suppose was near the regimental headquarters and by the time I got there it was dark, so this must have taken about an hour or more. I don't remember being in a great deal of pain, but I am sure my head ached and the nurses were very good about putting me down and gave me something to make me sleep and indicated that they would take care of it in the morning.

The next day, July 25th, I can remember laying on a cot outside of the tent waiting to be operated on, which entailed the removal of shrapnel from my head. I was really a very lucky guy and was shown the helmet later which had a hole about the size of a half dollar on the left side of the helmet, but the helmet liner which was made of plastic diffused the fragment that went through the steel portion of the helmet into small segments and it was these small segments that lodged into the top of my skull. The helmet liner saved my life, for if the helmet alone had been only there the large segment would not have diffused and certainly would have killed me, so from then on I was a great admirer of the helmet liner which we all took for granted.

M1 Army helmet lining

So, laying on the cot I looked and all of a sudden, the sky was black. It was a beautiful, sunshiny day, but the sky was black because it was filled with bombers who were in the process of trying to open the front so that the infantry could again get moving and the American 8th Air Force came over enmasse to do just that.

July, 1944

After the operation I was taken back to my tent since I had been given a full anesthetic. I took a few hours to recuperate, but I don't remember anything particularly painful about the recovery. Later that night, the cots began to fill up with wounded; most of whom had been hit by our own bombers during this massive air raid and some of them were quite belligerent to say the least. It seems that because of the tremendous number of bombers, that some of the bombs obviously did not land where they were supposed to and hit our lines.

I remember one big, good looking, blonde second lieutenant who was terribly upset because his was the lead tank for the attack which was to take place following the bombing. He noticed some dust explosions around him as the tanks were formed ready to move and at the last minute he ducked into the tank and closed the turret, but not before a piece of shrapnel caught him in the arm from one of the bombs from the 8th Air Force. He was furious and that's putting it mildly.

There was so many wounded from this unfortunate occurrence that it was necessary to bring the wounded in 2 1/2 ton trucks as there were not enough ambulances available for the numbers to be transported.

The skull heals fast and within a few days I was up and around and the wound was healing rapidly. During this interim, the Germans launched a counter offensive right in the area where my regiment was near the town of Mortain. And it was a full-scale offensive and was causing havoc with the American infantry and things were not going so well. As a matter of fact, they were going poorly. Again, there were a large number of wounded and the word was put out to the evacuation hospitals to send all personnel who could walk back to their units immediately. With a bandage still on my head and hardly able to wear a helmet, I was ordered back to my platoon and believe me I was not excited about going back this soon.

After you have been hit and realize that it can happen, it changes your mental attitude drastically toward the question of

M4 Sherman tank photo credit: BonesBrigade at English Wikipedia, (slightly cropped by this author) https://commons.wikimedia.org/w/index.php?title=File:TankshermanM4.jpg&oldid=464151560 (accessed October 30, 2020)

survival. My mental attitude was very bad and I was terribly depressed. I would even go so far as to say I was scared to death and wanted no more of this war, but that's not the way it's going to be, so back to my platoon I went. The next two or three days were very hard because the fighting was intense and my mental attitude was almost to the state of being frantic; but somehow, we survived and stopped the counter offensive and although there was a lot of casualties; luckily, I was not one of them.

After turning the situation around and causing the Germans to begin retreat, we again moved out on the back of the Sherman tanks and headed across the flats plain area of France; which was what we had been hoping to do for several weeks.

When General Eisenhower[58] chose the Normandy area for the invasion he did so at great peril, but the purpose of this location was to surprise the Germans. He succeeded in that but he caused the allies severe casualties; particularly the American infantry divisions in getting up to the area on D-Day and then the hedgerow country was another obstacle which delayed the real offensive for about six weeks.

But now the offensive is on and the tanks are rolling and shooting everything in sight; spirits are up and all we have to do

---

[58] Wikipedia contributors, "Dwight D. Eisenhower," *Wikipedia, The Free Encyclopedia*, https://en.wikipedia.org/w/index.php?title=Dwight_D._Eisenhower&oldid=975871657 (accessed September 1, 2020), "Dwight David "Ike" Eisenhower (October 14, 1890 – March 28, 1969), was an American army general who served as the 34th president of the United States from 1953 to 1961. During World War II, he became a five-star general in the Army and served as Supreme Commander of the Allied Expeditionary Force in Europe. He was responsible for planning and supervising the invasion of North Africa in Operation Torch in 1942–43 and the successful invasion of Normandy in 1944–45 from the Western Front."

July, 1944

is try to keep up with the tanks of General Patton[59]. His is the Third army and it is running across France at a pace unprecedented in modern warfare between the tanks and the infantry mopping up and the Air Force shooting everything in sight from freight trains to army depots to troops along the highways. It is a sorry sight for the German army.

To get a more thorough understanding of this, I decided to dig up some more information about Patton's rapid march across Europe and here is what Wikipedia.org[60] had to say about it:

> "Sailing to Normandy throughout July, Patton's Third Army formed on the extreme right (west) of the Allied land forces, and became operational at noon on August 1, 1944, under Bradley's Twelfth United States Army Group. The Third Army simultaneously attacked west into Brittany, south, east toward the Seine, and north, assisting in trapping several hundred thousand German soldiers in the Falaise Pocket between Falaise and Argentan.
>
> Patton's strategy with his army favored speed and aggressive offensive action, though his forces saw less opposition than did the other three Allied field armies in the initial weeks of its advance. The Third Army typically employed forward scout units to determine enemy strength and positions. Self-propelled artillery moved with the spearhead units and was sited well forward, ready to engage protected German positions with indirect fire. Light aircraft such as the Piper L-4 Cub served as artillery spotters and provided airborne reconnaissance. Once located, the armored infantry would attack using tanks as infantry support. Other

---

[59] Wikipedia contributors, "George S. Patton," *Wikipedia, The Free Encyclopedia*, https://en.wikipedia.org/w/index.php?title=George_S._Patton&oldid=973990962 (accessed August 31, 2020), "George Smith Patton Jr. (November 11, 1885 – December 21, 1945) was a general of the United States Army who commanded the U.S. Seventh Army in the Mediterranean theater of World War II, and the U.S. Third Army in France and Germany after the Allied invasion of Normandy in June 1944. From his first days as a commander, Patton strongly emphasized the need for armored forces to stay in constant contact with opposing forces. His instinctive preference for offensive movement was typified by an answer Patton gave to war correspondents in a 1944 press conference. In response to a question on whether the Third Army's rapid offensive across France should be slowed to reduce the number of U.S. casualties, Patton replied, 'Whenever you slow anything down, you waste human lives.' It was around this time that a reporter, after hearing a speech where Patton said that it took 'blood and brains' to win in combat, began calling him 'blood and guts'. The nickname would follow him for the rest of his life. Soldiers under his command were known at times to have quipped, 'our blood, his guts'. Nonetheless, he was known to be admired widely by the men under his charge."

[60] Wikipedia contributors, "George S. Patton," *Wikipedia, The Free Encyclopedia*, https://en.wikipedia.org/w/index.php?title=George_S._Patton&oldid=985570230 (accessed October 31, 2020)

armored units would then break through enemy lines and exploit any subsequent breach, constantly pressuring withdrawing German forces to prevent them from regrouping and reforming a cohesive defensive line. The U.S. armor advanced using reconnaissance by fire, and the .50 caliber M2 Browning heavy machine gun proved effective in this role, often flushing out and killing German panzerfaust teams waiting in ambush as well as breaking up German infantry assaults against the armored infantry.

The speed of the advance forced Patton's units to rely heavily on air reconnaissance and tactical air support. The Third Army had by far more military intelligence (G-2) officers at headquarters specifically designated to coordinate air strikes than any other army. Its attached close air support group was XIX Tactical Air Command, commanded by Brigadier General Otto P. Weyland. Developed originally by General Elwood Quesada of IX Tactical Air Command for the First Army in Operation Cobra, the technique of "armored column cover", in which close air support was directed by an air traffic controller in one of the attacking tanks, was used extensively by the Third Army. Each column was protected by a standing patrol of three to four P-47 and P-51 fighter-bombers as a combat air patrol (CAP).

In its advance from Avranches to Argentan, the Third Army traversed 60 miles (97 km) in just two weeks. Patton's force was supplemented by Ultra intelligence for which he was briefed daily by his G-2, Colonel Oscar Koch, who apprised him of German counterattacks, and where to concentrate his forces. Equally important to the advance of Third Army columns in northern France was the rapid advance of the supply echelons. Third Army logistics were overseen by Colonel Walter J. Muller, Patton's G-4, who emphasized flexibility, improvisation, and adaptation for Third Army supply echelons so forward units could rapidly exploit a breakthrough. Patton's rapid drive to Lorraine demonstrated his keen appreciation for the technological advantages of the U.S. Army. The major U.S. and Allied advantages were in mobility and air superiority. The U.S. Army had more trucks, more reliable tanks, and better radio communications, all of which contributed to a superior ability to operate at a rapid offensive pace."

Frequently we are told to take a little town or a hold out for the Germans have not yet retreated and we do so. Once in a

July, 1944

while they decide to stay and fight then this causes problems. Finally, we get to the town of Chateaudun. We're now in the middle of August and this town required a lot of fighting because they didn't give up and they stayed and fought.

This was a tragic moment for me because my dearest friend who had been with me through the replacement depots and into the 35th infantry division was killed. His name was O.T. Willrich from Texas. He attended Texas A & M and we were together at Fort Benning and in the 87th Infantry division at Fort Jackson and he and I were in charge of 200 GI enlisted men on the ship going overseas. We were very close.

His company commander was a sadist and seemed to seek pleasure in sending people on suicide missions and this is what he did with T. Unfortunately, he got caught between machine gun fire and was killed just before we got to Chateaudun. He was in the next company abreast of mine. His was company G, and I was in company F. I remember sitting under a tree and crying, and bewailing the fact that T was killed and I thought in such a useless manner.

Chateaudun was a pretty good sized town and this was my first experience with the FFI known as the Free French taking over after the town had been liberated and first thing they did was corral all of the girls that had been sleeping with the Germans and shave their heads and march them down the main drag of town and it was not a pretty sight. The French were quite belligerent to these girls, they threw things at them and kicked them and I often wonder how their life was spent following those days because they were certainly looked upon in a most degrading manner.

We were taking lots of prisoners during the month of August and lots of supplies. We would come upon whole caches of liquor. This would consist of calvados, cognac mostly, and all types of wine and most of it was very strong.

So, things were going great until there was a gas supply problem. You must remember tanks use gas and the gas had to be driven to them at night sometimes as much as 50 to 100 miles.

These huge trucks full of 2-and-a-half-gallon gas tanks would go in convoy and they were known as the red ball express. And would they move! Most of these convoys were driven by blacks and they know how to drive fast.

Well, of course as the supply lines lengthened the time element became more critical in getting the gas to the tanks each night and the supply was dwindling until Eisenhower was faced with a dilemma; namely to either supply the British with gas to keep them moving which meant slowing down Patton or shutting off the British entirely and allowing Patton to continue. He chose the former alternative which caused the 3rd army to slow down to a screaming halt.

This was most unfortunate for the American infantry divisions under the 3rd army, as it allowed the enemy time to regroup. This they did. I think that had there been gas for the 3rd army that the war would have been over before Christmas of 1944; but such was not the case.

So, the going got tougher and each day instead of making maybe 5, 10, or 15 miles on foot or on the back of tanks going even further or even going in two and half ton trucks now we were back on foot and moving slowly and the resistance was increasing tremendously. With lots of mortar fire, lots of artillery, and as I found out, lots of snipers.

We are now well into the month of September and the weather is getting a little nippier. The temperatures are dropping considerably at night and yet it's sort of like our Indian summer at home. We are assigned to work with the tanks and in this type of maneuver the tanks go forward ahead of us and blast anything in sight and then we come in later and mop up. We were stopped near a stream on September 15th trying to determine what our next movement would be and I was leaning down, kneeling sort of, in a squatting position talking to the tank commander when all at once I heard this blast and it knocked me over and I realized I had been hit. Blood was gushing out of my right arm so obviously that is where the hit had come from and apparently it was a sniper. I immediately retreated back to a safer area and the tank commander, who reminded me of the movie star Preston Foster, really was livid and he opened up with everything those tanks had through all the brush and all the trees and all the undergrowth hoping to get the sniper. Whether he did or not I never found out. Once again, I was very lucky as my arm had been resting on my thigh and had the bullet been an inch or two to the left would have gone right through me and I am sure it would have killed me.

So, back to another hospital I go and this time they gave me a local anesthetic and removed part of the bullet from my arm, but the surgeon said it was probably better to leave it in there and then gristle would grow around it and as time went on I would never feel it. So, to this day I have part of a German bullet in my right arm and the surgeon was right, it didn't bother me after the healing process was accomplished and I have no problem with it. As a matter of fact, I can barely see the scar anymore but that's been 40 some years ago.

For therapy in the hospital they had me carry a bucket of sand around to build up the muscle tissue and lessen the chance of having a crooked arm. This wasn't very funny as that bucket was very heavy and it hurt like hell, but I did what the Dr. ordered and after a couple of weeks I was able to again return to my unit.

So, now we're into October and the weather is turning bad, wet, cold, clammy, and overcast sort of like our November weather in Illinois and in Pennsylvania—just not very good and sleeping out was no fun because our foxholes rain would get in at night and our ponchos were not sufficient to keep us dry and it was a miserable time.

This time when I returned to the division I was assigned to a new company and it was Company B and we called it Baker Company. In those days we used the phonetics Able for A, Baker for B, Charlie for C, Dog for D, so if you were in one of those companies you were known by that phonetic name and I was in Baker Company. This was a different battalion. I am now in the first Battalion and E, F, G, and H were 2nd battalion. So, I was a long ways away from my pals and I missed them. But I got acquainted with the members of my platoon and they were a good bunch of guys, but I was not at all happy with the company commander.

Since I was the new kid on the street, he gave me all the rotten assignments. His name was Gardner, a former football player from one of the Ivy League schools. He was really a cocky guy and thought he could win the war single handedly, which he found out later didn't happen.

We're kind of in a holding area living in some houses and the army is preparing for a big offensive and I remember it occurred on election day which had to be around the 7th or 8th of November, 1944. Prior to the jump off, which was to be at dawn, someone was to go around and secure all the bridges and this was not a particularly welcome task but naturally I was selected as this was a rather dangerous mission. So, I gathered my group and what we would do is travel to all the areas where there was the possibility of blowing up a bridge and drop off a group with a machine gun, a mortar, and half a dozen troops probably, and we did this all night and had no problem.

After I had everybody situated, I found a farm house occupied by a French family and asked if I could get a little shut eye and they put me in an upstairs bedroom and I'll never forget the down comforters that were on that bed. Probably the most beautiful sight I had ever seen was jumping into that bed after removing my dirty clothes and falling asleep into a dead slumber. I hardly heard the huge 155-millimeter artillery guns being fired nearby. I was in a deep sleep and I think I slept probably several hours before waking up.

So, now we're well into the second day of that attack and I was trying to find my outfit. I remember it was a Saturday and it was raining miserably. I finally was apprised of their approximate location so I worked my way up to the line and find a sad, sad sight. Sometime during the preceding 24 hours they had been pinned down by machine gun fire and were really in a hot spot. Now these German machine guns were vicious instruments and could spit those bullets out in a more rapid rate

July, 1944

than our 30 calibers and they had the entire company pinned down apparently for most of the day and into the night so that nobody could move.

Well, according to the story I heard later Captain Gardner couldn't stand it any longer and he decided he was going to make a move and I presume was going to throw a hand grenade near the area where the machine guns were and apparently he had not moved more than a foot or two when they mowed him down. That was the end of Capt. Gardner and there he lay dead along with many of the other members of the company when I arrived.

This is an unknown newspaper article found among my dad's memoirs: "It's a Tough War (continued) Two Americans lie dead on a mountain trail. The French troops now fighting on the hill have covered them with blankets and a burial party is on its way to remove them to a cemetary. Total U.S. casualties in Italy up to last week were 2,985 killed, 12,504 wounded, 3,721 missing."

The action was obviously over and the company had moved on. I vividly remember that my feet were terribly wet and that Capt. Gardner had goulashes on and I didn't have any, so I removed the goulashes and left him there. When we were in

France in 1977, I looked up his grave in one of the national cemeteries and thanked him again for the goulashes.

Well, we kept plugging along inch by inch and mile by mile and trying to get a momentum going which would cause the enemy to again retreat but we weren't succeeding very well. I think the worst part of it was the weather because we are now in the rainy season, and it was muddy. The jeeps get stuck and the tanks get stuck and we get stuck and everybody is in a lousy mood and constantly wet and now we come into a new little plight that none of us had thought about and that is called trench foot.

This was a malady that was caused by wet feet and poor circulation and if this continued in many instances long enough the feet got black and they had to send these boys back to the evacuation hospital for treatment and in some cases amputation, so now we're in a new ballgame with everything else going wrong and the fear of trench feet on the horizon. It was impossible to keep your feet dry for any length of time and unfortunately the army had done a lousy job of supplying us with enough goulashes and wet proof items for our feet. Suddenly those goulashes of Gardner's were the most precious item in my wardrobe.

Somewhere in this time frame I remember getting a 3-day pass to go into the city of Nancy where they had a R and R program for the members of the infantry who had been on the line for a long period of time. I don't remember much about it except the beds were warm and the bath felt fantastic and the food was delicious and the drinks were excellent and in one of those areas I remember being in a large kind of a beer hall and literally ran into Roy Brown who was an SAE at Illinois when I was there. He was in the field artillery and we had a great reunion for a few hours drinking beer and recounting our great times in college and telling each other how we were winning the war. An unbelievable coincidence.

So, after a little fun and games it was back to the outfit where I immediately caught cold and it was a dandy. You know nature

July, 1944

is a wonderful thing and our bodies were used to the elements and the oils of our skin had formed an immunity so that we really didn't get cold or catch cold or the flu; but once I got cleaned up and lost that immunity first thing I did was catch a dandy cold and was sick as a dog for few days but finally recovered.

Chapter Eleven: Coming Home

I don't remember much else exciting until we get around the Christmas season. Oh yes, I do remember one night we had a night attack and my platoon was scheduled to be the lead platoon for the division on crossing the Roer River; which was swollen and flooded because of the rains. Well, this was a dandy little adventure. We had those little boats that kind of looked like the rubber boats you see out in Vail, Colorado going down the Eagle River and it was our task to take these little boats and get them across the river and secure a foothold and establish a position so that the rest of the company and the rest of the division could follow. Well, that was all peachy keen except that the boats would fill up with water immediately and tremendous weight of all the gear we had to carry didn't help any and we had one hell of a time getting across that river. Then to top things off, the Germans spotted us and began shoving mortar and machine gun fire at us and it turned out to be one chaotic operation.

We finally did secure a new foothold, but not until we lost a couple of boats and some men. It was a hair-raising experience and I don't want to go through that again. Of course, we are all sopping wet from top to bottom but obviously we made it all right and did the job we were supposed to. I think I could have figured out a better way to do that if we had it to do all over again.

Many of the nights in this timeframe we would end up in old bombed-out houses or even maybe sleep on the top floor while the French slept in the basement. Frequently we would not have to be in a foxhole and that was a plus. We even managed to scavenge up some chickens and some pigs and butcher them and pluck the chickens to have a little extra food to eat; so, life wasn't all bad. It's amazing what you can do when you have to. American ingenuity is unbelievable.

First Hand

As of December 18, 1944, my father was promoted to 1st Lieutenant "By command of Lieutenant General PATTON:"

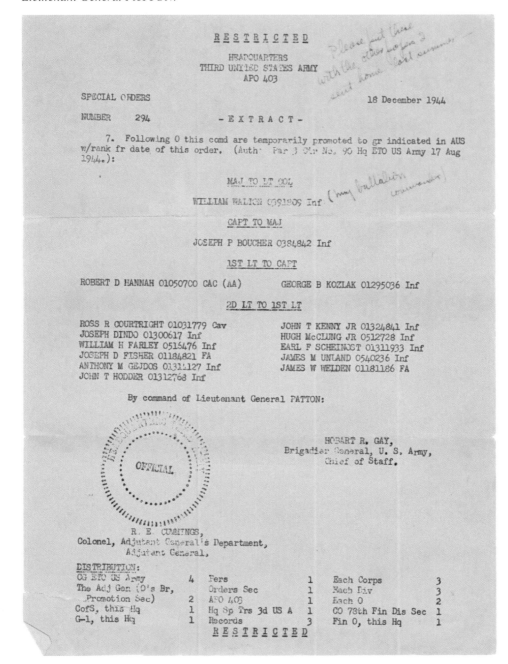

So, that's the way the war went and I remember another instance when we were told to take an area (I think it was a small town) and the guy that was running the company was Guilford from Detroit. One hell of a guy. But we started moving along and all of a sudden we see a company of German tanks coming at us and somebody in our unit started to panic and the next thing I know the whole damn company is running backwards retreating and Guilford yells for me to go get them and so I'm out there shooting my 45 caliber pistol in the air telling these characters to stop and turn around and I finally get them stopped and in the meantime Guilford sat up on top of the hill and directs artillery fire into the tanks. I went back up with him and I'm telling you that guy was something else. He was a cool customer. He just sat up there while those tanks were shooting at him and directed the artillery fire from our radio-based artillery and managed to turn that column around and send them another direction. For this he got a silver star; which was richly deserved.

Our division had been in the line constantly since they went into action back in the middle of July so it was time for a rest and we were sent to the city of Metz for a little R and R and to give us a chance to get our act together again.

I remember moving to the barracks where the Germans had been and I've never seen anything so filthy in my life. They had purposely defecated all over the barracks and the stench was unbelievable; so, we spent the first day cleaning up their mess and trying to make the place civilized again. I'll never forget that. Here I thought the German people were civilized and I find out they are the typical animals I suppose all soldiers get to be when they are losing a war.

Well, by now it's almost Christmas and the Battle of the Bulge began on December 16th; so, John O'Brien, my dear friend from New York City and I got in a jeep and drove approximately 30 or 40 miles to the city of Nancy where John had made the acquaintance of a French family. This family had invited us to spend Christmas with them if we were in the area and so we took a chance that they would be there and John knew his way pretty well and I remember we had a delightful day on Christmas of 1944 with this French family in an apartment in an area that was still in pretty good shape, that is, not bombed or blown to pieces by artillery.

John could speak just enough French to get by and was a big help because I couldn't speak any and we managed to communicate as best we could and they were a family of two young girls and a father and a mother who were elderly (or so it seemed like at that time) but were most hospitable to us and we sang and drank and ate and had a memorable time.

The only problem was that it was colder than hell riding in that jeep with no top and the temperature was hovering around zero which caused our feet to nearly freeze going and coming but it was really worth the effort and we enjoyed it.

While we were gone, the rest of the outfit had a real bash as the cognac and calvados which had been back in the kitchen came up and I guess they had a very wonderful drunken Christmas day all immersed in sentiment about not being at home. At least it was a lot better than some of our buddies who were up in the Bastogne area getting blown to bits by the Germans.

So, the day after Christmas it was on the road again and this time we had to go along with most of the rest of Americans to help relieve the pressure on the counter offensive which was known as the "Battle of the Bulge." We were sent up into the mountains and put into a holding pattern until called into action.

I vividly remember New Year's Eve. The platoon was scattered around in some houses and I said that we had to have a little party so I got into the jeep and drove down the mountain which was covered with ice and snow to the kitchen where I knew there was still some cognac and got back in the jeep and started back up the mountain to our area and my command post when suddenly the jeep went completely out of control.

The next thing I know I'm laying down in the jeep. My helmet is off, my rifle is thrown out. Fortunately, the liquor didn't break but the jeep is in a mess; not turned over but not in very good shape either beside the road and the next thing I know there are three rifle barrels pointing at my throat wanting to know who the hell I am. And give me the password, they said. I couldn't remember it!

Well, I managed to get out of that mess but these guys were really trigger happy because the Germans during this offensive had dropped lots of English-speaking troops of theirs in the back of the columns and caused havoc in many instances. They could speak good English and knew the Yankees from the Cubs and they managed to kill a lot of people way back in the kitchens and the regimental headquarters and disrupt the entire operation. So, these guys were not about to have some cocky smart 2nd Lieutenant tell them what was going on, but I talked by way out of it and got my jeep back on the road and managed to get back to the command post where we proceeded to have a very fine New Year's Eve. And that was the end of the party.

New Year's Day we were ordered to pack up and move out as we were given an assignment of relieving the 101st Airborne infantry division which had attained fame by holding onto the town of Bastogne and it was in this tremendous battle that the famous reply to the German surrender demand was given by General McAuliffe and his reply in one word was "nuts." So, they held out and the 101st did a magnificent job.

General George Smith Patton, Jr.

Several days later (probably one or two days at the most) we were in the town of Bastogne and I remember vividly that it was a clear, cold day and I was riding in a jeep and noticed that there was a great commotion up in front as this other jeep approached from a different direction with a man standing up in the jeep holding onto a bar and it was no other than the famous George Patton with his gleaming steel helmet and his six shooters at his side, his calvary boots and breeches, and he was indeed a sight. He proceeded to the parade crowd. There was a ceremony with a band as the general presented medals to the heroes of the 101st.

I don't think there was a building left standing in the town of Bastogne; which was an entirely different sight than Judy and I saw in 1977 when we revisited Bastogne; now a thriving city of probably 100,000 population. The reason that the Battle of the Bulge centered around Bastogne was that 3 or 4 roads came into the town and it was a strategic point to control, but the 101st held on and began to drive the Germans back away from the town. Now, our task was to continue pushing the Germans back again reentering the area on the offensive rather than be on the defensive; which was caused by this last plunge by Hitler to divide the allies and he had hoped to march to the sea and cause further havoc amongst our troops.

This new campaign of the Battle of the Bulge was probably the toughest we endured. The weather was frightfully cold and we were out in the woods sleeping in shallow foxholes and the temperature got down to 10-15 degrees below zero every night and it was necessary that a sentry go around and awaken everybody to get them up and circulate themselves, particularly their feet, in the middle of the night or the feet would be frozen; and in some cases probably the entire body would be frozen.

So, it was no Sunday school picnic. We didn't have much warm chow and we just kept plugging along and I remember my birthday, January 5th, 1945. I was 23 years old and I thought this was really a sad way to spend one's birthday; plodding along dodging the shells hoping not to get hit and continuing to push the Germans back. It was tough fighting because we were in the woods most of the time and meant you could not call on the artillery to assist and it was hand grenades and small mortar fire that we used constantly and machine guns that would gradually tear away at the enemy and push him back.

A low point in the campaign came on January 15th when we were really bottled in and pinned down by machine gun fire and mortars from two different directions. I remember we were in a valley and approaching a little town and were supposed to go in from the rear of the town which Company A took the frontal part of the town. We thought our assignment was going to be the less hazardous one, but as it turned out it was just the opposite. "A" company was able to secure their objective while we spent the day just trying to survive and the company commander was hit. Since I was the executive officer of the company, it fell upon me to then take command; which I did and gradually we worked our way out of the problem and I really don't think it was until night that we were able to move forward and secure a position in the area which was assigned to us. Casualties that day were horrendous from mortars and machine guns and when we finally got our troops gathered back together, we were probably at about 1/5th the strength that we normally should have been.

I vividly remember 43 years later the exact day of this debacle in which the company lost about half of the personnel. It was January 15, 1945 and as I mentioned, I was the company commander by the process of elimination. The 1st Lieutenant, whose name is no longer important, was severely wounded in the back and buttocks and so I took over and we finally got into this old own and the back part of the town which had been so well defended by the Germans.

We were exhausted. We found some old buildings which served as a shelter for the night and grabbed some cold K-rations to eat as we had no hot food, and everybody was ready to keel over and hit the sack wherever we could. However, such was not to be, as the battalion commander, Colonel Walton, was on the radio commanding me to get up to the battalion command post immediately. So, I jumped into the jeep with my driver who was a little Italian boy from New Jersey with the nickname of Dago. Dago and I proceeded to go to the back roads with no lights on, of course, and somehow managed to find where the Colonel was holing up.

In the room were the other company commanders of the battalion along with the members of the Colonel's staff and he began to tell us what we were going to be on the attack. He looked at the map and designated the areas we were to take in the line of attack and I sat there knowing full well that Baker Company (mine) would certainly not be in the attack because of the terrible beating we had taken that day.

I was wrong. I was stunned to hear him say that Baker Company would be on the left flank in the attack and I sat there in a complete stupor. Finally, he looked at me and in a very gruff voice gave me holy hell for not paying closer attention to what was going on because he said that I better know the line of march and all the particulars so that I could perform properly in the morning.

I don't think in my entire life has my morale been so low. We left the meeting and headed back to what was left of our company and I was forced to tell them the great news about being in the attack in the morning.

My recollection is that they took it very well, probably better than I did, and so the next morning off we went into another battle. This time we were luckier and did not suffer as many casualties. I remember being up in a three-story building directing artillery fire and also being able to direct a couple of P-47 airplanes which were our combat support.

Let me take a minute to tell you about these P-47's. They were a single engine and heavily armored plane designed to take a considerable amount of flak from anti-aircraft fire and believe me they really did. Many times, I'd see them go over the horizon

1940's era P-47NThunderbolt (public domain photo)

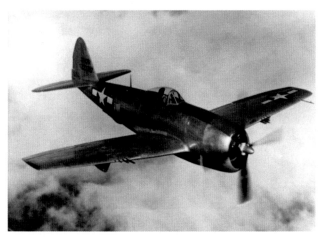

and drop one of their 500 lb. bombs and see all the sky lit up with red tracer bullets from the enemy anti-aircraft guns and assumed immediately that the plane would crash. But within a second or two, out of the flak would come this huge roar and this P-47 would head skyward once again. I really didn't have much love for the Air Corp, but I sure did have a tremendous amount of admiration for the guys who flew those P-47s and helped the infantry.

But, back to the action in the middle of January. Now, it's getting to the place where we had pretty much eliminated the opposition and the resistance was not nearly as severe as it had been a few days prior. So, for all the practical purposes with the offensive that the German's threw at the American forces beginning December 16th now finished, and after the loss of many, many thousands of young men on both sides, that phase of World War II had ended.

Public domain image of CCKW 2 1/2 ton GMC 6x6 long wheelbase cargo truck with winch (in production from 1941 - 1945)

I think I mentioned earlier that our General Baade had an amazing talent for getting us into action wherever it might be. Now, orders came down that we were to get into our big troop carrier trucks which were 2 1/2-ton vehicles and head south to the Vosges mountains where another counter attack was taking place. Again, I was dumb founded that we were so lucky as to have to go find another area of the war, but off we went and this is in the southern part of France where the Germans were trying to counter attack and fierce fighting was taking place.

First Hand

The mountains were probably 5,000 feet high and it was very cold; and of course, lots of snow, and the fighting was similar to what we had outside Bastogne. We were down there approximately two or three weeks and the same kind of closed-in fighting and suffering. Some casualties, but it was not as severe as it had been in January. So, after the Germans were again thrown back and that problem was solved, we did have a day or two of rest. Then, the next thing I know we were all told to get on railroad box cars because we were going now from the southernmost part of France to clear up into the northern part, into Holland, to prepare for a huge crossing of the Rhine River.

While this sounded like it might be a horrible experience, it actually turned out to be not so bad. You will remember that all of us had bed rolls which consisted of a G.I. blanket encased by a waterproof covering. The train had a kitchen, so we had hot food; and there was a little stove in one end of each car so it wasn't terribly cold. As the company commander, I decided I was going to live the life of luxury if there was any at this particular point in time. So, I literally stayed in the bedroll for the four or five days that it took for us to go through the war-torn zones and get to our destination; which was up in the Dutch country near the Rhine River. I had plenty of service and my boys brought me my food, we played cards, and I read. I mostly slept for several days and it was a really restful experience.

Of course, every time a train stopped, out would jump a bunch of G.I.'s and they would start foraging for food and frequently would come back with a chicken or two and sometimes some green vegetables. Once in a while they would find a train with supplies, and anything they could steal. There were no scruples in the infantry. By this time, we are getting into the month of March, 1945. The weather is not as severe now, and the snow is gone. It's still very wet out but spring is coming and life seems to be worth living once again.

We were holed up in a small village in Holland and all of us had a dry place to sleep. Inside a building of some type we spent several days getting new troops assigned to us for replacements and to build up our strength both physically and with ammunition, weapons, and more manpower. Lots of young replacements came over from the states and some of them came from difference branches of the service. The Battle of the Bulge drained the replacement camps in the U.S. and now we were receiving boys from the coast artillery who had been given a quick refresher course in the infantry and were sent over to be infantry men rather than be part of the coast artillery. Apparently, there was not as much need for coast artillery troops as there were for those in the infantry; and this was understandable.

I remember we had a lot of inspections and the idea was to dress up the troops again and get their clothes cleaned and looking decent; but most particularly to make sure their weapons were in good working order; which meant we had frequent weapons inspections.

Well, I remember one such inspection when the company was lined up and I was inspecting the rifles of the platoon when a shot went off. I heard this horrible scream in the back file of the next platoon. Some kid had been fooling around with his pistol to get it ready for inspection and the thing went off and shot him in the foot. And I want to tell you that is about the dumbest thing I have ever seen or heard of during my entire time in the service.

None of us were looking forward to the river crossing of the Rhine because we assumed the Germans would be heavily fortified on the opposite side of the river and it could very well be a huge disaster, but we lucked out. Our division had a relatively easy crossing, and as I recall our company was not one of the main first point companies, but got across the river without any casualties. And, the German resistance was not as great as we had originally feared. But as time went on the resistance became greater as we moved into the Motherland and the Germans were not anxious to have us take over their country.

The fighting goes on as always with the tanks supporting the infantry and I particularly remember a combat tank company made up of blacks only. Now, as I mentioned earlier, the blacks' place in the army was mostly in the non-combat areas of driving trucks, working in the kitchens, and being in the supply depots. However, there were combat units of blacks and this particular company of young black men in the tanks were sensational. I often wondered if they had an inferiority complex which caused them to be less fearful than their counterparts of whites. These guys were fearless and we became greats pals because we knew that with them supporting us, we would be in good shape.

Another branch of service was the cavalry. Now, this was the branch that I was supposed to be in after college, but because my name was at the end of the alphabet I ended up in the infantry and at that time thought that was too bad. I should have been in the cavalry. However, after watching what the cavalry had to do I was glad I was in the infantry because their mission was to go out in the front of the front lines of the American troops and scout in little half-track vehicles; which gave them very little protection and the casualty rate of these cavalry half-tracks was terrific.

Many a day we would come across their blown-up vehicles and their bodies strewn around the area when the German .88 had caught them and caused their death. So, we plugged along and kept going at a fairly decent rate; probably somewhere between the fast pace after St. Lo and the very slow pace in the Battle of the Bulge.

I remember one night we had a night attack and I always hated night attacks because you couldn't see anything and you never knew what was going to happen next. We were to take a town called Huck and we had to come up with some kind of a buzz word to identify ourselves without letting the enemy know where we were. We came up with one that was a little raunchy; which I won't repeat here but you get the point. The going was tough and the enemy was not about to let us take this town. I remember we had a tough time that night and had several wounded because of the confusion that always takes place in a night attack. I think that was the night I decided to smoke a pipe. Back in those days I was a heavy cigarette smoker and would often have to get up in the middle of the night to have a cigarette, but I decided that maybe a pipe was better because you could smoke a pipe at night without the flame being seen; which you could not do with a cigarette.

So, I lit this pipe up and held the bowl in my hands and smoked it most of the night. The next morning my tongue was so swollen that I could hardly speak. And that was the end of my pipe smoking.

Well, we kept moving and it was getting into the first of April when we got close to the city of Cologne. Now, we knew this was going to be a tough fight because this is a principal city in Germany and one of the first of the large cities to come under fire from the allies; and we were getting near the out-skirts so the going is really getting tough. I vividly remember that it was Palm Sunday and around the middle of the morning we were waiting for our order to move out. It was a bright, sunny day and I heard the radio come on and it was the Colonel wanting to see me. So, Dago and I head back in the jeep to the battalion headquarters and he makes this announcement, "Jim, I have two things to tell you. The first is that your promotion to captain will be here in a few days. The second is that your orders to go home are here now. Which do you wish to take?" And my reply was, "Colonel, are you kidding? Thank you for seeing that I finally became a captain, but I will forgo that and head for home."

I was overjoyed. They had a system in the army at that time called a point system whereby you received points for various accomplishments such as a bronze star or silver star; or being wounded; plus, the number of combat missions you had served in. Because I had been hit twice and been awarded the bronze star and silver star, as well as serving in five major battles, my points were quite high. I was eligible for a 30-day leave back to the states. Now, you remember that the war was not over yet and it was assumed that I would go home for 30 days and return back to my unit.

Well, within a matter of an hour I was out of there with bag and baggage, what little I had, heading for transportation to take me all the way back to the coast and to Le Havre where a ship would then take us home. I think this was April 6th, which is John's birthday, and I didn't get home until a month later; but it really didn't make any difference. I was out of combat and headed in the right direction.

We got to Le Havre and were given clean clothes and, of course, we got to shave and shower and clean up and waited around there for several days; during which time President Roosevelt died. Every time I hear the Star-Spangled Banner, I think of the time they played it at the formation to commemorate his death while we were in Le Havre. It was a chilling feeling knowing that the President had died and here you were a part of the war which he had directed and you were still alive. I was grateful for that, but sorry that the old man had passed on. Finally, we embarked toward home and my recollection was that it was about a two-week voyage.

This ship was jammed with guys similar to me and there was a large contingent of Air Corp personnel who had flown their required missions and were headed home. Now, you will recall that the infantry was never too excited about the Air Corp because we felt they lived the good life jumping into a plane and flying from England over to France and returning every night to cocktails, dinner, dancing, women, and whatever. We thought that was kind of a sloppy way to fight the war in as much as we were in the slop ourselves all the time.

So, there was not much camaraderie between the two branches of service. I met a guy from New York who had been overseas for 3 years fighting in combat. His name was Finkelstein. A Jewish boy from New York who was one of the sharpest card players I have ever seen before or since. This was the beginning of gin rummy and he taught me how to play; but I never have been very good at it despite his teachings. He was sensational and every night he would get these Air Corp guys in a gin rummy or poker game, which he also knew how to play very well, and I would go back and get in my berth in the bottom of the ship and be sound asleep and he would always come and wake me up to tell me how much money he had won. I can tell you that between Le Havre and New York he won thousands of dollars. I often wonder whatever happened to that guy because he was certainly a sharp card player.

Well, we did have good food and we ate in a mess hall but it was terribly boring and terribly slow and finally I recall at around dawn one morning, Finkelstein came down and shook me awake. The tears were rolling down his cheeks and he said, "Jim, come on, get up." So, I threw some clothes on and went up to the deck and there is New York Harbor and the great lady (the Statue of Liberty) looking at us as we approached our dock. Finkelstein was bawling like a little kid because he had been gone so long. This was his hometown and he was just absolutely ecstatic.

Well, we all said good-bye to each other and began heading towards home. That's

USS New Mexico moored in the Hudson River near the Statue of Liberty in June of 1934 (public domain photo, courtesy of the U.S. Navy via navsource.org)

the last I've seen of any of that crowd. After going through the normal inspections and whatever they did to us, I remember we got on a train and headed for Chicago. It was now about the 2nd or 3rd of May, 1945. The train finally pulled into Chicago and they took us out to Fort Sheridan; which is out by Waukegan, Illinois. Again, we went through a processing procedure which I think took overnight; but finally, I was out and had a 30-day leave so I'm now on a train from LaSalle Street Station heading towards Champaign, Illinois to see my wife, Judy.

She knew I was getting close but had not been brought up to date as to exactly when I was going to show up; except that I think I did tell her it was going to be either a Monday or a

Tuesday. When I got into Champaign, I caught a cab and took it over to the Chi Omega house where she was staying until I got back into town.

Now, the Chi Omega house has a beautiful circular staircase and it was in this very area that we were married about two years earlier. Some little girl told her I was downstairs and I can still see her running down the stairs; she missed the last five steps and flew into my arms. You can well imagine the tremendously poignant and loving reunion after such a long separation; and one which had been filled with so many moments of anxiety.

We spent that night and the next day in the apartment we were sharing with Eleanor Munger. Coincidentally, Eleanor's husband Stan, who was in the Navy, had hit the West Coast and Eleanor was meeting him for their reunion. So, we had the apartment all to ourselves and soon thereafter my dad and mother came down to take us back to Pekin; and it was certainly very soon because I know my mother was anxious to see her little boy who had just returned from the war.

We drove back to Pekin and stayed there for several days; during which time the war in Europe ended. Well, all of a sudden, I was a hometown hero because there weren't too many veterans returning back home yet and since I had been in the thick of things, I was suddenly given a lot of recognition. I spoke to the Pekin Rotary Club, among other things, and was kind of enjoying all of the adulation being thrown my way. We saw the relatives in Delavan and renewed acquaintances before taking off again.

One thing we did during that interim was to drive down to the Ozarks by ourselves and spend a few days just laying around, fishing, and just relaxing. I remember going over to Uncle Ralph and Aunt Bernice's house in Joplin, Missouri and having a delicious meal of steak. During the war, even some of the Americans suffered somewhat because steak was at a premium and you had to have a lot of stamps in order to get good red meat. But Uncle Ralph ran a grocery store and I can still see

Coming Home

Aunt Bernice frying up that steak on the stove in their apartment and it was indeed delicious.

Since the war was over it was, of course, not very wise for the army to send me back to Europe. So, they decided I would go to San Antonio, Texas instead and join another unit and go into a training camp to help train the soldiers who would then go to Japan, including me. From San Antonio, Judy and I went to Tyler, Texas to a place called Camp Fannin. This was my first experience in Texas in the summertime, and of course, this was before air conditioning so it was hot; and I do mean hot.

We managed to get a little apartment and we always kidded about it because it overlooked the garbage area of the apartment complex. We became great friends with a couple by the name of Arny and Doretta Alger who had a little baby boy named Doug. He was the cutest thing we had ever seen before or since. Doug was probably a year and a half to two years old and he put in a miserable summer in the heat because they were on the third floor and it was like an oven up there day and night.

Arny and I would head out to camp every morning at around five o'clock and get back home around six o'clock at night. This went on during the months of July and into August; and then suddenly President Truman decides to drop the atom bomb on Hiroshima and then on Nagasaki; and suddenly the war was over.

I will always remember the night of the armistice when the four of us realized that neither of us were going to have to go to Japan. If the war had proceeded according to schedule in Japan, it's impossible to imagine what the casualty rate would have been. I have to tell you that I'm not too sympathetic with the Japanese for lamenting the fact that we dropped those bombs on them because while we did cause a tremendous number of casualties to the Japanese people, we saved an untold number of American lives. And since I'm an American, and since I've been to one battle area for a year and know what was in store, I have to say that I'm sure glad that Truman made that decision.

We spent two or three more months at Camp Fannin before being separated from the service, and when I knew I was going to get out I called my dad and said, "Gee, suddenly the war is over. What am I going to do now?" He suggested that I come home and he would send me out to Hartford to the insurance school at Aetna and then I could come home and try the insurance business. If I liked it, good; and if not, I could try something else. And that's what we did.

We had an old Plymouth Coupe that we drove with all of our belongings from Tyler, Texas to Pekin, Illinois to begin our life anew; and it's where we've remained ever since.

I think that just about winds it up. I was so lucky in so many ways to have survived and I used to worry most about losing my eyesight; which fortunately did not happen. I think often of the many friends that I left behind that did not have the opportunity to live another 40-plus years like I have, and who have missed all the greatness of this country, of their families, of their loved ones, and to me this is the big sacrifice that constantly haunts me because they have not had what I had and still have.

Coming Home

DEPARTMENT OF THE ARMY
OFFICE OF THE ADJUTANT GENERAL
WASHINGTON 25, D. C.

IN REPLY REFER TO
AGPO-AD 201 Unland, James M. 18 March 1952
O 540 236 (19 Jul 51)

SUBJECT: Letter Orders - Bronze Star Medal

TO: Captain James M. Unland
42 Park Avenue
Pekin, Illinois

1. By direction of the President, under the provisions of Executive Order 9419, 4 February 1944 (Sec. II, WD Bul. 3, 1944), you have been awarded the Bronze Star Medal for exemplary conduct in ground combat against the armed enemy while assigned as Second Lieutenant, 320th Infantry Regiment, on or about 20 August 1944, in the European Theater of Operations.

2. Authority for this award is contained in paragraph 18, AR 600-45, and General Orders Number 9, Headquarters 320th Infantry Regiment, dated 20 August 1944, which awarded the Combat Infantryman Badge.

3. It is not the policy of the Department of the Army to announce retroactive awards of the Bronze Star Medal in General Orders.

BY ORDER OF THE SECRETARY OF THE ARMY:

Adjutant General

First Hand

The preceding Bronze Star letter to James M. Unland states: "1. By direction of the President, under the provisions of Executive Order 9419, 4 February 1944 (Sec. II, WD Bul. 3, 1944), you have been awarded the Bronze Star Medal for exemplary conduct in ground combat against the armed enemy while assigned as Second Lieutenant, 320th Infantry Regiment, on or about 20 August 1944, in the European Theater of Operations. 2. Authority for this award is contained in paragraph 18, AR 600-45, and General Orders Number 9, Headquarters 320th Infantry Regiment, dated 20 August 1944, which awarded the Combat Infantryman Badge. 3. It is not the policy of the Department of the Army to announce retroactive awards of the Bronze Star Medal in General Orders. BY ORDER OF THE SECRETARY OF THE ARMY: Signed by Adjutant General Walter Hess"

Coming Home

```
                    HEADQUARTERS 35TH INFANTRY DIVISION
                         APO 35      US ARMY

GENERAL ORDERS                                  12 April 1945
NUMBER    26
                                                    Section
    *          *          *          *               *

SILVER STAR -- Awards  - -  - - - - - - - - - - - - - - - -II

        II - - SILVER STAR.  Pursuant to authority contained in AR
600-45, dated 22 September 1943, as amended, and Memorandum 34,
Headquarters Ninth United States Army, 8 September 1944, as
amended, a Silver Star is awarded to the following officers and
enlisted men:

    *          *          *          *               *

        First Lieutenant James M Unland, 0540236, Infantry, United
States Army, for gallantry in action near Weselhof, Germany on
6 March 1945.  When his men, part of whom were riding tanks, en-
countered heavy enemy machine gun, rifle and mortar fire during
an attack, Lieutenant Unland, commanding Company B, 320th Infantry,
ordered all troops except those in the lead tank to seek cover.
He then ran three hundred yards through enemy fire, mounted the
lead tank and directed the combined infantry-armored force from
his exposed position in a successful assault on a fortified
building.  His daring and resourceful leadership resulted in the
capture of twelve prisoners, two light machine guns, a mortar and
eight rifles, and undoubtedly prevented numerous casualties.
Entered military service from Illinois.

    *          *          *          *               *

            BY COMMAND OF MAJOR GENERAL BAADE:



                                    MADDREY A SOLOMON
                                    Colonel, GSC
OFFICIAL                            Chief of Staff



/s/ Julius Cahn Jr
    JULIUS CAHN JR
    1st Lt, AGD
    Asst Adj Gen
```

First Hand

The preceding Silver Star letter to James M. Unland states: "II - - SILVER STAR. Pursuant to authority contained in AR 600-45, dated 22 September 1943, as amended, and Memorandum 34, Headquarters Ninth United States Army, 8 September 1944, as amended, a Silver Star is awarded to the following officers and enlisted men: First Lieutenant James M Unland, 0540236, Infantry, United States Army, for gallantry in action near Weselhof, Germany on 6 March 1945. When his men, part of whom were riding tanks, encountered heavy enemy machine gun, rifle and mortar fire during an attack, Lieutenant Unland, commanding Company B, 320th Infantry, ordered all troops except those in the lead tank to seek cover. He then ran three hundred yards through enemy fire, mounted the lead tank and directed the combined infantry-armored force from his exposed position in a successful assault on a fortified building. His daring and resourceful leadership resulted in the capture of twelve prisoners, two light machine guns, a mortar and eight rifles, and undoubtedly prevented numerous casualties. Entered military service from Illinois. BY COMMAND OF MAJOR GENERAL BAADE: Signed by Colonel Maddrey A. Solomon (GSC), Chief of Staff

THE UNITED STATES OF AMERICA

TO ALL WHO SHALL SEE THESE PRESENTS, GREETING:

THIS IS TO CERTIFY THAT
THE PRESIDENT OF THE UNITED STATES OF AMERICA
AUTHORIZED BY ACT OF CONGRESS, JULY 9, 1918, HAS AWARDED

A SILVER STAR

TO

Captain (then First Lieutenant) James M. Unland, 0 540 236, Infantry

FOR
GALLANTRY IN ACTION

near Weselhof, Germany, 6 March, 1945

GIVEN UNDER MY HAND IN THE CITY OF WASHINGTON
THIS 18th DAY OF March 1952

THE UNITED STATES OF AMERICA
TO ALL WHO SHALL SEE THESE PRESENTS, GREETING:
THIS IS TO CERTIFY THAT
THE PRESIDENT OF THE UNITED STATES OF AMERICA
HAS AWARDED THE

PURPLE HEART

ESTABLISHED BY GENERAL GEORGE WASHINGTON
AT NEWBURGH, NEW YORK, AUGUST 7, 1782
TO

Captain (then Second Lieutenant) James M. Unland, O 540 236, Infantry

FOR WOUNDS RECEIVED IN ACTION

European Theater of Operations, 24 July 1944

GIVEN UNDER MY HAND IN THE CITY OF WASHINGTON
THIS 18th DAY OF March 1952

First Hand

Across the top, from left to right, are my father's Silver Star, Purple Heart, and Bronze Star.

Coming Home

MILITARY RECORD AND REPORT OF SEPARATION
CERTIFICATE OF SERVICE

1. LAST NAME - FIRST NAME - MIDDLE INITIAL Unland James M	2. ARMY SERIAL NUMBER O 540 236	3. AUS. GRADE 1stLt	4. ARM OR SERVICE Inf	5. COMPONENT ORC
6. ORGANIZATION Co "A" 83rd BN 15th Regt. Camp Fannin, Texas	7. DATE OF RELIEF FROM ACTIVE DUTY 27 Nov 1945	8. PLACE OF SEPARATION Separation Center Camp Fannin, Texas		
9. PERMANENT ADDRESS FOR MAILING PURPOSES 807 Dacon St Pekin, Illinois	10. DATE OF BIRTH 5 Jan 1922	11. PLACE OF BIRTH Delavan, Illinois		

12. ADDRESS FROM WHICH EMPLOYMENT WILL BE SOUGHT	13. COLOR EYES	14. COLOR HAIR	15. HEIGHT	16. WEIGHT	17. NO. OF DEPENDENTS
See 9	Blue	Brown	6'1"	160	1

18. RACE	19. MARITAL STATUS	20. U.S. CITIZEN	21. CIVILIAN OCCUPATION AND NO.
WHITE X	MARRIED X	YES X	Student (College) X.02

MILITARY HISTORY

SELECTIVE SERVICE DATA	22. REGISTERED: YES X	23. LOCAL S. S. BOARD NUMBER	24. COUNTY AND STATE Champaign Illinois	25. HOME ADDRESS AT TIME OF ENTRY ON ACTIVE DUTY Same as 9

26. DATE OF ENTRY ON ACTIVE DUTY	27. MILITARY OCCUPATIONAL SPECIALTY AND NO.
21 Jan 1944	Infantry Unit Commander 1542

28. BATTLES AND CAMPAIGNS
Northern France   Rhineland   Ardennes   Normandy   Central Europe

29. DECORATIONS AND CITATIONS
Silver Star   Purple Heart with One OLC   Combat Infantry Badge in ETO 1944
EAME Theater Campaign Medal with Five Bronze Stars

30. WOUNDS RECEIVED IN ACTION
24 July and 15 Sept 1944   ETO

31. SERVICE SCHOOLS ATTENDED None	32. SERVICE OUTSIDE CONTINENTAL U. S. AND RETURN		
	DATE OF DEPARTURE	DESTINATION	DATE OF ARRIVAL
	6 June 1944	ETO	14 June 44
33. REASON AND AUTHORITY FOR SEPARATION RR 1-5 Demobilization	21 Apr 1945	USA	5 May 1945

34. CURRENT TOUR OF ACTIVE DUTY						35. EDUCATION (years)		
CONTINENTAL SERVICE			FOREIGN SERVICE			GRAMMAR SCHOOL	HIGH SCHOOL	COLLEGE
YEARS	MONTHS	DAYS	YEARS	MONTHS	DAYS			
0	11	7	0	11	0	8	4	4

INSURANCE NOTICE
IMPORTANT IF PREMIUM IS NOT PAID WHEN DUE OR WITHIN THIRTY-ONE DAYS THEREAFTER, INSURANCE WILL LAPSE. MAKE CHECKS OR MONEY ORDERS PAYA...

36. KIND OF INSURANCE			37. HOW PAID		38. Effective Date of Allotment Discontinuance	39. Date of Next Premium Due (one month after 38)	40. PREMIUM DUE EACH MONTH	41. INTENTION OF VETERAN TO
Nat. Serv.	U.S. Govt.	None	Allotment	Direct to V.A.				Continue / Continue only / Discont.
X			X		30 Nov 45	31 Dec 45	*6.60	X

43. REMARKS
Lapel Button Issued
ASR Score (2 Sept 45)   76

44. SIGNATURE OF OFFICER BEING SEPARATED
/s/ James M. Unland 1st. Lt Inf

46. PERSONNEL OFFICER
CARROL J. HOWARD /s/ Carrol J. Howard
1ST Lt. Inf.

WD AGO FORM 53-98
1 November 1944
This form supersedes all previous editions of WD AGO Forms 53 and 280 for officers entitled to a Certificate of Service, which will not be used after receipt of this revision.

First Hand

Letter of gratitude from the Office of the Commanding General, Jacob Devers.

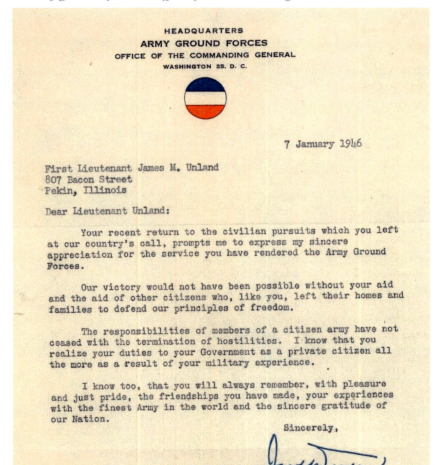

Jacob Loucks Devers,[61] according to Wikipedia, "was a general in the United States Army who commanded the 6th Army Group in the European Theater during World War II. He was involved in the development and adoption of numerous weapons, including the M4 Sherman and M26 Pershing tanks, the DUKW amphibious truck, the Bell H-13 Sioux helicopter and the M16 rifle."

---

[61] Wikipedia contributors, "Jacob L. Devers," *Wikipedia, The Free Encyclopedia*, https://en.wikipedia.org/w/index.php?title=Jacob_L._Devers&oldid=972451886 (accessed September 3, 2020).

Coming Home

GRACE UNITED METHODIST CHURCH
Pekin, Illinois

April 17, 2010   11 A.M.

A Celebration of the Life
Of
James M. Unland

Organ Prelude   Gayle Cooper, Organist

Words of Greeting & Grace (responsive)

    Dying, Christ destroyed our death. Rising, Christ restored our life. Christ will come again in glory. As in baptism *Jim* put on Christ so in Christ may *Jim* be clothed with glory. Here and now we are God's children, what we shall be has not yet been revealed; but we know we shall be like him as he is.

    Jesus said, I am the resurrection and I am life, those who believe in me, even though they die, yet shall they live, and whoever lives and believes in me shall never die.

    Friends we gather here to praise God and to witness to our faith as we celebrate the life of *James M. Unland*. May God grant us grace and peace through Christ Jesus, our Lord.

Prayer

Old Testament   Ecclesiastes 3:1-8

Psalms   Psalm 23

Solo   "How Great Thou Art"   Connie Moser

Eulogy   James J. Unland

Homily   Rev. Gary L. Ford

Military Background Remarks   John L. Unland

Military Honors Ceremony

Solo   "I'll Be Seeing You"   Connie Moser

*Benediction (responsive)

    We feel much the pain of separation; we are conscious of our loss, but we have a deep Christian faith and hope in Jesus Christ that nothing can separate us from the love of God.

    We have given thanks to God for the privilege of sharing life with *Jim Unland*. We have affirmed our faith in Jesus Christ and his victory over death.

    Now let us go forth, recognizing that being rooted and grounded in the love of God and knowing the love of Christ that surpasses all knowledge we remain in the hollow of God's hand.

    The Lord Bless you and keep you, the Lord make his face to shine upon you, and be gracious unto you; the Lord lift up the light of his countenance upon you, and give you peace.

    In your going out and coming in, in your lying down and in your rising-- in your labor and in your leisure--in your laughter and in your tears-- now and forever more.

    Amen and Amen.

Postlude   Organ

+ + + + +

Immediately following this Memorial Service you are invited to the Pekin Country Club to greet the Unland family.

Coming Home

In Tom Brokaw's book, The Greatest Generation, *he describes how my dad's generation and those who fought in World War II returned from their military service and proceeded to build our great nation. As you read the following program which talks about some of my dad's many life accomplishments, you will see how he embodied this "Greatest Generation" by continuing his civic focus throughout his adult life; not for "fame and recognition" as Brokaw put it, but because it was the "right thing to do." And, quite frankly, I believe he did it because he loved it.*

James M. Unland

January 05, 1922 - March 19, 2010

A treasured husband, father, grandfather, friend and avid golfer, Jim Unland of Paradise Valley, Arizona and Central Illinois, died on March 19, 2010. Jim is survived by his wife Frances, his two sons John and Jim, his grandsons Logan and Tyler and his daughters-in-law, Linda and Judy.

Jim was born in Delevan, Illinois on January 5, 1922. He attended Pekin High School and the University of Illinois, graduating in 1943. At the U. of I. he was a member of the Alpha Tau Omega Fraternity. He married Judith Johnston of Morton, Illinois in June of 1943 and, shortly thereafter, entered the Army's officer training program.

In the summer of 1944 Jim entered the European Theatre as a Company Commander of the 320th Infantry. In the process of liberating numerous cities and towns with his unit, he was wounded several times, each time returning to combat. He was awarded the Purple Heart with Cluster, the Bronze Star, the Silver Star and six Battle Stars and was honorably discharged in October 1945. He continued his military involvement after returning to Illinois, serving as a Company Commander in the 123rd Illinois National Guard through 1949. Jim often related his war experiences with friends and family, memories that have been captured in both written and audio diaries.

Following World War II he went into the insurance business in Pekin, Illinois with his father, J. Logan Unland. Over the years he also owned all or portions of other local businesses including Space Age Travel, Inc. in Peoria and Carriage Corner in Pekin.

He and his wife Judy were heavily involved in Central Illinois activities and politics. Jim ran for Congress in 1956 in the 18th Illinois Congressional District Republican primary and was Chair or co-Chair of several Republican presidential campaigns in the Central Illinois area.

In addition to his activities in the insurance business, Jim served on numerous civic boards including serving as: member of the Illinois Board of Higher Education during the 1970's and 80's; Vice Chairman of the Bradley University Board of Trustees; a co-founder and Board Chair of the Everett McKinley Dirksen Congressional Research Center; Chairman of the Route 121 Committee; Chairman of the Central Illinois Interstate Highway Committee; President of Pekin Rotary Club; County Chairman of the USO; County Chairman of the Red Cross Blood Program; Division Chairman of two Pekin Hospital Fund Drives; County Chairman of the American Cancer Society; County Chairman of the Heart Fund; Chairman of the Pekin United Fund; President of the Central Illinois Planning Corp.; Finance Chairman, Grace Methodist Church; Chairman of the Women's Western Open Golf Tournament; Board Member of both the Pekin and Peoria Chambers of Commerce; member of the American Legion, a Son of the American Revolution, a 32nd Degree Mason and a member of the Pekin Country Club, Peoria Country Club and Paradise Valley Country Club.

He also served on several corporate boards including Cilcorp, the First National Bank of Pekin, the Commercial National Bank of Peoria, the Midwest Financial Group and Bird Farm Sausage.

Jim lived in Central Illinois until 1994. His wife Judy had died in 1992. He met Frances Guenther in Paradise Valley in late 1993 and they married in early 1994 at which time Jim relocated to Paradise Valley.

First Hand

This is my father's bible that he carried with him all throughout the war—1944-1945. Though tattered and torn, he never got rid of it. I'm certain there was a good reason for that—although he was never able to tell me the story behind it.

"His Last Words" The last several years of my dad's life were challenging to say the least. Though his mind was sharp, his physical state required him to be bedridden or in a wheelchair. I was with him for the last two days of his life when my intuition had told me to fly from my home in Colorado to Phoenix to visit him. He was in the hospital and, though on morphine, was pretty lucid. In a meeting with his wife—my stepmother—we decided that it was time for him to go into a hospice facility. He had said many times during the previous years that he wanted to die; so I suggested that the time was upon him and I would be the one to tell him that we thought he should consider hospice. I left the meeting, walked into his room, and said, "Dad, what do you think about going into a hospice facility at this point?" He paused and said, "I think that's a good idea. I have led a full life and I have helped everyone that I could." I then rode with him in the ambulance from the hospital to the hospice facility—and on that ride I looked at him and asked, "Dad, are you sure you're ok with this?" In an unusually strong voice for his condition, he answered back, "Why wouldn't I be?" Which was so typical of him. Those were the last words I ever heard him speak. He passed away the very next day in hospice.

Chapter Twelve: A Few More Stories

"GRATITUDE AND TEARS IN BELGIUM"

Sometime in the mid 90's, I traveled to Europe to interview several organizations on behalf of my client, DuPont. I traveled to Italy, France, Spain, and Germany for this work. One of my last stops was in Belgium in a town near Leige. I mentioned to the owner of the company and his son, who also worked with him, that my father had been in World War II, in the 3rd Army under General Patton and had been in the Battle of the Bulge in efforts to liberate Europe from the Nazis. When I mentioned this, the father jumped out of his chair—literally jumped—and came over to me and gave me a huge hug with tears streaming down his face. He said, "I was 12 years old when your dad and General Patton's army liberated our town. I remember those terrible days only too vividly. And please tell your father how grateful my father, myself, and my family are to him."

I was both shocked and moved by this and tears welled up in my eyes and I said, "Sir, I will definitely relay this to my Dad." Which I did. This really brought home to me the impact of my father's effort in a very personal and real way.

"RETRACING MY DAD'S ROUTE IN EUROPE"

Years ago, Linda and I took a trip to France, and we decided to retrace some of my dad's route during his time in the war.

In his memoir and in many stories he told me as a young boy, he talked about the "hedgerows" and how dangerous it was to be walking along in those "hedgerows," and how the Germans would hide in the hedgerows and pin people down between them. Until I actually saw them for myself, I had no idea just how dense they were and how difficult they must have been to maneuver through. We walked along some of them and was overcome with an enormous sense of dread thinking how small we felt next to them; and how small my father must have felt knowing that at any moment the enemy could have opened fire on him from the other side.

Hedgerow photo by John & Linda Unland

We first went to the museum in Normandy, which was breathtaking, and it showed what the GIs wore and we learned a lot about the invasion from a wonderful guide.

I told the guide that my father had landed at Utah Beach weeks after the invasion and he took us down to Utah Beach so that I could stand there on that same beach; with the water lapping up against the shore, imagining him walking on that very same sand so many years ago.

The guide told us that in all likelihood my father walked through the hundred-yard path up to what was then considered one of the ally corridors. I think there were three corridors which the allies had secured movement from the beaches into interior France. I stood there looking at that path, thinking that there he was at 23 years old—walking with his gear and his rifle and his helmet—having landed at Utah Beach and marching up these

100 yards into safety along this corridor. And here I am walking that same path at the age of 63 that he had walked when he was 23; and at that moment all of my animosity toward him and all of the feelings that I had harbored against him for his behavior of forsaking me and my family for other people, I just let it all go on that walk. I just forgave him. I just let it all go because I decided it was time to honor him for what he did and how courageous he was in his life and in this battle.

First Hand

Like any relationship between a father and son, he disappointed me at times in my life as I'm sure I disappointed him. But as I walked in his steps (about 100 yards through the sand on Utah Beach) and realized that I was re-tracing the path he had followed on his way to help liberate France under the command of General Patton, I was humbled by the enormity of the burden he must have felt with each step he took; and any animosity I felt towards him simply melted away.

And on this same trip, Linda and I drove down to this village called St. Lo, which is referred to in my dad's diary. We drove down to the village where in my father's diary he talks about the 35th infantry regiment taking the town and liberating Saint-Lo. He wrote about having to take the high ground that the Germans occupied and about a church at the highest point of the town; and how it was necessary for the allies, and for him and his 35th Infantry Division to take this high ground. We drove into the town because it was part of his infantry experience. Just as we entered the town there was a plaque—in red, white, and blue—that says, "Thank you 35th Infantry Division of the Third Army for liberating Saint-Lo" on some date.

So that's another story of my dad's trek through Europe on his way to the Battle of the Bulge; and how I was able to get a small sense of it simply by walking up that path on Utah Beach. And again, this trip gave me a much better understanding of my dad—having "walked in his shoes"—so to speak. I gained some deep admiration for him that I never thought I would ever have and I was finally able to put my mixed feelings for him aside.

A Few More Stories

"MAKING PEACE BEFORE HIS INEVITABLE DEATH"

When my dad was gravely ill, I asked him where he would like his ashes placed when he died. He was then living in Phoenix, Arizona, and I was living in Colorado and would fly down to see him once a month, at least. In our discussions he was very matter of fact and not despondent at all.

On one such trip he mentioned to me that the first place he would like his ashes scattered—or the most important place—was at our family's graveyard plot in Delavan, Illinois, where he was born and where his grandparents and my mother are buried. Then he said he also wanted his ashes placed near my mother's memorial at the Betty Ford Garden in Vail, Colorado. They had a condominium there and spent many, many summers in Vail; and absolutely loved the area.

The next place he wanted his ashes placed was on our property in Driggs, Idaho. He loved the Teton mountains and wanted some ashes placed there. And I said, "Okay, got it." Then I remember him sitting back and thinking and getting very emotional. And finally he said, "I also want some of my ashes placed on my best friend in the Army's grave site. My best friend in the Army was O.T. Willrich." And I said, "Okay dad, I'll do that. Where was he from?" And he said, "Well, he's from a small town in Texas." But he couldn't remember the name of the town. I told him I would do my best to find it—and he did give me some geographic bearing, though I can't remember what it was—but the

conversation stopped there and I promised him I would do my best to carry out his wishes.

And then I said to him, "Dad, how would it be if I placed some of your ashes in the American cemetery in Luxemburg?" (which is where thousands of American soldiers are buried who fought in the Battle of the Bulge) But then I added, "How about if I sprinkled some of your ashes on General Patton's grave?" (General Patton is buried there because he wanted to be buried with his men) When he heard me say that, he looked at me with these huge, wide eyes and said, "Really? You would do that for me?" Of course, I responded, "Yes, I'll do that for you. If that's what you want me to do. I'd be happy to." And then he said, "John, that's a great idea. I would love that."

He passed away maybe six months after that, but in between that time he called all of his friends and told them, "John is going to put my ashes on General Patton's grave site in Luxembourg. Isn't that fantastic?" He was so excited about the fact that he would be back with his commanding general at his grave site. And he certainly didn't let me forget that I promised to do that—though it did take me a number of years to keep my promise and honor all of his requested locations.

He died in 2010, but it wasn't until 2019 that I was finally able to take the trip to Luxembourg. Back in 2007 I had a stroke, and I still suffer from many invisible deficits including partial blindness. I still lose my sense of place and time very easily and I struggle daily to remember things. I'm not going to dwell on that, but I do still have some serious deficiencies.

One of the things that I did a lot of during my career was travel. I traveled all the time by myself on business; rented cars, flew on planes, checked into hotels, hailed taxis, made all the reservations and so forth. But since my stroke in 2007 I hadn't been able to travel anywhere alone—nowhere—because it was too intimidating for someone who was still partially blind and didn't always know where he was or what time of day it was to travel away from home. I couldn't even drive a car anymore.

So, I decided that not only was I going to take this trip to Luxembourg—but I was going to go all by myself. This was something I needed to do for both my father and for me. Taking this trip and putting his ashes on Patton's grave in that cemetery would not only be fulfilling a dream and a wish of his, but also for me, it would be completing a mission of my own. I wanted very much to cross this last hurdle of regaining my validity and sense of independence and a trip overseas was something I always knew would be the ultimate challenge for me to overcome.

So, I arranged all the facets of this trip to Luxemburg—the hotels, the flights, the trains—and then flew into Paris for four nights by myself. I then took the train to Luxembourg, checked into my hotel, and taxied out to the American cemetery where thousands of soldiers from the Battle of the Bulge are buried along with General Patton.

In my pocket I carried a tablespoon full of my father's ashes, which I sprinkled at the edge of General Patton's grave site on a beautiful sunny day—and once again, I reconciled my differences with my father and honored him in the way he wished to be honored; an honor that I was very proud to bestow upon him.

First Hand

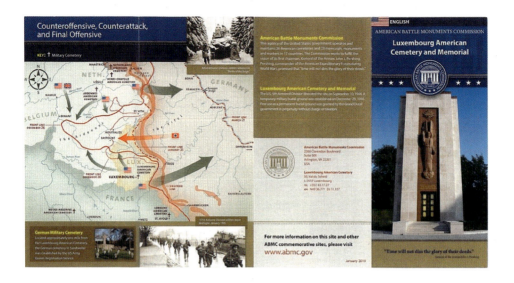

"REUNITING MY DAD WITH O.T."

The other piece of this story was tracking down O.T. Willrich's grave site. During my career I worked with a wonderful woman, Susan McAninley, who could find pretty much anything. And so, I asked Susan if she could try to find the grave site of O.T. Willrich. I gave her all the information that I'd received from my father, which wasn't much. But sure enough, she found his grave site in Texas.

Now, an important part of this story that I haven't explained yet is this: The reason it was so important for my dad to have his ashes near his buddy O.T. is because O.T. was killed when he and my father were together. O.T. was assigned to a very difficult mission but my father was not; and on that mission O.T. was killed.

My dad had always wondered since 1945 whether he had written O.T.'s parents a letter explaining to them how O.T. had died and the importance of their relationship. He wondered that up until a month before he died. He told me a few times, "John, I don't know if I wrote his parents. I just don't remember if I did that."

Well when Susan discovered the grave site, she also contacted this town's small library and asked them questions about O.T. They told her that, "Oh, yes, we have a memorial to O.T. here in our library and we'll send you some pictures." So, they sent pictures of O.T. himself and his trunk that he used to ship his military gear over to Europe and back. They had a bit of a shrine set up for him—and in their shrine they had a letter from my father that he had written to O.T.'s parents back in 1945 describing O.T.'s death and their relationship. The library was kind enough to send us a copy of that letter and I have included it within the pages of this book so that you can read it for yourself.

When I received the letter, I called my father and said, "Dad, you're not going to believe this but I'm going to read you something." He was gravely ill then, lying in bed. I read him the letter—and when I finished there was a long pause—and all he said was, "I did the right thing."

First Hand

```
To:                              From:

Mr. & Mrs. Willrich              Lt. J. M. Unland - 0540236
La Grange, Texas                 Co. F., 320th. Inf.
                                 A.P.O. 35 - % Postmaster
                                 New York, N. Y.
                                 Sept. 16, 1944
```

Dear Mr. & Mrs. Willrich -   (Please write sometime and send me Pat's address - Thank you)

No doubt you are surprised to receive a letter from me, not knowing who I am, but after serious consideration I feel that you would undoubtedly like to know the circumstances behind the death of your boy. "T" (as I called him) and I became acquainted in Aug. 1943 at Fort Benning and were in the same platoon in OCS, the same regiment in 87th Div., the same replacement company from Fort Meade until France and were lucky enough to be assigned to same battalion in 35th Div. - I tell you this to let you know that I knew him very well and considered him my closest friend in the Army.

It was on Aug. 16 that our battalion had as its mission, the town of Chateridum. "T"'s Co. was on our left and had advanced under heavy fire to the edge of town where they were pinned down. Our artillery laid in a terrific barrage after which we were all to advance to the town. After the barrage lifted, "T" leading his platoon which was the forward platoon in the battalion started to advance. It was necessary for him to cross a deep ditch before hitting the first building and it was in this ditch that the Germans had their machine guns on both flanks. He no sooner hit the ditch than they opened fire and fatally wounded him. He died in the arms of his platoon sergeant. I found out about it the next day and immediately talked to his men. They told me "T" was the best officer they had ever had and that he did everything in his power for their welfare & safety. Everyone who ever knew him considered him a wonderful man and officer. Please accept my deepest sympathy in your hour of need and be thankful his soul rests in peace. May God bless you both.

Jim Unland

A Few More Stories

So, there's another piece of his history. Somehow Susan found this letter. All she had was the name "O.T. Willrich" and that he was born in Texas—maybe she had a little bit more than that but not much. I then shipped my father's ashes down to my Aunt Sue who lived in Dallas and she drove them to O.T.'s grave site and placed them there for my dad.

This is a note that Susan wrote to me during her search:

> It appears that O.T. is Otto Thomas Willrich Jr., born in 1923 in LaGrange, Fayette County Texas.
> He is probably buried in Texas. My guess is he is in a military cemetery near his family's home, or buried in the family plot nearby.
>
> **The search:**
>
> 1. checked out info@abmc.gov (American Battle Monuments Commission which lists American Cemeteries in France) and sent a query. There was no entry for anyone with the Willrich name.
>
> On reading guestbook entries, I learned other soldiers who were in these units were buried in Lorraine and Epinal in France. D-Day casualties were mostly buried at the American Cemetery at Colleville-Sur-Mer.
>
> 2. Did query on Willrich family site on Ancestry,com 5/21/09. Waiting for a reply. (This may take a while…sometimes responses take months…depends on when a family member decides to check the site).
>
> Also found birth record on Ancestryry.com that seems to fit your father's description exactly. This must be our guy.
>
> Birth record:
> O.T. Willrich Jr. (Otto Thomas) born in LaGrange, Fayette Co, Texas in 1923
> It checks out because it also shows up on death record.
>
> 3. Signed guestbook with query on www.htmlgear.tripod.com (site has a lot of info on Saint Lo battles and the 35th Division, 320th Infantry.) Sounded like a hellhole. Fighting in the hedgerows.
>
> 4. Signed guestbook with query for 35th Infantry division website (www.35thinfdivassoc.com). Thee guys all seem to be located in Kansas. Lots of other queries of people looking for veterans.
>
> 5. Birth and death records on Ancestry.com. This site has been around for a while and originally was run by the Mormons who are heavily into family trees. Here it is.

First Hand

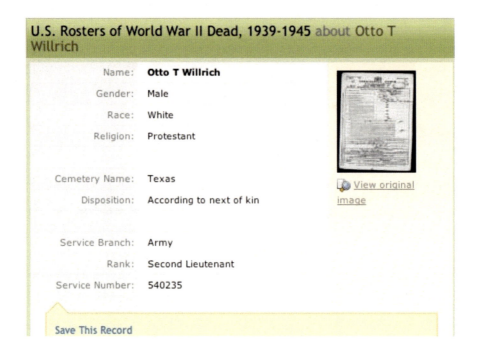

Male, white Protestant
Cemetery Name: Texas
--disposition according to next of kin
Service Branch: Army
Rank: Second Lieutenant
Service #: 540235

So next I'll check out military cemeteries in Texas. Internment there seems more likely than internment in family plot...a lot of families who lost sons preferred military cemeteries). Most likely the cemetery was close to LaGrange.
Alternately, O.T.'s body may have been shipped from France to a family plot. If someone on the family message board answers me I'll know for sure.
Also knowing the Service # is a big help.

A Few More Stories

Lt. O.T. Willrich

A Few More Stories

I think it's important to note again that my trip to Europe accomplished both goals of re-establishing my independence by doing what I used to do and also honoring my dad by putting his ashes with his commanding General, George Patton; it was a double accomplishment. He would have been proud of me just as I was proud of him.

When I went to Luxembourg and placed those ashes on Patton's grave site, I also took copies of my father's medals and placed them next to General Patton's memorial for a photo. As I was doing this, two young men walked up behind me and asked me if they could help me take the photo. They asked me what I was doing and I mentioned to them why I was there. They were both in the U.S. Air Force out of Colorado and had made the trip to see the grave sites of World War II in Europe and Normandy, and this was one of the places they chose to visit. They almost had tears in their eyes when they realized I was the son of a World War II veteran of the Battle of the Bulge.

That was another very special moment on a very memorable trip; which concludes the stories of the World War II era. And class is dismissed.

*White House/Watergate Diary:
As Written by John Unland
1974/1975*

Chapter Thirteen: My Time at the White House During Watergate and Beyond

An Internship to Remember

In order to give readers some important context around this portion of the book, to follow is some important background information on the Watergate scandal which was in full swing when I arrived at the White House for my internship program in June of 1974:

According to information available on Wikipedia.org, "The Watergate scandal was a political scandal in the United States involving the administration of U.S. President Richard Nixon from 1972 to 1974 that led to Nixon's resignation. The scandal stemmed from the Nixon administration's continuous attempts to cover up its involvement in the June 17, 1972 break-in of the Democratic National Committee headquarters at the Washington, D.C. Watergate Office Building. After the five perpetrators were arrested, the press and the U.S. Justice Department connected the cash found on them at the time to the Nixon re-election campaign committee. Further investigations, along with revelations during subsequent trials of the burglars, led the U.S. House of Representatives to grant its judiciary committee additional investigation authority to probe into 'certain matters within its jurisdiction', and the U.S. Senate to create a special investigative committee. The resulting Senate Watergate hearings were broadcast 'gavel-to-gavel' nationwide by PBS and aroused public interest. Witnesses testified that the president had approved plans to cover up administration involvement in the break-in, and that there was a voice-activated taping system in the Oval Office. Throughout the investigation, the administration resisted its probes, which led to a constitutional crisis.

Several major revelations and egregious presidential action against the investigation later in 1973 prompted the House to commence an impeachment process against Nixon. The U.S. Supreme Court ruled that Nixon must release the Oval Office tapes to government investigators. The tapes revealed that Nixon had conspired to cover up activities that took place after the break-in and had attempted to use federal officials to deflect the investigation. The House Judiciary Committee then approved articles of impeachment against Nixon for obstruction of justice, abuse of power, and contempt of Congress. With his complicity in the cover-up made public and his political support completely eroded, Nixon resigned from office on August 9, 1974. It is believed that, had he not done so, he would have been impeached by the House and removed from office by a trial in the Senate. He is the only U.S. president to have resigned from office. On September 8, 1974, Nixon's successor, Gerald Ford, pardoned him.

There were 69 people indicted and 48 people—many of them top Nixon administration officials—were convicted. The metonym Watergate came to encompass an array of clandestine and often illegal activities undertaken by members of the Nixon administration, including bugging the offices of political opponents and people of whom Nixon or his officials were suspicious; ordering investigations of activist groups and political figures; and using the Federal Bureau of Investigation, the Central Intelligence Agency, and the Internal Revenue Service as political weapons. The use of the suffix "-gate" after an identifying term has since become synonymous with public scandal, especially political scandal.[62]"

Then there was the "Smoking Gun" tape which was released on August 5th, 1974. (Official White House response and Press Release is included within the pages of this book)

Also found on Wikipedia.org was this information: "On April 11, 1974, the House Judiciary Committee subpoenaed the tapes of 42 White House conversations. Later that month, Nixon released more than 1,200 pages of edited transcripts of the subpoenaed tapes, but refused to turn over the actual tapes, claiming executive privilege once more. The Judiciary Committee, however, rejected Nixon's edited transcripts, saying that they did not comply with the subpoena.

Sirica, acting on a request from Jaworski, issued a subpoena for the tapes of 64 presidential conversations to use as evidence in the criminal cases against indicted former Nixon administration officials. Nixon refused, and Jaworski appealed to the U.S. Supreme Court to force Nixon to turn over the tapes. On July 24, 1974, the Supreme Court ordered Nixon to release the tapes. The 8–0 ruling (Justice William Rehnquist recused himself owing to having worked for Attorney General John Mitchell) in United States v. Nixon found that President Nixon was wrong in arguing that courts are compelled to honor, without question, any presidential claim of executive privilege.

The White House released the subpoenaed tapes on August 5. One tape, later known as the "smoking gun" tape, documented the initial stages of the Watergate coverup. On it, Nixon and H. R. Haldeman are heard formulating a plan to block investigations by having the CIA falsely claim to the FBI that national security was involved. This demonstrated both that Nixon had been told of the White House connection to the Watergate burglaries soon after they took place, and that he had approved plans to thwart the investigation.

---

[62] Wikipedia contributors, "Watergate scandal," Wikipedia, *The Free Encyclopedia*, https://en.wikipedia.org/w/index.php?title=Watergate_scandal&oldid=975846960 (accessed November 10, 2020).

My Time at the White House During Watergate and Beyond

In a statement accompanying the release of the tape, Nixon accepted blame for misleading the country about when he had been told of White House involvement, stating that he had a lapse of memory.

Once the "smoking gun" transcript was made public, Nixon's political support practically vanished. The ten Republicans on the House Judiciary Committee who had voted against impeachment in committee announced that they would now vote for impeachment once the matter reached the House floor. He lacked substantial support in the Senate as well; Barry Goldwater and Hugh Scott estimated no more than 15 Senators were willing to even consider acquittal. Facing certain impeachment in the House of Representatives and equally certain conviction in the Senate, Nixon announced his resignation on the evening of Thursday, August 8, 1974, effective as of noon the next day.[63]"

---

[63] Wikipedia contributors, "Nixon White House tapes," *Wikipedia, The Free Encyclopedia*, https://en.wikipedia.org/w/index.php?title=Nixon_White_House_tapes&oldid=972004948 (accessed November 10, 2020)

The flag of America as she continues to protect freedom

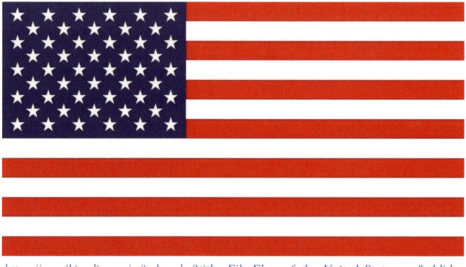

https://en.wikipedia.org/w/index.php?title=File:Flag_of_the_United_States.svg&oldid=981746251 Current flag of the United States of America

Chapter Fourteen: My Personal Diary of My White House Days

In the spring of 1974, I was enrolled as a student at Colgate University, but was actually living in London and attending the London School of Economics on an exchange program when I applied for an internship at the White House during the Nixon administration. I had an interest in politics and thought an internship would be a good opportunity. I was accepted, and subsequently received a telegram on Memorial Day 1974 indicating that I was expected to report to Washington D.C. in four days. I packed up my belongings, shipped them to my home in Pekin, Illinois, and flew to D.C. The first thing I did when I arrived was to get my long hair cut. Then my dad told me to go straight to Brooks Brothers and buy some business clothes—which, of course, I did.

This was my international ID during my time in England: a month studying architecture at Oxford University and then on a student exchange program at the London School of Economics.

June 3rd 1974—

Arrived at White House old Executive Office Building (EOB) (which is the large building adjacent to the actual White House complex where the President resides and the West Wing and Oval Office are located) at 8:30, one half hour before I was due in room 450. I took a long stroll around the White House grounds and again was entranced by its beauty. It is, by far, the most beautiful building in Washington.

Old Executive Office Building (public domain photo)

Oval Office photo by John Unland

At 9:00 I walked through the main entrance at which I was cleared and went up to room 450. Inside was Pam Powell and all the interns. The room is that at which many news conferences are held and is decorated throughout with pictures of the Nixon family. Pam had us introduce ourselves and we then filled out several forms—tax, security questions, etc. for about two hours. We had a lecture from Secret Service on security matters and told to use common sense. Then we were assigned our jobs. I work for Mr. William Baroody, Jr.[64], who, in a large sense, filled in for Charles Carlson's tasks and was given additional responsibility. I was surprised to find that I was assigned directly to a Senior Staff

---

[64] Wikipedia contributors, "William J. Baroody Jr.," *Wikipedia, The Free Encyclopedia*, https://en.wikipedia.org/w/index.php?title=William_J._Baroody_Jr.&oldid=955830189 (accessed September 17, 2020), "William J. Baroody Jr. (November 5, 1937 – June 8, 1996) was an American government official best known for running the White House Office of Public Liaison under President Gerald Ford and, later, the American Enterprise Institute (AEI)."

Official, but think I'll channel most of my work through Wayne Valis.[65]

Wayne took me around to meet Mr. Baroody's staff, and to meet Mr. Baroody himself. He helps set the philosophical tone of the Administration. Naturally, I'll learn more of his tasks as summer wears on. He used to be Ass't Sec. of Defense under Laird[66] and he, Wayne, and Laird all worked together.

The office of Baroody is 4 doors down from Nixon's personal office in the EOB—187 office, where he works mostly. Wayne & Mr. Baroody gave me an office on the 4th floor—spent remainder of the day getting office in shape & reading speeches of Laird, Baroody, & materials related to Baroody's operations. Then to ORS (Office of Revenue Sharing) to pick up materials related to revenue sharing & new federalism (located in the Treasury Building adjacent to the White House). I really like Wayne—though a challenge to become friendly with & work with.

June 4th—

Arrived at 8:25 & went to Wayne's office—these offices are really beautiful! —to repeat. We shot the breeze until 9:00. Talked about White House prior to his arrival—April '72—said it was—and still is—laced with too many PR people on staff & not enough political minds. Talked of '72 campaign & said that the guys (Halderman, Erlichman, & others) who ran the show—PR from California —knew how to image-make & get those images across to voters, but they didn't really build the right kind of political campaign. This would have an immediate advantage to Nixon's re-election effort, but then the result was such a shallow base of general support. The '72 campaign was built with general widespread support through PR but not "authentic"

---

[65] Nancy Evaldson, "Wayne H. Valis Files, 1973-77," *FordLibraryMuseum.gov*, https://www.fordlibrarymuseum.gov/library/guides/findingaid/valisfiles.asp (accessed September 17, 2020), "Wayne Valis joined the White House staff during President Nixon's second term and performed duties in areas of public liaison, recruitment, legislative tracking and speechwriting under the direction of Melvin Laird and William J. Baroody."

[66] Wikipedia contributors, "Melvin Laird," *Wikipedia, The Free Encyclopedia*, https://en.wikipedia.org/w/index.php?title=Melvin_Laird&oldid=976743137 (accessed September 17, 2020), "Melvin Robert Laird (September 1, 1922 – November 16, 2016) was an American politician, writer and statesman. He was a U.S. congressman from Wisconsin from 1953 to 1969 before serving as Secretary of Defense from 1969 to 1973 under President Richard Nixon."

coalition political support. Bad for country & politics, says Wayne.

Then chatted about Watergate—Wayne came after break-in. Wayne critical of the Administration on several points of handling the case—and of Nixon. Said Watergate affects his work all the time every day. Not the implementation of policy—not the hard-core work—but presents itself as a roadblock in the form of everyone asking about it—reporters, etc. so that the work he is trying to implement & get across to areas of concern is delayed & frequently neglected. Talked to the press—very critical of press, but not in the same manner as Nixon. Says Nixon and those close to him—Ziegler[67]—see press attacking them & take it as a personal slap, personal criticism, which it is. But, says Wayne, the Administration tries to build support for itself by telling the American people that the press has a vendetta against them.

Wayne feels this type of "complex" about the press & support-building by the Administration is "disgusting." He believes what the Administration should do is to hit the press legitimately—attack their objections and criticism. Example—if & when they show programs and write stories about cost overruns in the defense dept, inept bureaucracy, etc., the Administration should hit back & talk about the USSR's increasing their nuclear Polaris sub fleet that legitimately authorizes spending on defense, show the programs in defense against those of other nations to give the people a sense of the real security America has. Hit press legitimately and rally support. Wayne went on to say "Of course, now it's too late to do this—Watergate and press are too formidable, it seems, to overcome on a legitimate basis, if at all."

---

[67] Wikipedia contributors, "Ron Ziegler," *Wikipedia, The Free Encyclopedia*, https://en.wikipedia.org/w/index.php?title=Ron_Ziegler&oldid=975315519 (accessed September 18, 2020), "Ronald Louis Ziegler (May 12, 1939 – February 10, 2003) was the eleventh White House Press Secretary and Assistant to the President, serving during United States President Richard Nixon's administration."

My Personal Diary of My White House Days

[Richard M. Nixon, head-and-shoulders portrait, facing front]. From the Presidential File Collection, [between 1969 and 1974]. Library of Congress Prints & Photographs Division. https://www.loc.gov/item/96522669/

**Many images (such as the one immediately following this note) are scans of actual documents and photos from my days at the White House.

Others will be given proper credit (such as the one immediately preceding this note) when necessary.

First Hand

These are remarks in April of 1974 by President Nixon regarding Watergate before I arrived at the White House. As you can tell by the last two paragraphs, the Watergate scandal was already in high gear.

FOR IMMEDIATE RELEASE   APRIL 29, 1974

OFFICE OF THE WHITE HOUSE PRESS SECRETARY

THE WHITE HOUSE

ADDRESS BY THE PRESIDENT
ON LIVE TELEVISION AND RADIO

THE OVAL OFFICE

9:01 P.M. EDT

        Good evening.

        I have asked for this time tonight in order to announce my answer to the House Judiciary Committee's subpoena for additional Watergate tapes, and to tell you something about the actions I shall be taking tomorrow -- about what I hope they will mean to you, and about the very difficult choices that were presented to me.

        These actions will at last, once and for all, show that what I knew and what I did with regard to the Watergate break-in and cover-up were just as I have described them to you from the very beginning.

        I have spent many hours during the past few weeks thinking about what I would say to the American people if I were to reach the decision I shall announce tonight. And so, my words have not been lightly chosen; I can assure you they are deeply felt.

        It was almost two years ago, in June 1972, that five men broke into the Democratic National Committee headquarters in Washington. It turned out that they were connected with my Re-Election Committee, and the Watergate break-in became a major issue in the campaign.

        The full resources of the FBI and the Justice Department were used to investigate the incident thoroughly. I instructed my staff and campaign aides to cooperate fully with the investigation. The FBI conducted nearly 1500 interviews. For nine months -- until March 1973 -- I was assured by those charged with conducting and monitoring the investigations that no one in the White House was involved.

        Nevertheless, for more than a year, there have been allegations and insinuations that I knew about the planning of the Watergate break-in and that I was involved in an extensive plot to cover it up. The House Judiciary Committee is now investigating these charges.

                              MORE

                                                  (OVER)

June 4, 1974 (continued)

Spent most of yesterday reading on materials related to the philosophy of the Nixon Administration. I was quite amazed to find that the administration which is regarded as having no philosophy—the pragmatic, hard-hitting administration—really is laced with philosophical threads. Indeed, Mr. Baroody, Jr., is part of a think-tank for philosophical linkages from the Administration to the public.

The basic, very, very general philosophy running throughout the administration is: have those whose problems are at hand give the federal government sufficient input to acknowledge their abilities in assisting with problem solving.

Take general revenue sharing as an example. The federal government allocates a hunk of money per state based upon the formula (population, per capita income, tax factors, etc). The State government then gets one third of the hunk and the localities and county governments divvy up the other two thirds based, again, on similar factors. But the crux is here: The Fed. keeps hands off on how the monies are spent per respective area, (i.e. law enforcement, environmental programs, etc.). No monies are connected with attached strings except for these specific areas. This type of program—emblematic of the New Federalism[68], that it gets entirely away from Fed. control of monies through the old grants in aid and matching funds programs.

On the international level—Vietnamization—let those nearest the problem solve the problem with American assistance and their own initiative. Indeed, debatable on how much initiative etc. is not American. Yet, still the philosophy is there.

Until recently, I fear that the average American was unaware of the correlation of a philosophy in the two areas. I was, until today.

---

[68] Wikipedia contributors, "New Federalism," *Wikipedia, The Free Encyclopedia*, https://en.wikipedia.org/w/index.php?title=New_Federalism&oldid=951139839 (accessed September 17, 2020), "New Federalism is a political philosophy of devolution, or the transfer of certain powers from the United States federal government back to the states."

June 5, 1974

Today, was in Wayne's office and given task to write 500-word article for Mr. Baroody's use for the American Retail Federation. Speech has to deal with Nixon Administration's views on inflation and on the energy situation. Naturally, had to be pro-business. I didn't know the first thing of what to do. Sent for articles and speeches, etc. and got overview of what inflation was all about. Then called Jim (my brother, who was living in Chicago) to cut him into the action. He aided a good deal and, if nothing else, cleared me up on increased production and its relationship to inflation. Then pieced article together, which was to be ready at noon. I had not written the first draft by noon! Wayne had an extended lunch break and I had until two to finish it. I think it was OK. Called Jim back to read it to him and he thought it was "great." We'll see. Looking forward to feedback from Wayne.

4:00, had intern meeting. All had to tell our jobs, etc. and what we were doing. Some had rather menial jobs. Mike (my office mate was a guy by the name of Michael Mulligan from Newburyport, MA, a town I had never heard of. Mike (who also works with Mr. Baroody as an intern) and I get along well and are lucky in jobs we have. Parties galore, etc. Just act nicely, smile, etc. Off to greet Cathy.

The entire office staff with whom I worked during my tenure at the White House.

June 6, 1974

Came to work to find that Wayne was in middle of two crises at 8:30 A.M. Had to get article out that I had written for Baroody the previous day and also had to get Presidential Proclamation on D-Day out. Were in constant state of panic until 2:00 P.M.

Article naturally had been dissected by pros and came out looking somewhat similar to that which I had written. But we had to have it whipped into final shape by 11:00 A.M. Wayne took care of that.

He gave me responsibility for coming up with a rough draft on the D-Day thing. So, I set out to the conference room on the first floor of our office space and wrote what I felt was a pretty good draft. At 10:30, Wayne and I hashed it over and he suddenly tells me he wants it to be in Ziegler's office by 11:00. Baroody and Wayne each had to go over it and time was short. Wayne pressured one of his secretaries into typing it and she was so nervous that she made copious mistakes and broke down crying. She put the icing on the cake and we didn't get it in by 11:00. Next was to get it out to the Veterans, at least. Got ahold of a list of 35 Vet organizations and telegraphed it. They would have been sensitive to the fact that the President of the United States didn't recognize the 30th Anniversary of the invasion that began the drive for victory in WWII. It was a mess. I can't believe that, of all the people in the White House, no one thought to write up a Proclamation on D-Day, after the 1,000 French came to this country to commemorate our efforts, and we, in our feeble attempt missed the 11:00 News Conference. Weak and unorganized.

Spent the rest of the day going over letters Wayne wanted me to work on. I had to, for the first time, officially defend the President against calls for resignation in a letter to a big-wig Representative in Pennsylvania who wrote Baroody. It was a logical letter and didn't say much that I didn't personally agree with. Of course, I would have deleted or moderated much if it had been my own letter.

First Hand

This is a draft memo from me to Mr. Baroody defending the President against impeachment.

MEMORANDUM

Impeachment

THE WHITE HOUSE
WASHINGTON

Dear Mr. ~~_____~~,

Thank-you for your letter dated in May concerning your views on the present political situation in the country. I must apologize for the delay in my response.

Indeed, it is the right of every citizen in America to voice his opinion on Watergate, its possible ramifications on American government, and to offer his personal solutions to the situation as he sees it. In my position, I appreciate the divergence of opinions, weighing each of them against my own.

There are those who feel that because of Watergate, the government has come to a standstill- that the President spends undue time protecting only his personal interests and image, neglecting the interests of the country. Your letter indicated concern that the President is "surrounded" and "emeshed" in scandle and should step down "as quickly as possible."

In my judgement, the President is in complete control of the Executive branch of this government. Internationally, he and Secretary Kissinger have nearly pieced together the complexed puzzle of a Mid-East peace. The President's trips to the Mid-East and th the USSR will provide the needed dialogue essential in easing world tensions. Domestically, President Nixon has taken strong initiatives in many areas, especially in the nation's two most pressing problems: inflation and energy. Much administratively backed legislation on energy, education, trade, health, and other areas is now in Congress pending action. ~~The point is that the President is leading this country in a determined~~

My Personal Diary of My White House Days

MEMORANDUM

THE WHITE HOUSE
WASHINGTON

The point is that the President is leading this country in a determined manner. Those who advocate the President's resignation or stepping aside are recommending a grave, high-risk gamble. The President's primary interest now, as it always has been, in not "image", but America. Through America's history, generation after generation has placed high value in the laws and institutions of this country. Our pluralist institutions have served us well, and our Constitution is a strong one. You, also, expressed concern over the survival of our institutions. Within the Constitution of the United States lies the appropriate proceedure for dealing with the problems as they have now arisen in America. The President of the Unived States is entitled, like any other American, to defend himself through due process of law, against acquisitions he believes to be erroneous and against charges he believes he is innocent of. Not only is President Nixon entitled to such rights, but to resign- to be hounded from office-because of moral indictments, mis-interpreted motives, attitudes, profanity, or for his "life-style", would certainly weaken the office he has commanded during the past six years.

We all must affirm and reaffirm our beliefs in our institutions, for by doing so we a reaffirm our beliefs in ourselves as a just, lawful people. Two hundred years ago America devised the greatest governmental system the world ha ever known. To damage the key elements of our Constitytion now, through inappropriate action, would tarnish the Presidency and the nation for years to come.

213

June 7th

Finished Wayne's letters. Worked from 7:15 - 1:00.

Walked over to the South lawn and stood around, sick that I didn't bring my camera. I was standing about eight feet from Ron Ziegler, Alexander Haig[69], Vice President Ford, and of all people, Henry Kissinger[70]. I was right at the door and the Cabinet was on the White House lawn with the helicopter—Presidential seal—on the White House lawn also. Marines and other branches of the military had guards at attention with red carpet in front of the copter. Security was intense—even on the White House lawn. Men in the bushes, etc. I would hear, over their intercoms, voices stating exactly where the President was, how many seconds it would take for him to get into the elevator, come down to the lawn, etc. "He's in the elevator and will be down in twenty seconds." Out walked the President, his wife, kids and husbands. All shook hands with the Arab and Israeli diplomats and with the Cabinet and the Vice President. Then the President spoke a few words of how this mission[71] would build upon that of Kissinger's efforts (shuttle diplomacy[72]) and would bring all the involved nations closer together with each other and with the U.S. He needs to justify this trip (to get out of Washington, D.C. at the height of Watergate). Good timing. Then Ford spoke. Then, the President started for the copter and

---

[69] Wikipedia contributors, "Alexander Haig," *Wikipedia, The Free Encyclopedia*, https://en.wikipedia.org/w/index.php?title=Alexander_Haig&oldid=979041244 (accessed September 27, 2020), "Alexander Meigs Haig Jr. (December 2, 1924 – February 20, 2010) was the United States Secretary of State under President Ronald Reagan and the White House chief of staff under presidents Richard Nixon and Gerald Ford."

[70] Wikipedia contributors, "Henry Kissinger," *Wikipedia, The Free Encyclopedia*, https://en.wikipedia.org/w/index.php?title=Henry_Kissinger&oldid=979500968 (accessed September 27, 2020), "Henry Alfred Kissinger (born Heinz Alfred Kissinger; May 27, 1923) is an American politician, diplomat, and geopolitical consultant who served as United States Secretary of State and National Security Advisor under the presidential administrations of Richard Nixon and Gerald Ford."

[71] On June 16-17, 1974, President Nixon became the first U.S. President to visit Israel. (https://www.nixonfoundation.org/2014/06/6-16-74-president-nixon-becomes-first-president-visit-israel/)

[72] Wikipedia contributors, "Shuttle diplomacy," *Wikipedia, The Free Encyclopedia*, https://en.wikipedia.org/w/index.php?title=Shuttle_diplomacy&oldid=980362913 (accessed September 27, 2020), "In diplomacy and international relations, shuttle diplomacy is the action of an outside party in serving as an intermediary between (or among) principals in a dispute, without direct principal-to-principal contact. Originally and usually, the process entails successive travel ("shuttling") by the intermediary, from the working location of one principal, to that of another. The term was first applied to describe the efforts of United States Secretary of State Henry Kissinger, beginning November 5, 1973, which facilitated the cessation of hostilities following the Yom Kippur War."

My Personal Diary of My White House Days

the crowd cheered, etc. Beautiful morning. He and Mrs. Nixon got into the copter and all waved him good-bye.

Walked back with Dr. Marrs (Deputy Assistant Secretary of Defense for Reserve Affairs). Wish I could work for him, for I would get more recognition for what I am doing. Do like him. Got assignment from Wayne to do packet on energy bills, initiatives of the President, and how Congress and democrats torpedoed all his efforts.

Monday, June 10th—

After President and party left, went back and worked with Dr. Marrs—really swell man and knowledgeable on Indian affairs—Administration's liaison with tribes.

Then, talked with Wayne. Gave new assignment—put together Nixon Administration energy proposals and the way it has dealt with this crisis[73] (the oil embargo of 1973). Then, checked original proposals with bills as they now are in Congress. Draw conclusions concerning responsibility of Democratic-controlled Congress, shedding favorable light on the Administration and assessing blame on Congress where blame is due.

Tues. June 11th

In early—7:15. Took out all materials I had gathered day before—all President's energy speeches, etc. and tried to get some degree of order and idea of proposals. Then, went to Federal Energy Office, soon to be F.E. A.[74], and talked to a Mrs.

---

[73] Wikipedia contributors, "1973 oil crisis," *Wikipedia, The Free Encyclopedia*, https://en.wikipedia.org/w/index.php?title=1973_oil_crisis&oldid=979076866 (accessed September 27, 2020), "The 1973 oil crisis began in October 1973 when the members of the Organization of Arab Petroleum Exporting Countries proclaimed an oil embargo. The embargo was targeted at nations perceived as supporting Israel during the Yom Kippur War. The initial nations targeted were Canada, Japan, the Netherlands, the United Kingdom and the United States with the embargo also later extended to Portugal, Rhodesia and South Africa. By the end of the embargo in March 1974, the price of oil had risen nearly 300%, from US$3 per barrel to nearly $12 globally; US prices were significantly higher. The embargo caused an oil crisis, or "shock", with many short- and long-term effects on global politics and the global economy."

[74] Wikipedia contributors, "Federal Energy Administration," *Wikipedia, The Free Encyclopedia*, https://en.wikipedia.org/w/index.php?title=Federal_Energy_Administration&oldid=874603880 (accessed September 27, 2020), "The Federal Energy Administration (FEA) was a United States government organization created in 1974 to address the 1970s energy crisis, and specifically the 1973 oil crisis. President Nixon established the Federal Energy Office (FEO) in December 1973, which was tasked with coordinating the American response to the embargo. In June 1974, the FEO was superseded by the FEA under the Federal Energy Administration Act of 1974 and Executive Order 11790."

Tucker, a hard-core bureaucrat. She was of little assistance, but did try. In afternoon, to the Hill to meet with the Republican Research Committee. Guy by the name of Jack helped me out somewhat. It will be difficult to find out where the bills are, who sits on the particular committee, and to what end the members acted responsibly and to what end the President's original proposals were responsible.

Back at office for meeting with Bruce Herschensohn[75]—hard-core Nixon supporter and talked about the media. Attacked somewhat, but was objective in his remarks, and I agreed with them considerably, though not with handling of Watergate...and transcripts.

Wednesday, June 12th

Jim's birthday. He's 24. Incredible, but still young. Surely glad we are brothers.

Worked on speeches, but not an overly productive day. Had lunch with Pam Powell and Sandy on top of Exchange, which has a really nice view of the city—Washington Monument, Jefferson Memorial, top of E.O.B., top of White House and Capitol. Afternoon, got a new project from Wayne: have to put together a few op eds (opposite editorials) for Mr. B. Will be sent to the New York Times, etc. to oppose the day's editorials, if against the Administration. Called planting stories, I guess. Didn't do much else all day. I was a dud.

June 13th—Thursday

Ug. Haven't done much. In at work at 8:00 and must find a way to get in here earlier. Did some work on the op eds, but not much. Ate lunch with Wayne and Kris.

Then talked of lobbying on the impeachment vote. He (Wayne) said that a way to do it would be to get ahold of all the big businesses in the Members' districts and find out who the big

---

[75]Wikipedia contributors, "Bruce Herschensohn," *Wikipedia, The Free Encyclopedia*, https://en.wikipedia.org/w/index.php?title=Bruce_Herschensohn&oldid=951103863 (accessed September 27, 2020), "Stanley Bruce Herschensohn (born September 10, 1932) is a conservative American political commentator, author and senior fellow at the Pepperdine University School of Public Policy in Malibu, California. Herschensohn quickly rose to prominence in the Republican Party, becoming a consultant to the Republican National Convention in 1972 and joined the Nixon administration on September 11, 1972. He served primarily as a speech writer."

boys of the businesses are, then tell them to put the squeeze on the members for voting against impeachment. And, could find out how much government money goes into each district and act accordingly in negating the funds to the district. How that is accomplished, I don't know.

Had a really terrific tour of the White House. Lasted two hours. We went everywhere but the East Wing and the residence. The Nixon's were gone, so we did get into the Oval Office. I was a bit surprised, for I imagined it much larger. It was very light and lively. Mrs. Nixon decorated it and it was light, but can't hand her much for the birds she scattered about the shelves and empty spaces. But there I was—in the office of the most powerful man in the world. In the office where many men have wanted to be, but so few have been. There I was, looking out onto the same view as many presidents—as the Kennedy brothers, etc. I was touching the President's chair, etc. I was in awe. There was no doubt.

President Richard M. Nixon & then-Representative Gerald R. Ford in the Oval Office prior to the nomination. (Wikimedia Commons, the free media repository. 6 Mar 2015, 12:28 UTC. Accessed 25 Aug 2020,
https://commons.wikimedia.org/w/index.php?title=File:Photograph_of_President_Richard_M._Nixon_and_Representative_Gerald_R._Ford_in_the_Oval_Office_Prior_to_the_Nomination..._-_NARA_-_186969.tif&oldid=152281930)

One interesting thing was the phone. It was a normal phone, but had only three exchanges. One for "Woods," and one for "Haig," and one for "Kissng." Those are the three most important people, I suppose. Then into the Cabinet Room. The President's chair is the tallest in the middle and the other chairs go out left and right according to the age of the office. Sec. Kissinger sits next to the President. There is a phone everywhere possible the President could want to be. Lots of big decisions have taken place there. A big portrait of Ike (President Eisenhower) hangs over the table. Then to the Roosevelt room where smaller meetings are held. Quite a lovely room. Incidentally, the Vice President sits right across from the President in the Cabinet Room.

We meandered throughout the White House for two hours. Saw the controversial portrait of Jackie Kennedy, which, the more one gazes at it the more one is accustomed to it. Then wound up back at the North portico where there was the marvelous portrait of President Kennedy with his arms crossed on his chest pondering, looking at the floor. There were others up on the stairwell going to the private residence and I thought I would go look at the one of Herbert Hoover. I was about to climb onto the steps when the guide shouted at me warning me not to go up. I cowered back down to the group and then was told that the steps were alarmed and I would have sounded off a major White House alarm scare.

Home to pack for Rehoboth beach—going with Mike.

June 14

Today was spent mostly in celebration of Wayne's birthday. A group of us went out to lunch—Wayne, Leslie, Kris, and a gal named Debbie, and myself. We took Wayne to some dive near 16th Street. Then, in the afternoon spent one hour eating cake that Kris made. Ridiculous to spend so much time. The office and Mr. Baroody wrote a cute poem commemorating Wayne's personality and his efforts to the staff. It was well framed. Also, being Flag Day, the office and Mr. Baroody gave him a copy of the President's Proclamation. Worked a touch on the energy project, but didn't get far.

Then, in P.M., Mike and I changed and jumped into my Jeep Waggoneer and were off to Rehoboth Beach (Delaware, a popular resort on the East Coast on the Atlantic Ocean). Good weekend—no women, but good weekend.

I am amazed at how my mind is practically totally dedicated to my work this summer, not that that is anything new, but that, after a rather bumpy time attending the London School of Economics in England during the oil embargo (and being lonely), it feels so good to get back to the type of work that I love so… and to be involved in something worthwhile, where I feel that I am an asset and somewhat needed. It is a great feeling to be working in the White House.

June 17

I had to rush a National Managers Association article to Wayne as soon as I could get it in, as the deadline for the issue was in May! I worked one draft out, which didn't quite fit the picture, then was told to do another, which, in a strange way, is a compliment. But, couldn't get it all put together in time, as so many events crowded out the needed time.

A new intern, Tom Eggleston, came onboard—Dartmouth basketball man and a truly nice guy. I also was working on some op eds for Wayne. Day was productive in other ways. Mike and I worked on our speeches for a better part of the day, which are to be given tomorrow.

In evening, we went to hear Dean Rusk[76] speak sponsored by the American Enterprise Institute[77]. Good talk on the American Revolution and the future of this nation. Then, at a reception

---

[76] Wikipedia contributors, "Dean Rusk," *Wikipedia, The Free Encyclopedia*, https://en.wikipedia.org/w/index.php?title=Dean_Rusk&oldid=976652736 (accessed September 18, 2020), "David Dean Rusk (February 9, 1909 – December 20, 1994) was the United States Secretary of State from 1961 to 1969 under presidents John F. Kennedy and Lyndon B. Johnson. Rusk is one of the longest serving U.S. Secretaries of State, behind only Cordell Hull."

[77] Wikipedia contributors, "American Enterprise Institute," *Wikipedia, The Free Encyclopedia*, https://en.wikipedia.org/w/index.php?title=American_Enterprise_Institute&oldid=977699657 (accessed September 18, 2020), "The American Enterprise Institute for Public Policy Research, known simply as the American Enterprise Institute (AEI), is a Washington, D.C.–based think tank that researches government, politics, economics, and social welfare. AEI is an independent nonprofit organization supported primarily by grants and contributions from foundations, corporations, and individuals."

following, I introduced myself to Mr. Rusk and spoke of John McNaughton, whom he knew and who was one of my father's best friends from Pekin, Illinois. He also talked about the worthiness of the intern program, saying, "We old fogies have done one thing for you youngsters: we have left you plenty of problems to solve." True. Very nice, humble man.

My Personal Diary of My White House Days

This is an example of some of the notices sent to the interns regarding upcoming seminars held for our benefit during the summer of 1974.

THE WHITE HOUSE

WASHINGTON

June 17, 1974

MEMORANDUM FOR THE WHITE HOUSE SUMMER INTERNS

FROM: SANDY LAUGHLIN

SUBJECT: Seminars for the weeks of June 17 and June 24, 1974.

Mr. Joe Bartlett, House Minority Clerk, has kindly agreed to give a Capitol tour for the Interns on Tuesday, June 18, 1974 at 10:00 a.m. sharp. You should meet Sandy Laughlin and Linda Bartlett on the House steps promptly at 9:50 a.m. for a picture taking session and also to receive your Congressional Passes which you may use for the duration of the summer.

The Secretary of Agriculture, the Honorable Earl L. Butz has agreed to speak to the Interns on Wednesday, June 19, 1974 at 4:00 p.m. in Room 450 EOB. Other members of the White House Staff are invited, therefore we recommend you come early.

Senator Barry Goldwater is speaking to the Rupublican Women's Forum at 12 noon on Thursday, June 20, 1974 at the Capitol Hill Club, 300 First Street, S.E. If you plan to stay for lunch, you should notify to Republican National Committee, and be expected to pay $4.00 for cost of the luncheon.

Mrs. Anne Armstrong, Counsellor to the President will speak to the Interns at 4:30 p.m., Thursday June 20, 1974 in the Roosevelt Room. You should be outside the West Wing entrance at 4:20 p.m.

Attachments

June 18

This morning I was at work at 7:00. I have found a neat parking place which is free and right across the street from the Executive Office Building. As I came in and walked past the President's personal office in the E.O.B., I asked the guard if it would be possible to peek in for a look. He said he would show me the office, but to keep it quiet, for no one but staff and appointments are to be allowed in. So, in we went. The reception room is nice, with pictures of the First Family on the wall. Then, one enters the President's own office, which is beautifully decorated. The carpet is yellow and the walls are light. The desk isn't as large as that in the Oval Office and has a beautiful red leather chair behind it. Again, there are the porcelain objects in cases on the walls. On the north wall, there are pictures and on the east wall hangs the President's collection of gavels. There may be twenty at the most. He also has some in the Oval Office and in the Cabinet Room. There was a small round table that is so familiar in many pictures when the president has his feet up on the top talking with Sec. Kissinger and writing on his legal pads. On the way out, we again went through the reception room which, as I understood from the guard, is the Cartoon Room. On the wall hang about fifty cartoons from Mr. Nixon's Vice-Presidential days and earlier days of his public service. Quite a thrill for me to be in there, for he spends 50% of his time in Washington there in that office. Beautiful.

At 9:00 I had typed up a collection of op-eds for Wayne and was to speak to a group of high-school kids from Wilmington, Delaware. Mike and I waited for about an hour and then they showed up. The kids didn't ask many questions, but the teachers did. Rather disappointing, for the lack of governmental interest stemming from a government class bothered me. They left, and then up to work on some remarks for the Washington Sertoma Club, which was to be addressed by Mike and I at noon.

The Sertoma Club is like a normal service club, but the members were so much older than I had expected. I gave my remarks, which centered on the need for affirmation on the institutions of government in this country, and some of the audience slept through it. They, as an audience, weren't overly eager to hear from a young person working in the White House and I, as a speaker, responded with the same degree of enthusiasm they gave me—none. It was rather sad, and my fault for not putting all I had into it, but I just didn't have too much! A bad shot.

I recorded Mike and my speeches and spent the rest of the day listening to them, trying to figure out all the bad elements in my methods of presentation. I called Jim and he gave me a reassuring chat that I wasn't as dumb as I felt at the time and gave me very helpful pointers on how to deal with working peer-group pressure—maintain a shell of quasi-isolation around yourself and your endeavors. Good advice, which I sub-consciously knew, but needed to be brought out by one hell of a guy. His talk has set me in the proper frame to keep plugging at my work, regardless of the little amount of feed-back from Wayne and Mr. Baroody.

Took Mike home after asking a girl by the name of Kathy Campbell out on Saturday night. Mike was after her and I beat him to the punch this time. Think amends need to be made somehow without losing the prize. Then, worked on the management article and talked with Ellen, who is sweet.

Got two tickets to the National Symphony on Saturday night with Kathy.

Wednesday, June 19, 1974

Today, time was spent on Energy Packet. Have much to go on getting it succinctly organized and coherent, but have broken ground, barely. So many Presidential statements, information to hack over, viewpoints to coalesce, let alone politics behind it. All is confusing. Had lunch with the ORS crowd and really had a blast. Afternoon seminar with Secretary of Agriculture Butz[78].

---

[78] Wikipedia contributors, "Earl Butz," *Wikipedia, The Free Encyclopedia*, https://en.wikipedia.org/w/index.php?title=Earl_Butz&oldid=970718345 (accessed September 18, 2020), "Earl Lauer "Rusty" Butz (July 3, 1909 – February 2, 2008) was a United States government official who served as Secretary of Agriculture under Presidents Richard Nixon and Gerald Ford. His policies favored large-scale corporate farming and an end to New Deal programs, but he is best remembered for a series of verbal gaffes that eventually cost him his job."

Naturally, everything sounded rosy. He talked of figures that when he was born 65 years ago, 45% of this country's labor force worked on the agricultural front. Now, the % is 5. These reduced figures dealing with the necessity of producing food releases society's people to build a better nation in other areas. Food is the necessity of life. With greater efficiency in production, greater resources to build on other fronts. 64 years ago, 45% of the population was producing food for 90 million people; today, 5% for 200 million. Also talked on the effectiveness of food surplus in diplomacy, especially in the Mid-East. Says that to hold prices, need to increase production to allow maximum output by farmers so that the government doesn't have to subsidize them. Anyway, this increased production routine makes for a large surplus market for the farmers. They need an export market when in full production and the USSR, the Mid-East, other nations and perhaps even the People's Republic—from all these nations, food may be used as a diplomatic tool. Interesting.

Then, after his chat, we all went out to greet the President from his return from the successful Mid-East trip. That was quite the ceremony. The power this one man has just completely makes me in awe of him. What really makes me in awe of him is that he knows how to use it effectively in diplomacy and understands the nature of diplomacy, the international world scene, and its relation to American interests both from a domestic view and international, for the two are never separated.

As I watched him come down from the helicopter with his wife following, I weaseled my way

into the front of the line about twenty feet from where the President gave his return remarks and took several photos which I hope come out. (During my time at the White House, I was rarely without my camera)

It was really a thrill to stand so close to the President of the most powerful, most rich nation in the world's history and his helicopter was on the South Lawn as the press rolled the cameras. The Cabinet, except for the Secretary of State (who was in Canada), was present.

President Nixon photos by John Unland

Then, after work, went out with a girl named Kathy Campbell who is really nice, but didn't say three words the entire evening.

June 20th

I swear that this crew celebrates anything and everything. Two birthday parties. One for a secretary in Mr. Baroody's office and the other one for Pam Powell, who is deserving of a good drink and a cake, for she's done a great job with this program. Day was spent again trying to work on energy jazz. Wayne is knee-deep in the politics of impeachment, so I haven't seen him in a good while. Mike and I went to Mike Farrell's (Special Assistant to the President) office in the East Wing for a visit—beautiful office and nice staff. He's in charge of the Visitor's Office and has a truly great job. Then, seminar with Anne Armstrong[79] in the Roosevelt Room in the West Wing. Beautiful place and is where the senior staff meets every morning at 8:30—right across from the Oval Office and Cabinet Room. She's a really charming lady, but didn't talk too much on what she does. Talked about her day's schedule and of a cabinet meeting with the President. She said that all the Congressional leaders gave him a standing ovation after his briefing—they really still respect him and the Office of Presidency when the chips are down. Must talk to her about my idea concerning speakers during bicentennial.

My dad and me at the White House.

Then, Mike and I went home to find that Dad had driven up with Ralph Venovich of Congressman Michel's office. We all went to the Marine Dress Parade ceremony in tribute to Les Arends[80] given by the

---

[79] Wikipedia contributors, "Anne Armstrong," *Wikipedia, The Free Encyclopedia*, https://en.wikipedia.org/w/index.php?title=Anne_Armstrong&oldid=959828987 (accessed September 18, 2020), "Anne Legendre Armstrong (December 27, 1927 – July 30, 2008) was a United States diplomat and politician. She was the first woman to serve as Counselor to the President and as United States Ambassador to the United Kingdom; serving in those capacities under the Ford, Nixon, and Carter administrations. She was the recipient of the Presidential Medal of Freedom in 1987."

[80] Wikipedia contributors, "Leslie C. Arends," *Wikipedia, The Free Encyclopedia*, https://en.wikipedia.org/w/index.php?title=Leslie_C._Arends&oldid=970678140 (accessed September 18, 2020), "Leslie Cornelius Arends (September 27, 1895 – July 17, 1985) was a Republican politician from Illinois who served in the United States House of Representatives from 1935 until 1974. He remained loyal to Richard M. Nixon during the Watergate scandal, and indicated that he would not vote to impeach Nixon."

Secretary of Defense Schlesinger.[81] Saw Mrs. Armstrong there and asked to talk with her about my idea, she said O.K. So, O.K. The entire evening was just incredibly impressive—Marine precision. Just beautiful. The drum and bugle corps was the greatest, also taps played by a Marine on top of the roof with soft light on him in the dark. Great respect for the armed services, augmented when one sees an event such as that. If they had passed a sign-up sheet, I would have signed. Home to bed. Great to see my Dad, but realize that we all have our lives to lead and mine, hopefully, will be centered here in Washington. Much on my little mind. We are a family of true individuality.

After seeing the Marine performance and weighing my interests and academic endeavors, I have essentially decided that the thrust of my life will be spent in service to this country in one way or another.

Friday, June 21, 1974

Work today was unusually good. I did quite a number of things—wrote a speech, an op-ed, and worked with Tom Eggleston on Energy stuff. With energy stuff, it is more a matter of coordination than anything else; the Republican National Committee has a research staff working on energy attack, the Congressional Republican Committee has a small staff working on it—The Republican Research Committee, and there are those in the F.E.O. (Federal Energy Office) who are knowledgeable of dealings with Congress on energy issues.

And, now, the White House is doing its thing. What one would call Governmental Overlap. Dad came in today at 2:30 and he and I hiked around the White House. He met the entire Baroody crew and naturally everyone liked him; especially the women. They all thought he was "cute." While we were in the White House library, we bumped into Pam Powell and she took Dad and I up to the Oval Office, Cabinet Room, and to the

---

[81] Wikipedia contributors, "James R. Schlesinger," *Wikipedia, The Free Encyclopedia*, https://en.wikipedia.org/w/index.php?title=James_R._Schlesinger&oldid=977727125 (accessed September 18, 2020), "James Rodney Schlesinger (February 15, 1929 – March 27, 2014) was an American economist and public servant who was best known for serving as Secretary of Defense from 1973 to 1975 under Presidents Richard Nixon and Gerald Ford."

Roosevelt Room. I always enjoy seeing those three rooms more than any others. And I think Dad did enjoy seeing them. Then, he went his merry way with Congressman Michel and I did a touch more work. Days are measured as to their merit in terms of productivity. This was a good day.

In the P.M. Mike M. and I went to a cocktail party one of the interns was giving and then out to Mr. Baroody's for dinner. I spent most of the evening playing the piano, as I wasn't in the mood to mingle with the crowd. Very nice evening, as I hadn't played the piano in such a long time.

Nixon's Rating Slumps to 26 Pct.

New York — (AP) — A Harris poll taken early this month, before President Nixon's trip to the Middle East, indicated Mr. Nixon's standing with Americans dropped back to its all-time low after a brief surge.

In surveys during April and May, Mr. Nixon got a positive rating of 31 percent and 32 percent respectively. However, a sampling during the first four days of this month indicated Mr. Nixon's rating had slipped back to record low March figures — 26 percent positive and 71 percent negative.

Harris said Mr. Nixon adopted an underdog image and took his case to the people, producing the April and May figures. But by June, said Harris, the public had a "long hard look" at the tape transcripts and Mr. Nixon's continued refusal to obey subpenas.

Article published in The Philadelphia Evening Bulletin on June 21, 1974.

This is an indication of the public's distrust of the President during Watergate.

Saturday, June 22

Vegetated all day. In the evening, had a date with Kathy Campbell. Went to the Kennedy Center to see the National Symphony and sat in the Presidential Box. Indeed, could have done worse.

Monday, June 24, 1974

Today was a good day. Woke up at 8:45—did I fly out of bed! I usually am at work at 7:15! I wrote two speeches today: one to be given by Mr. Baroody to a group of Young Marines[82]—loaded it with patriotic language as it was a Presidential acknowledgement of the 75th anniversary of the V.F.W. which is to go into their program at their convention in August. Then, let Tom take over on Energy packet, for I am swamped with "projects." Want to get my hands into that, however.

Also talked to Pam Powell about my Bicentennial speaking idea and she did like it quite a bit. Must write up a good proposal to both Pam and to Mrs. Armstrong and try to at least sell the idea to them. Finances will be the problem. I pray.

Then, we had a meeting of the interns, at 4:45. Mike and I have the reputation of being the "Bobsy Twins." They all need a focus—the group needs a focus—on someone, and we really don't care about the kidding. They think we're a couple of real hot tickets and we go along with them. Nice group. I was placed on the historical committee—keeping track of who meets with whom and what other important transactions might take place. Linda Bartlett is on the committee, whom I really like. Should be fun.

---

[82] Wikipedia contributors, "Young Marines," *Wikipedia, The Free Encyclopedia*, https://en.wikipedia.org/w/index.php?title=Young_Marines&oldid=967713861 (accessed September 27, 2020) "The Young Marines is a youth program in the United States and Japan open to all youth between the ages of 8 to 18 or completion of high school (whichever is later, not to exceed 20 years of age). The Young Marines are different from Junior ROTC units, in that they are not part of a high school and are a 501(c)3 non-profit instead of a government agency. Generally, units meet on local military bases or other locations such as American Legion, VFW, Fire or Sheriff Dept. etc. where a building serves as their headquarters and classroom."

My Personal Diary of My White House Days

This is an invitation to all the interns for the departure ceremony of the President as well as an invitation to Senator Howard Baker's speech (he was also a family friend).

THE WHITE HOUSE

WASHINGTON

June 24, 1974

MEMORANDUM FOR: THE WHITE HOUSE SUMMER INTERNS

FROM: PAM POWELL
SANDY LAUGHLIN

SUBJECT: Schedule for the week of June 24, 1974.

The President and Mrs. Nixon will leave the South Lawn of the White House Tuesday, June 25, 1974 at 8:10 a.m. for their visit to Belgium and the Union of Soviet Socialist Republics. You and your friends are invited to see them off. Guests accompanied by a White House or EOB pass holder will be admitted through the Southwest gate on Tuesday, June 25, 1974 beginning at 7:40 a.m. Please plan to be in place by 8:00 a.m.

Senator Howard Baker is speaking at the Capitol Hill Club's luncheon on Wednesday, June 26, 1974 at 12:00 noon. Each of you should have received a memorandum from Christina Wagner with the details.

John Nidecker, Special Assistant to the President, has agreed to speak to the interns on Wednesday, June 26, 1974 at 3:00 p.m. in Room 459 OEOB. He has been with the President in all his campaigns since 1956, and therefore is one of the few people who can speak about the personal aspects of the First Family. This is a most fascinating man, therefore we urge you all to come if possible. A White House photographer will be on hand for a group picture.

We have tentatively schedule a White House photographer to take a group picture along with individual shots for your press releases. This sessions will probably take place on Thursday, June 27 in the afternoon.

Tuesday, June 25th

Kathy Griffith and I hustled to say good-bye to President and Mrs. Nixon this morning at 7:30. She was a sketch with her camera and all her giggles. We had a good time. The President looked in fantastic shape—rested, a bit tan from somewhere (probably a tube tan), and was in good spirits. There weren't more than 200 White House staffers to say farewell to him on his way to Russia and the official ceremony was to take place at Andrews Air Force Base. So, he told us he wished we all could come along, but that we can't—no room, so get back to work. Away we went. It was a cool, fresh, a bit of a cloudy morning. I do love that helicopter. I took a few pictures—camera not functioning well and I think that I'll get another.

Wrapped up Young Marine points after alteration. Then listened to a taped speech by Mr. Baroody to a group of Defense-interested folks—really super talk. He's good.

Mom coming out tomorrow and really looking forward to seeing her. Have tons of work, but will get it done here. Amy (mom's nickname) and I always have a blast. She's a great character.

Wednesday, June 26

Still have been getting to work by 7:00 A.M. and is a good feeling. Lets me do work, plus items such as this diary. Always have a doughnut and coffee. Did revision of Young Marine speech today, putting in touches that young Marines will, when they become full Marines, be protectors of the peace, not soldiers in battle, because of President Nixon's peace efforts. Ta Da!

Then, at 11:30, the Great Amy came to the 17th street entrance with her two bags, ready to play in the big city. What a character she is. We went to the Capitol Hill Club to the meal and to hear Senator Howard Baker speak. He was his usual, low-keyed eloquent speaker and both mom and I shook his hand and spoke to him briefly. He actually remembered who we were. Such a nice guy. Left Amy about 1:30 and then back here. At speech also met Harold Collier[83] who really enjoyed Dad at last weekend's golf outing. We had an intern meeting and heard Mr. (John) Nidecker speak. He is an Assistant to the President and covers a wide spectrum of activity for the President. He is in charge of parties such as the Easter Egg Hunt, the Santa Claus of the White House, etc. Just a good guy.

Back home to Amy at 7:00 and she and Kathy and I went to the Tombs[84] for dinner and had a great time.

Thursday, June 27

Worked all day on a leadership speech for Baroody and on a defense speech, which is a biggie. Wayne naturally got me all confused as to what I was exactly to do. I thought he wanted to have a defense speech written, taking the main points from a speech that Baroody had given months ago. But, as I found out after wasting hours, he just wanted the tape transcribed, which Leslie did.

Then, we went over her transcription and compared it to the tape, which was fun indeed. I easily can see how the people who transcribed the Transcripts had a tremendous difficult time; Baroody was speaking into the microphone and we could barely make out his comments, let alone trying to do so from a mic hanging from a chandelier in an office.

---

[83] Wikipedia contributors, "Harold R. Collier," *Wikipedia, The Free Encyclopedia*, https://en.wikipedia.org/w/index.php?title=Harold_R._Collier&oldid=961855944 (accessed September 27, 2020), "Harold Reginald Collier (December 12, 1915 – January 17, 2006) was a Republican member of the United States House of Representatives from Illinois."

[84] "The Tombs," http://tombs.com/ As of September 27, 2020, their website reads in part: "Situated on the edge of Georgetown University's campus, The Tombs is a neighborhood restaurant by day and a popular gathering place for Georgetown students by night. Along with 1789, The Tombs is built in a Federal-style townhouse dating from the mid-1800s."

Also worked on an A.E.I. project to get (Ted) Kennedy[85] and (Ed) Muskie[86]. The A.E.I. just finished a comprehensive study stating that we will have a surplus of doctors by that time and the problem will be with distribution of them, not a shortage.

This place has been a pressure cooker all week long and I have had a difficult time finding out which project has priority and which is to be done in what manner. Communication is difficult—even between two people. A.E.I. stuff was to go to Clawson, Cole, and Timmons and they were going after Kennedy and (Jacob) Javits[87].

---

[85] Wikipedia contributors, "Ted Kennedy," *Wikipedia, The Free Encyclopedia*, https://en.wikipedia.org/w/index.php?title=Ted_Kennedy&oldid=979501518 (accessed September 27, 2020), "Edward Moore Kennedy (February 22, 1932 – August 25, 2009) was an American politician and lawyer who served as a U.S. Senator from Massachusetts for almost 47 years, from 1962 until his death in 2009. A member of the Democratic Party and the Kennedy political family, he was the second most senior member of the Senate when he died and is the fourth-longest-continuously-serving senator in United States history. Kennedy was a brother of President John F. Kennedy and U.S. Attorney General and U.S. Senator Robert F. Kennedy and was the father of Congressman Patrick J. Kennedy."

[86] Wikipedia contributors, "Edmund Muskie," *Wikipedia, The Free Encyclopedia*, https://en.wikipedia.org/w/index.php?title=Edmund_Muskie&oldid=980009073 (accessed September 27, 2020), "Edmund Sixtus Muskie (March 28, 1914 – March 26, 1996) was an American statesman and political leader who served as the 58th United States Secretary of State under President Jimmy Carter, a United States Senator from Maine from 1959 to 1980, the 64th Governor of Maine from 1955 to 1959, and a member of the Maine House of Representatives from 1946 to 1951. He was the Democratic Party's candidate for Vice President of the United States in the 1968 presidential election, alongside Hubert Humphrey. Muskie ran with Humphrey against Nixon in the 1968 presidential election, only to lose by 0.7 percentage points – one of the narrowest margins in U.S. history."

[87] Wikipedia contributors, "Jacob Javits," *Wikipedia, The Free Encyclopedia*, https://en.wikipedia.org/w/index.php?title=Jacob_Javits&oldid=962699704 (accessed September 27, 2020), "Jacob Koppel Javits (May 18, 1904 – March 7, 1986) was an American politician who represented New York in both houses of Congress. In the House and Senate, Javits established himself as a liberal Republican. Despite his unhappiness with President Richard Nixon over the Vietnam War, Javits was slow to join the anti-Nixon forces during the Watergate scandal of 1973–74. Until almost the very end of the affair, his position reflected his legal training: Nixon was innocent until proven guilty, and the best way to determine guilt or innocence was by legal due process."

White House Interns Class of 1974 (though we hardly knew each other at this point, and I wasn't yet dating Linda, somehow the three of us stood right next to each other for this photo.)

Friday, June 28th

To work early and began on yesterday's projects. Lots to do here. We had a group picture taken this A.M.—what a group. Naturally it had to rain for our shot.

Worked on Defense speech, going over Leslie's goofs and adding this and that. One thing I can say is that I have learned a good deal about the issues and philosophies of this Administration. It would be to his advantage if other Americans knew one fourth of what I did about his work. Had lunch with Wayne. Afternoon spent in anticipation of a relaxing weekend with Mom and Dad in Virginia near Winchester at a wedding.

At 4:00, went to hear Baroody give the prepared remarks I did for the Young Marines...he didn't use more than a paragraph. Wayne and I just looked at each other and laughed. These young guys gave Baroody a plaque and a lamp with a Bulldog and a Marine on it. Baroody didn't do a hot job. Should have given them a little house, regardless of how busy he was. He accepted the speaking engagement and should have done it right. Rather disappointing.

Back to Georgetown Inn to greet Dad and Mom—had a drink and then dinner at Jour et Nuit on M. St. Really fun to be with them.

My Parents - Jim & Judy Unland

July 1, 1974

Today I did what was almost an impossible task for my little mind. Wayne said that Mr. Baroody wanted some talking points for a meeting he is having with business leaders next week. He gave me the following topics: energy, inflation, capital formation, pension legislation, tax cuts, and tax incentive legislation. I knew nothing about any of them. But, after sifting through documents, speeches, and articles, I managed to come up with a ten-page summary on those topics in fairly good form. Don't know how he liked them but I was happy I got them finished.

Also did some defense statistic updating and it took me two days of bureaucratic phoning and haggling to get three statistics from the Defense Department. The White House personnel cannot call directly to the Defense Department; a protocol set by Melvin Laird when he was at the White House. He put that into effect so that people like Haldeman[88] and Erlichman[89] types couldn't call up to get further appropriations and push their weight around to get action. White House now screens calls and have to be OK'd. Vickie Allen (my brother's girlfriend) came to town today also. Fun.

July 2, 1974

Wayne and I talked to Baroody today about projects. Off the cuff remark was that we, staff, had to keep him informed of what the government was doing, for he didn't know or have time to

---

[88] Wikipedia contributors, "H. R. Haldeman," *Wikipedia, The Free Encyclopedia*, https://en.wikipedia.org/w/index.php?title=H._R._Haldeman&oldid=978655613 (accessed September 27, 2020), "Harry Robbins "Bob" Haldeman (October 27, 1926 – November 12, 1993) was an American political aide and businessman, best known for his service as White House Chief of Staff to President Richard Nixon and his consequent involvement in the Watergate scandal. After he left the Nixon administration in April 1973, Haldeman was tried on counts of perjury, conspiracy, and obstruction of justice for his role in the Watergate cover-up. He was found guilty and imprisoned for 18 months."

[89] Wikipedia contributors, "John Ehrlichman," *Wikipedia, The Free Encyclopedia*, https://en.wikipedia.org/w/index.php?title=John_Ehrlichman&oldid=979501074 (accessed September 27, 2020), "John Daniel Ehrlichman (March 20, 1925 – February 14, 1999) was counsel and Assistant to the President for Domestic Affairs under President Richard Nixon. Ehrlichman was an important influence on Nixon's domestic policy, coaching him on issues and enlisting his support for environmental initiatives. Ehrlichman was a key figure in events leading to the Watergate break-in and the ensuing Watergate scandal, for which he was convicted of conspiracy, obstruction of justice, and perjury and served a year and a half in prison."

keep up with happenings. Worked on defense material and Toffler speech which has to be redone.

In evening, about 7:30, I went down to see Wayne to wish him goodbye, for he was taking off for the 4th weekend. He was working on a Presidential Memo on Impeachment. He, at first, said I couldn't read the memo, for if leaked, could be very hazardous to the momentum of the impeachment efforts. I ended up reading the whole thing, which will not be reprinted here, but which, if leaked, could have caused some flak about the country and the press would have eaten up the memo with delight. It concerned White House efforts in drumming up support for the President throughout the country via various men, women, and groups. Shots are being called from the White House.

July 3rd, 1974

Got here early to type up report for Wayne. Then, went to hear the Vice President at 9:15 in the treaty room on the 4th floor. We all got there and waited for 15 minutes until he arrived. He walked into the room and thought we were White House Fellows, not interns.

My Personal Diary of My White House Days

THE WHITE HOUSE
WASHINGTON

June 25, 1974

MEMORANDUM FOR: ALL WHITE HOUSE/O.E.O.B. STAFF

SUBJECT: <u>Annual Fireworks Display</u>
<u>Thursday, July 4, 1974 - 8:00 p.m.</u>

The President and Mrs. Nixon have requested that the South Lawn be open to you and your families to view the "4th of July" fireworks display which is held annually at the Washington Monument.

The fireworks display, which is part of a larger program on the Monument grounds, is expected to begin at 9:00 p.m. We will begin admitting White House and E.O.B. pass holders and their families through the Southwest Gate at 8:00 p.m.

Michael J. Farrell
Special Assistant to the President
Office of White House Visitors

July 4, 1974

Pam Powell had a party last night at her apartment in the Towers. The party was somewhat entertaining. Mike, Kelly, Trevor, John S., and I joked around a good deal and tortured the women with our good looks (joking). I sat in one seat the entire evening, but saw many people. After the party, Michael and I went to the Sheraton Park Hotel, stripped down, and went for a mid-night swim. A true delight. The White House would have loved it if we had gotten caught by the police. Ug. Kids today.

First Hand

I awoke at 9:30 A.M. and turned on the radio to the D.C. classical station only to hear John Phillip Sousa[90] for fifteen minutes on the morning of the 4th. How marvelous!! I just soaked in every note of those truly great marches.

July 4, 1774. Two hundred years ago today, the American colonists were under the strain of confusion in their relation to Britain. The Boston Tea Party[91] had occurred. The Coercive Acts[92], Quebec Act[93], and amendments to the Quartering Act[94] had sharpened the blade of conflict. In New England, the popular

---

[90] Wikipedia contributors, "John Philip Sousa," *Wikipedia, The Free Encyclopedia*, https://en.wikipedia.org/w/index.php?title=John_Philip_Sousa&oldid=980155768 (accessed September 27, 2020), "John Philip Sousa (November 6, 1854 – March 6, 1932) was an American composer and conductor of the late Romantic era known primarily for American military marches. He is known as "The March King" or the "American March King", to distinguish him from his British counterpart Kenneth J. Alford. Among his best-known marches are 'The Stars and Stripes Forever' (National March of the United States of America), 'Semper Fidelis' (official march of the United States Marine Corps), 'The Liberty Bell', 'The Thunderer', and 'The Washington Post'."

[91] Wikipedia contributors, "Boston Tea Party," *Wikipedia, The Free Encyclopedia*, https://en.wikipedia.org/w/index.php?title=Boston_Tea_Party&oldid=967206061 (accessed September 27, 2020), "The Boston Tea Party was a political and mercantile protest by the Sons of Liberty in Boston, Massachusetts, on December 16, 1773. The target was the Tea Act of May 10, 1773, which allowed the British East India Company to sell tea from China in American colonies without paying taxes apart from those imposed by the Townshend Acts. American Patriots strongly opposed the taxes in the Townshend Act as a violation of their rights. Demonstrators, some disguised as Native Americans, destroyed an entire shipment of tea sent by the East India Company."

[92] Wikipedia contributors, "Intolerable Acts," *Wikipedia, The Free Encyclopedia*, https://en.wikipedia.org/w/index.php?title=Intolerable_Acts&oldid=977122142 (accessed September 27, 2020), "The Intolerable Acts were punitive laws passed by the British Parliament in 1774 after the Boston Tea Party. The laws were meant to punish the Massachusetts colonists for their defiance in the Tea Party protest in reaction to changes in taxation by the British Government. In Great Britain, these laws were referred to as the Coercive Acts. The acts took away self-governance and rights that Massachusetts had enjoyed since its founding, triggering outrage and indignation in the Thirteen Colonies. They were key developments in the outbreak of the American Revolutionary War in April 1775."

[93] Wikipedia contributors, "Quebec Act," *Wikipedia, The Free Encyclopedia*, https://en.wikipedia.org/w/index.php?title=Quebec_Act&oldid=980318012 (accessed September 27, 2020), "The Quebec Act 1774, formally known as the British North America (Quebec) Act 1774, was an act of the Parliament of Great Britain setting procedures of governance in the Province of Quebec. The Act had wide-ranging effects, both in Quebec itself as well as in the Thirteen Colonies. In Quebec, English-speaking immigrants from the Thirteen Colonies objected to a variety of its provisions, which they saw as a removal of certain political freedoms."

[94] Wikipedia contributors, "Quartering Acts," *Wikipedia, The Free Encyclopedia*, https://en.wikipedia.org/w/index.php?title=Quartering_Acts&oldid=956646798 (accessed September 27, 2020), "The Quartering Acts were two or more Acts of British Parliament requiring local governments of the American colonies to provide the British soldiers with housing and food. Each of the Quartering Acts was an amendment to the Mutiny Act and required annual renewal by Parliament. They were originally intended as a response to issues that arose during the French and Indian War and soon became a source of tensions between the inhabitants of the Thirteen Colonies and the government in London. These tensions would later lead toward the American Revolution."

leaders—the Adams's, James Otis[95], Dr. Joseph Warren[96], Paul Revere[97], etc. —were struggling to maintain their stature as leaders against unjust British actions, pleading "natural law" arguments for American rights. Outside of New England, the popular leaders were constantly clashing with more conservative to moderate factions in their respective colonies. There was much discussion of Congress to air grievances and to decide strategy against irritating British actions. The country and its people were confused, yet becoming daily more and more defined of their intent. Through discussion, debate, and confrontation among themselves and the British authorities, America was chartering her course in July of 1774.

July 4, 1974. The years of toil, dissatisfaction, and idealistic vision by our colonial ancestors produced what is not a perfect system of government—theoretically or practically—but is, comparatively, the greatest governmental system in the world. The key elements in the Constitution of the United States have ensured for our people the freedom, the liberties, and the dignity due each man on earth, yet given to so few.

Though the political climate is laced with suspicion and discontent, our political life in America is very healthy. As we grow daily, as people, we experience events which teach us to

---

[95] Wikipedia contributors, "James Otis Jr.," *Wikipedia, The Free Encyclopedia*, https://en.wikipedia.org/w/index.php?title=James_Otis_Jr.&oldid=968460885 (accessed September 27, 2020), "James Otis Jr. (February 5, 1725 – May 23, 1783) was an American lawyer, political activist, pamphleteer, and legislator in Boston, a member of the Massachusetts provincial assembly, and an early advocate of the Patriot views against the policy of Parliament which led to the American Revolution. His well-known catchphrase 'Taxation without Representation is tyranny' became the basic Patriot position."

[96] Wikipedia contributors, "Joseph Warren," *Wikipedia, The Free Encyclopedia*, https://en.wikipedia.org/w/index.php?title=Joseph_Warren&oldid=980009932 (accessed September 27, 2020), "Joseph Warren (June 11, 1741 – June 17, 1775) was an American physician who played a leading role in Patriot organizations in Boston during the early days of the American Revolution, eventually serving as President of the revolutionary Massachusetts Provincial Congress. Warren enlisted Paul Revere and William Dawes on April 18, 1775, to leave Boston and spread the alarm that the British garrison in Boston was setting out to raid the town of Concord and arrest rebel leaders John Hancock and Samuel Adams."

[97] Wikipedia contributors, "Paul Revere," *Wikipedia, The Free Encyclopedia*, https://en.wikipedia.org/w/index.php?title=Paul_Revere&oldid=978065232 (accessed September 27, 2020), "Paul Revere (January 1, 1735 – May 10, 1818) was an American silversmith, engraver, early industrialist, and Patriot in the American Revolution. He is best known for his midnight ride to alert the colonial militia in April 1775 to the approach of British forces before the battles of Lexington and Concord, as dramatized in Henry Wadsworth Longfellow's poem, 'Paul Revere's Ride' (1861). At age 41, Revere was a prosperous, established and prominent Boston silversmith. He had helped organize an intelligence and alarm system to keep watch on the British military."

better ourselves, to become better people and better citizens of this nation. And, as our country has grown, it too has learned from experience ways which can make it a better place to live and more responsible to its citizens.

There have recently been mistakes made which are to be seen as very painful and quite damaging. Yet, in the long run, these blunders should not only teach our politicians to respect the limits of greed and unjust actions, but should teach all of the Americans to be more responsible in choosing their leaders. To educate this nation's people, to make them immune to the gimmicks, the slogans, and the insincerity of phony politicians—this will be the great lesson from Watergate for all Americans. The large part of the guilt of Watergate not only falls with President Nixon and his staff members, but also upon the shoulders of all of us.

So, the connecting link between July 4, 1774 and July 4, 1974 is that we were embarking on a journey 200 years ago in need of experience and knowledge. Today, we still are in need of knowledge and experience, though we have learned so much and come so very far in the benefits granted each citizen of America. Ours is the greatest country in the history of the world—no question. We all must do our part, though small it is, to ensure its greatness and decency.

This evening, I picked up Vickie Allen (my brother's girlfriend) and she, myself, Elizabeth, and Billy Furse (family friends) went to 2517 Q. St. N.W. (my apartment) and ate hamburgers cooked on the grill. We had a blast. Liz and I really are at each other's throats in a chiding manner when we are together. Then, we all trotted to the White House to sit on the South Lawn to view the fire-works display across the street at the Washington Monument. It really was fun. We sat next to

Father McLaughlin[98] and played with his dog, Oliver, though I didn't know who it was until the day after.

A good day—swimming, reading, pictures, Blue Ridge Mountains, friends, and fire-works. Puts one in a jolly frame of mind!

July 8, 9, and 10.

Lumped all of these together for I didn't do a darn thing during the three days worthy of the ribbon on the typewriter. Was doing a speech for Dr. Marrs and some jazz for Wayne, but have been frustrated and uneasy for a week. Will never take days off again—lose momentum at work. My mind is just now beginning to take hold again.

July 11

I forgot what I've been working on today. Guess…Ah! The mind may falter, but dare not fail. I took the speech I was working on defending the President into Dr. Marrs. He read it and said, "do you believe this?" To which I responded, "Yes, sir." Shocker, as the speech dealt with the core of the Nixon Administration philosophy. He sounded as though he didn't believe it.

Afternoon went rapidly…We had a seminar this morning—Bradley Patterson, who is Len Garment's[99] chief aide. Really good speaker, but a bit verbose. Nice guy, indeed. Mike and I had to scoot from the seminar in order to try to meet a Press Conference in the press room of the West Wing. We got there and listened to all the press guys mull over their Vietnam stories—impressive coverage and dangerous, too.

---

[98] Wikipedia contributors, "John McLaughlin (host)," *Wikipedia, The Free Encyclopedia*, https://en.wikipedia.org/w/index.php?title=John_McLaughlin_(host)&oldid=958495377 (accessed September 27, 2020), "John Joseph McLaughlin (March 29, 1927 – August 16, 2016) was an American television personality and political commentator. Through a friendship with Pat Buchanan, McLaughlin then became a speechwriter for U.S. President Richard Nixon. In 1974, after the resignation of President Nixon, he spent two months under President Gerald Ford's administration. In 1975, he left the priesthood."

[99] Wikipedia contributors, "Leonard Garment," *Wikipedia, The Free Encyclopedia*, https://en.wikipedia.org/w/index.php?title=Leonard_Garment&oldid=933515326 (accessed September 27, 2020), "Leonard Garment (May 11, 1924 – July 13, 2013) was an American attorney, public servant, and arts advocate. He served U.S. presidents Richard Nixon and Gerald Ford in the White House in various positions from 1969 to 1976, including Counselor to the President, acting Special Counsel to Nixon for the last two years of his presidency, and U.S. Ambassador to the Third Committee at the United Nations."

Then, about 11:30, the press camera men took off up to the Oval Office. Mulligan and I tagged along, naturally. We got to the top of the stairs and the Cabinet Room door opened, and there sat the President, Mr. Baroody, the President's economic aides, and several business men from around the nation. We just sat there with our mouths wide open trying to look like we belonged, which was so obvious that we didn't. Was really impressive to see the President in a working situation, rather than on the tube or on the campaign trail.

Went to lunch with Mia Taylor, a girl I met on the way home from work on the bus. Nice, expensive, and fruitless.

July 12

Did finish up some odds and ends, but slow. I thought I would put my mind towards other talents, so I did a fake Biographical Sketch on Trevor Vietor, which was fun. Also did a take-off on the Intern Memoranda that comes floating around here. I played. Was to meet Susan and Chris here, but guess they'll meet me at home.

July 15

Had pictures taken on the White House South Lawn for our press releases. Lots of joking. Then, began work on the Baroody speech for Opinion Research Corp. and will be tough—30 minutes on something I am totally fogged out on—dangerous climate for more governmental controls. Will have to  really dig for material but I'll learn a good deal.

July 16

Did a piece for Mr. Baroody for a manager's magazine on the government and the Nixon Administration. Getting old hat at this sort of work. Then, went to a meeting between interns and Mr. B. for which I was criticized for being the leader of the interns, talking too much, etc. I thought it was funny, for if I hadn't said the things I said, someone else would have. In my nature to command meetings.

I had some good ideas that I may follow up on. Just like to have things run smoothly and well organized.

Went to A.E.I. to see a Dr. Johnson for aid on the opinion research speech and he guided me to a chap in St. Louis...will be tough, for lots of research to do.

Then, went to Blanch Day's (Mike's Aunt) for dinner with Mike, John S., and Tom. Was a good time, especially when we all went to Tammany Hall—great bar.

July 17

Mike and I introduced Mr. Baroody to the interns, as it was his turn to speak to us. We really put on a show and it was quite humorous. Mr. B. went along with a few jokes and was a great part of the act.

The crowd loved our act. I still do get nervous in front of a crowd—just not enough experience as of late. Takes experience, too. No other way.

The afternoon was spent trying to get information on this controls speech. I'm just amazed that the White House doesn't have a logging of all of the Administration's positions on every issue facing them. But no such log is available. An office should be able to call somewhere, tell someone what they have to give a talk on, and get the Administration's view by someone in full. As it is now, each office has to scrape up the needed information on its own. Time consuming.

Went to see Wayne and he gave me a copy of the first draft of the President's nationwide speech on the economy. We both looked it over and decided, with Wayne's dramatics, that the speech was too technical and no color nor punch to it. He said that I had an hour to help remedy this situation and sent me upstairs to get clippings of our speeches that would help. When I returned, he called off the task—not enough time. I asked him if there was any possibility of an extension—no.

I left work convinced that the speech needed some of my flavoring and a bit sad that we didn't have an opportunity to color it up. Nixon's speeches are so drab—so lacking in heart-filled expressions and lacking in real contact with his audience. It is as though he put in an order for a speech on the economy, got it, and gives it point blank. Needs some souping up. But, a 22-year old Intern in the White House ain't going to do that!

July 18

Slept late and didn't get to work until 8:45. Saw Wayne as soon as I arrived and he relayed to me that we had until 11:00 to go over the Nixon speech, not to re-write it, but to add to or subtract from the content, making stylistic suggestions only. They are afraid to bend the nose of the speechwriters, I'm sure. He wanted me to go up, read it over again, and let him know if I had any suggestions. So, up I went, mad that we didn't get to re-write it and that Wayne didn't let me take it home with me to do over the night before.

By the time I got to my room, I was so burned up that this was the only thing we were going to do for this thing and that I had been solicited to aid in this and hadn't been given the opportunity to put in my two cents worth because of all these "deadlines," that I just glanced over the draft for content errors and for style, not really re-reading it. I thought for about thirty seconds about what I could recommend to Wayne and Mr. Baroody and picked up the phone and told Wayne that the only suggestion I had was that it should be re-written from head to toe, like we agreed it should. He became irritated at me and said, "Well if that is the only comment you have to make then go back to your work, if you are doing any." That was my two cents worth! He was mad and I was mad.

Didn't see Wayne the whole day. He's hot and cold. But I meant it. That draft was the worst thing I could have imagined to give to the American public and whoever wrote it in the speechwriter's staff should seriously think of another vocation.

Then, my day was highlighted by a great date in the evening with Spank (Linda's nickname) Smith.

We went to the National Gallery, to which she had never been, and then to Hogate's[100] for dinner. She's sharp, strong, good-looking and sweet. I had a great time.

Oh, before the date with Spank, I had an interview with the Washington Post about how it is to be an intern during the summer of the impeachment proceedings. I answered in good faith, truthfully, and not dodging Watergate in the slightest, calling it a serious problem. The White House will love that.

Linda Smith, who at the time this photo was taken worked as an intern in the First Lady's Press Office in the East Wing of the White House.

---

[100] https://www.flickr.com/photos/streetsofdc/12152234403 Hogate's Seafood Restaurant, 800 Water St, S.W. Washington, D.C. - now closed.

July 19

Today, the information on the controls speech came in and really is substantial. Had to rewrite a managers article I had written a few days before.

The Washington Post photographer came to take my pictures for the interviews of interns that supposedly is to be printed.

Talking on the phone in my office in the Old Executive Office Building 1974/1975

Screwed up my time and attendance cards again for my pay check for the fourth consecutive time. We have been paid four times.

Then left for the greatest weekend so far this summer—a weekend with Liz and Bill in Ashland, VA. I do love those two!

My paycheck was a whopping $1,037.60 every two weeks!

Monday, July 22, 1974

Got to work at usual time—7:00, but substantial workload has decreased and I basically am doodling around, (reading the Post) and eating breakfast.

Been trying to keep my nose in work, but can't seem to get psyched lately. Speech on governmental controls—something I know absolutely zero about. But, if I sit on it long enough and read enough material, I'll come up with ideas.

Got a call at 9:00 from Cathy Griffith who started telling me how I was a celebrity, a showboat, etc. I didn't know what her problem was...until I realized that the Post article and interview and picture of last week must have made the ink. Not only was my picture and this article in the Post, but on the front page of the Style section. I got grief all day: "Small home-town boy makes big time, eh?, May I have your autograph?, Where's Pekin?, Where's Illinois?" It was fun. (Linda (Spank) was also featured in the Post article.)

First Hand

In afternoon, got a call from some FM radio station in D.C. that wanted to interview the Interns—some of them—from the Post article. Spank and I got together to discuss things in general and decided to go ahead with it, knowing full well that the entire discussion would be Watergate oriented. She was doing an interview with "Mademoiselle" at the time I called—busy lady and a really great girl—solid, sensitive, and sharp. We decided to meet this "Fred" figure from the radio station to get a reading before the interview on Wed. We met him and he's going to give us a tough time.

Took Spank home and pondered the fact of a possible relationship, but fell asleep in the midst of thoughts.

My Personal Diary of My White House Days

Washington Post style section articles featuring myself, Linda (on the phone) and my good friend to this day, Kelly Duncan.

First Hand

SIDE STORY: During my time working in the White House, Linda also worked for the first lady's press office, and was housed in the first lady's suite of offices in the East Wing.

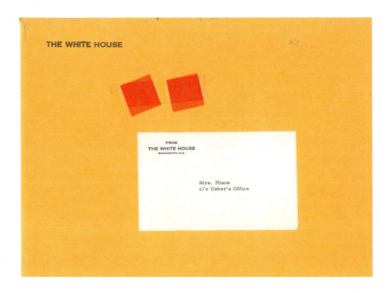

When we first started to date during our internship, and while she was still in the East Wing, she would attend state dinners. She would help with press arrangements for the state dinners that were held by the President and Mrs. Nixon or Mrs. Ford. At the end of each State dinner she would sneak out a bunch of cookies and take them back to her office in the East Wing. Within a day or so, I would receive cookies sent to me through the White House mail system, the inter-White House mail system.

The White House mail system in 1974/1975 consisted of staff pushing carts down hallways and stopping in offices to see if those in an office wanted to send a package to others within the White House. For example, if I wanted to send something to Linda, I would get an official White House mail envelope, put it inside, and if I felt it were important, I would put a red tag on it, meaning that it needed to get to the East Wing (or wherever), quickly.

I never sent Linda a red tag envelope. But after these state dinners she would put cookies in an envelope in the East Wing and send them to me in my office; and I would receive a red tag envelope thinking it was something somewhat important. I would open it up, and there would be a half dozen cookies that Linda had taken from the state dinner the night before. She did this five or six times and all of the interns and others on Mr. Baroody's staff got the biggest kick out of that.

One thought has been going through my mind for quite a while and that concerns "coalition politics" and its needed role in American political life. I would completely concur with Wayne that the basic problem within the Nixon Administration is that there existed and still exists a group of close aides which is naive about politics—Haig, Ziegler for examples—and who are paranoid, to degrees, of politics. Nixon likes to mold the political minds of his aides.

Tuesday, July 23

Ran an errand for Wayne to Jack Mills and met him. Dad had played golf with him on occasion and he is a fine man. He is working with Wayne on impeachment tabulation and, perhaps, doing some pinpoint lobbying. Then I went to the situation room of the West Wing to "dex" (a precursor to faxing) a copy of a management article to Baroody who is with the President in San Clemente. That room is amazingly sophisticated; it is the White House crisis room for international and domestic events. Computers, phones all over, and equipment of all kinds.

Ate lunch with Kelly, John S., and Tom Eg and one of the most amazing men in the Nixon Administration I have ever met, Dolf Droge (a foreign policy expert and confidant to President Nixon). He touched on the following:

1. New Federalism—the concept is so vitally important to involve state and local governments in policy decision making...let the Federal government assist them without strings attached. Then, if the aid and guidelines aren't enough, come back to D.C. for further help. Programs of the 30's needed FDR and he was the man for the job at the right time, but realities change—bureaucracy wallows in itself. Local governments have the talent and resources. Let's tap this talent and expand the local talent bank to raise the level of local governmental expertise and participation.

2. Nixon needed a Henry Kissinger for domestic affairs. He tried (John) Connally[101], but didn't work. Too bad, for Connally was a politician and a good one and perhaps could have straightened and pushed things into shape.

3. Impeachment—one ramification internationally could be dangerous. The North Vietnamese, once Nixon is in the Senate on trial with his hands tied, might very well step up military action, perhaps even launch an all-out invasion on the South. In

---

[101] Wikipedia contributors, "John Connally," *Wikipedia, The Free Encyclopedia*, https://en.wikipedia.org/w/index.php?title=John_Connally&oldid=973214507 (accessed September 20, 2020), "John Bowden Connally Jr. (February 27, 1917 – June 15, 1993) was an American politician. He served as the 39th Governor of Texas and as the 61st United States Secretary of the Treasury. He began his career as a Democrat and later became a Republican in 1973."

the mid-east, the Russians and Chinese, though at each other's throats now and with a Sino-Soviet[102] war imminent, could coalesce and break out war in this area and other areas in the world to give us a bad time. All hypothetical.

On the domestic side of the impeachment question, Droge suggested that the house "censure" the President in his execution of domestic responsibilities, taking him from certain powers applicable only to this case and this President, but to leave him alone internationally. The Democrats want Nixon in, in many ways, for they fear Vice President Ford being President for two years and his chances for '76 and '80. They want to see a crippled Nixon and make Ford straddle the fence for two years and nail him in '76.

---

[102] Wikipedia contributors, "Sino-Soviet split," *Wikipedia, The Free Encyclopedia*, https://en.wikipedia.org/w/index.php?title=Sino-Soviet_split&oldid=980047542 (accessed September 27, 2020), "The Sino-Soviet split (1956–1966) was the breaking of political relations between the People's Republic of China (PRC) and the Union of Soviet Socialist Republics (USSR), caused by doctrinal divergences that arose from their different interpretations and practical applications of Marxism–Leninism, as influenced by their respective geopolitics during the Cold War (1945–1991). In the late 1950s and early 1960s, Sino-Soviet debates about the interpretation of orthodox Marxism became specific disputes about the USSR's policies of national de-Stalinization and international peaceful coexistence with the Western world, which Mao decried as revisionism. Against that ideological background, China took a belligerent stance towards the West, and publicly rejected the USSR's policy of peaceful coexistence between the Eastern bloc and the Western bloc. In addition, China resented the closer Soviet ties with India, and Moscow feared Mao was too nonchalant about the horrors of nuclear war. In the Western world, the Sino-Soviet split transformed the bi-polar cold war into a tri-polar cold war, a geopolitical event as important as the erection of the Berlin Wall (1961), the defusing of the Cuban Missile Crisis (1962), and the end of the Vietnam War (1955–1975), because the rivalry facilitated Mao's realisation of Sino-American rapprochement with the 1972 Nixon visit to China. Moreover, the occurrence of the Sino-Soviet split also voided the concept of Monolithic Communism, the Western perception that the communist nations were collectively a unitary actor in post–Second World War geopolitics, especially during the 1947–1950 period in the Vietnam War, when the US intervened to the First Indochina War (1946–1954). Historically, the Sino-Soviet split facilitated the Marxist–Leninist Realpolitik with which Mao established the tri-polar geopolitics (PRC–USA–USSR) of the late-period Cold War (1956–1991) as well as the quad-polar geopolitics (PRC-UK-USA-USSR) until the Suez Crisis of 1956."

WATERGATE

The Tide Turns Back Toward Impeachment

In recent weeks President Nixon has had reason to believe that he was on the upswing in his battle to turn back the advance of impeachment. His trips to the Middle East and the Soviet Union were marked by some modest successes that reinforced his record of accomplishment in foreign policy. At home the impeachment drive seemed to be faltering in Congress, slowed by legalistic detail and partisan bickering. There were no new Watergate sensations, and the public appeared weary of the deepest political scandal in U.S. history.

Last week the mood in Washington changed abruptly. Impeachment once again picked up momentum in Congress. Despite some past mistakes, Rep-

BRACK—BLACK STAR

resentative Peter Rodino's Judiciary Committee was now seen to have performed remarkably well in virtually uncharted constitutional waters. As it wound up its examination of Nixon's "defense" witnesses—who turned out to be markedly unhelpful to the President —it seemed almost certain that a vote for impeachment would come by the end of the month. The previous week's minimum estimate of votes for impeachment (25 to 13) was now moving toward the maximum estimate (29 to 9). House Speaker Carl Albert and Democratic Floor Leader Thomas P. O'Neill have agreed that the full House come to a final vote no later than Aug. 23.

The President had his own day in court. Special Counsel James St. Clair squared off against Special Prosecutor Leon Jaworski before the Supreme Court in three hours of historic arguments about presidential privilege. At issue was whether the President must turn over 64 more White House tapes to Judge John Sirica for use as evidence in the trial of seven other Nixon aides (*see cover story next page*). It was not known just how damaging to the President's cause the withheld tapes might be. But Nixon, tempted to turn them over to avoid a confrontation with the courts, made the final decision to suppress them after spending two entire mornings listening to them.

While the suspense built up in anticipation of the court decision, it was a week of growing troubles for Nixon:

▶ A federal jury in Washington convicted John Ehrlichman, one of the President's two former closest advisers, of conspiring to violate the civil rights of Daniel Ellsberg's psychiatrist, and of lying to both the FBI and a federal grand jury about authorizing the break-in of the psychiatrist's office.

▶ The House Judiciary Committee released more than 4,000 pages of evidence that it has compiled so far on the Watergate break-in and cover-up. There was fresh and (for the President) damning new detail. The bulk of evidence indicated that Nixon was deeply involved in the cover-up—and even earlier than some of his critics had previously assumed.

▶ The Judiciary Committee also released a carefully transcribed version of the White House tapes containing some astounding discrepancies with the President's edited version. Conversations were shown to have been truncated or omitted entirely from the version of the tapes that the President had proclaimed to be finally telling the full story. Some of the dialogue contains exhortations to his aides to "stonewall" rather than tell the truth to investigators.

▶ The Senate Watergate committee finally published its report on the case. To Nixon, the most damaging part was an account of how his closest friend, C.G. ("Bebe") Rebozo, had probably used about $50,000 in campaign contributions—some of them carefully laundered to conceal the source—to pay for diamond earrings for the President's wife and other personal luxuries.

Those who believed that the President had not been hurt by last week's reports argued that only some major bombshell establishing the President's criminality would lead to his impeachment. Whether such an overwhelming piece of evidence exists—or if it does, whether he would allow it to be revealed —is doubtful. Moreover, the view that impeachment should occur only for an indictable crime is denied by most constitutional experts.

"[This doctrine] leaves the country without the means to assure responsible self-government in certain contingencies," Columnist William F. Buckley Jr. pointed out last week. "There are any number of activities, not formally proscribed by the law, which a President could legally undertake at indescribable cost to the Republic." Buckley imagined a number of fanciful actions for which a President should be indicted, such as commuting the sentences of all federal prisoners or taking a six-month vacation. Notwithstanding such *reductio ad absurdum*, Buckley says, the principle remains: "Congress has got to retain the right to pass judgment on gross presidential abuses: the true, and studied, disrespect for the sophisticated obligations of office."

Sheer Volume. The evidence produced so far would lead to an indictment of Nixon in almost any U.S. court. Yet what his supporters now seem to be demanding for impeachment is not merely an indictable offense but some piece of evidence that will make a prima facie case for conviction. There are growing signs in Congress that this strategy is losing ground. A move in the House among supporters of the President to convert the impeachment vote to a motion of censure—thereby allowing them to vote against Nixon without alienating many voters who still back him—is also likely to fail.

The White House clearly hoped that the sheer volume of the disclosures—218 pages of Judiciary Committee comparisons of transcripts, more than 4,000 pages of other committee evidence, the 2,217-page draft of the final Senate Watergate committee report, the long arguments before the Supreme Court —would further numb the minds of many Watergate-weary Americans. Press Secretary Ronald Ziegler dismissed the Judiciary Committee transcripts as part of "a hyped-up public relations campaign," and the Watergate committee allegations about the Rebozo fund as "warmed-over baloney."

The President may well be underestimating the public. When all 1,253 pages of the original White House transcripts were released in April, many Administration supporters hoped that the formidable mass of evidence would deter many people from inspecting it closely. But it turned out differently, and it probably will again.

THE PRESIDENT, CHAIRMAN RODINO, JOHN EHRLICHMAN & VOLUMES OF EVIDENCE FROM HOUSE JUDICIARY COMMITTEE

July 24th Wed.

Day of the radio interview and I have been a bit nervous—not because I panic in front of the mike, which I do a bit, but because I have been so torn on the various issues of Watergate and the President's handling of the case. I had to—I was forced to—reach some conclusions in my own mind on how I stood regarding his innocence or guilt, his effectiveness as a leader, and several questions that I had subconsciously avoided taking hard stances on. That is what made me nervous and tore me up during most of the day.

There is a beautiful park across from the White House and I ambled there pondering what I would say in regard to the dirt questions that would come. I came up with the following answers which, on July 24th, I believed sincerely:

A. On Nixon—I am not the type to cling to a man, defending him at all costs and believing in everything he does. I view a man based upon his politics, his ideas, and the goals he has set for his nation. So, while at the White House, I am serving the President from a conviction that his general policies are very sound, imaginative, responsible, and, most importantly, bring this nation up to the realities of the last third of the 20th Century. I am also serving the Republican Party, of which I am a member, and I also am serving, in a small way, my country, which is the most honored service of all.

B. On Watergate/Impeachment—Watergate definitely is a serious dilemma facing this nation. There are those in the White House who avoid conversations leaning towards Watergate and Impeachment and there are those who still say that Watergate is merely a hotel complex off of Rock Creek Parkway. So much is at stake; it is potentially devastating at worst and, at best, will make this country stronger in its institutional form of government. But there is no good = no real good—evolving from this crisis. So much is involved—from the technical legalities to the grand Constitutional questions; emotions are involved and are running high; politics in the barest sense are involved; the safety of the Presidency is involved; strong leadership is involved; and the psychological effects upon the American public in terms of politics and governmental trust is involved. The stakes are high. It is not an issue easily tossed aside in the slightest by the Administration, the Congress, or the public.

On impeachment, I'll say that objectivity is hard to come by in this town and if it can't come from this town, where the news breaks and is made, then objectivity throughout the nation is at a premium. There definitely is a rash bias on the part of leading papers here and in other parts of the country; this is countered by biased comments and, in some instances, lies, by the Administration. It's tough to know exactly which end is up, which set of "facts" are true, to form a valid judgement. Leaks, selected information, and the incredible fast pace of Watergate-related matters add to the difficulty in reaching an objective analysis on impeachment or other events. So, I'm just not going to make a judgement for the very valid reason of a lack of proper perspective and I only pray that those shoulders upon whom this burden falls be strong, that the minds be reasonable in weighing the international and domestic ramifications of a potential impeachment.

C. Nixon Doctrine and New Federalism—These are the two basic reasons why I, myself, am a Republican and support the President's imaginative, responsible leadership. These two philosophies have reversed thinking of over the past 30-40 years. Thirty years ago, centralized governmental power in Washington was the answer both domestically and internationally to bring us out of a depression and to guide us through a war. But, realities change. From these past policies, we now suffer from inflated expectations—believing, in an exaggerated way, that the Federal government and American technology can solve the social and human problems; more and bigger programs of the past are the source of irritation. We no longer are able to dictate to other nations solutions to their problems and in our interest; the bi-polar world has changed to a multi-polar world; nuclear arms are in the hands of several nations and blocks of nations. The Nixon

Doctrine calls for a creative partnership of aid and assistance between America and its allies to balance the interests of both.

On the domestic front, over the past 30-40 years, we have accumulated such centralization in Washington that we have neglected the voices of local municipalities and governments; we have amassed such an ineffective bureaucratic entanglement as to lose perspective of the real problems and needs of local citizens. Through New Federalism and the revenue sharing, the President has begun to bring these state, county, and local governments and their officials back into the mainstream of political life—to tap the resources and talent of localities throughout America so that they can solve their own problems, with aid from the Federal government. This nation was founded 200 years ago and has grown since, from local concern and local productivity. We must again return to this concept, tap local resources, and allow America to continue to grow.

D. <u>Coalition Politics/PR men</u>—If Nixon had utilized those who understood coalition politics in this nation, perhaps Watergate could have been avoided. If he had men who understood the ramifications of such a childish, weak stunt, who affiliated themselves not only with the President but with the Republican party and the American people, this might have been avoided. Never was the decision of an electorate so decided before the election; never in history was a Presidential incumbent sitting so high and in such a magnificent position politically in this nation's history. Paranoia by the PR boys and the political novices brought the house tumbling down. That's 20-20 hindsight. The point is that there is a need to return to the ABC's of American politics, though those ABC's have been changed to some degree by Watergate forever.

Well, if this were all that were on my mind today, I guess I would be lucky. The Supreme Court this morning came down with the 8-0 decision for the President to turn over the 64 tapes which he has been withholding. I was in Wayne's office when the decision was to be announced at 10:45 A.M., then strutted to Baroody's office to watch it on his TV with Maureen and Tom

Egg. To say the least, we were all on pins and needles, but again I was struck by the fact that I was open-minded somewhat regarding the decision, fearing that the Court would not limit its decision narrowly enough to the Nixon case specifically, thus not harming the President in any way. They, in my opinion, were a bit broad in their decision by narrowing their votes to encompass "criminal" charges, but at least it left the basic tenets of Executive Privilege untouched enough for my liking. Thus, I was in fair agreement with the decision, but did not emote the fact in the office of a Special Assistant to the President (Mr. Baroody). It was dramatic. Yet, what really sickened and depressed me deeply about the whole episode was watching the crowd behind Douglas Kiker[103], the correspondent, cheer and jump in elation when the decision was announced. It was as though I were watching a basketball game which had gone into over-time and the opposite team had won.

Never in my life did I feel instant depression overwhelm me in such a fashion as when I saw those Americans behaving in such an irresponsible, disgusting, juvenile fashion. What had this all come to when the world's most powerful man is on trial in the institutions our ancestors had died for in the nation which is the envy of the world? What has happened to any semblance of national maturity? Or was there ever any? It was then that I realized that Watergate indeed will leave a tarnish upon this nation which will take untold years to remove.

It was then that I realized the gut division in this country—the quiet, yet increasing division over Richard Nixon and Watergate. To be divided in the eccentric and emotional manner which this country recently went through during the Vietnam war is different and, in some aspects, less damaging to the national spirit, for the issue and the emotional outlets were more tangible.

---

[103] Wikipedia contributors, "Douglas Kiker," *Wikipedia, The Free Encyclopedia*, https://en.wikipedia.org/w/index.php?title=Douglas_Kiker&oldid=977582722 (accessed September 27, 2020), "Douglas Kiker (January 7, 1930 – August 14, 1991) was an American author and newspaper and television reporter whose career spanned some three decades...[He] became a reporter for the New York Herald Tribune newspaper and in his first week on the job rode in the press bus in the motorcade of President John F. Kennedy when Kennedy was assassinated in Dallas, Texas. He was also the commentator on the August 9, 1974 live broadcast of President Richard Nixon's departure from office in disgrace from the Watergate scandal."

But this is different. The division is still emotional and, watching the Supreme Court decision, still surreal. But it seems to possess the undulating, quiet tones of a deeper, more lasting divisiveness—a melancholy that will be so much more difficult to erase by whatever means are attempted. I need to clarify what I mean: Example: Watergate will, and has, quietly made Americans very distrustful of any politician and, perhaps, paranoid of politics. I still need to elaborate and clarify, which I will do. But the point is that such behavior threw me into shock.

Thursday, July 25

A day of sadness indeed. There have been many recently and will undoubtedly be more, the way things are going. It is quiet here—the President and staff are in San Clemente and the Supreme Court decision yesterday took the sting out of the complex. Yet, still I remain convinced that the legal evidence is not there to impeach the President. The Judiciary committee hearings have been on many TV's here and occupy the thoughts of some, but work is here to do and lingers over everyone's head. Watergate and impeachment are beginning to have an effect upon the work operations—slowing down.

Friday, July 26th

Again, not productive. Working on a new project, though—assimilating an information bank for Mr. Baroody on various topics. Don't think that I will get too far with it, but worth a try. Lunch with Spank and then we went to Lafayette Park to sit and discuss the morale and tone of the White House. We had just finished a hellish week—Post article and radio show had emotionally undone me as well as the Hogan[104] defection, Supreme Court decision, and impeachment hearings. Who should waltz up to us as we are enjoying each other's company amidst the quiet of the park? A Washington Post reporter who

---

[104] Wikipedia contributors, "Lawrence Hogan," *Wikipedia, The Free Encyclopedia*, https://en.wikipedia.org/w/index.php?title=Lawrence_Hogan&oldid=980281961 (accessed September 27, 2020), "Lawrence Joseph Hogan (September 30, 1928 – April 20, 2017) was an American politician who served as a Republican U.S. Congressman, representing the 5th congressional district of Maryland from January 3, 1969, to January 3, 1975. In 1974, he was the only Republican Representative to vote to recommend all three House articles of impeachment against President Richard Nixon."

had undoubtedly saw us coming out of the White House and/or our pictures in the Post. He began to ask us about what the atmosphere was in the White House. Spank didn't respond well to him, as she had had it with impeachment, etc. and she didn't want to voice her opinions. I did the best I could with him, but it was a strain to sound at all cheery, as though the events of the past week had not shaken the morale of the staff. I gave him lines that the Supreme Court decision had been an expected one and, in my view a fair one, and that the decision proves once again that the institutions of government in America work well, for the decision had taken only a short time to reach. Blah, Blah, Blah. I didn't even read the paper the next day to see if I was quoted (I didn't give my name—he didn't want it either). Just sick of it.

Went to the office and stared at the desk and chatted with the guys about the happenings.

My Personal Diary of My White House Days

Invitation by Julie & David Eisenhower to a reception for the interns in the White House Residence.

```
                    THE WHITE HOUSE
                      WASHINGTON
                     July 19, 1974


     MEMORANDUM FOR THE WHITE HOUSE SUMMER INTERNS

     FROM:         PAM POWELL
                   SANDY LAUGHLIN

     Julie and David Eisenhower called this morning to invite
     all the 1974 White House Summer Interns to attend a
     reception next Friday evening, July 26, 1974, at 6:00 p.m.
     This is one of the rare occasions when the Second Floor of
     the White House, the First Family living quarters, will be
     opened for a special event-- Just for you!!! You will also
     be allowed to drive in the Southwest Gate and park your cars
     on the circular driveway in front of the South Portico.
     Entrance will be through the Diplomatic Reception Room. As
     usual, men should wear coat and tie and women may wear either
     a short of long dress. THIS IS GOING TO BE " THE " EVENT OF
     THE SUMMER, SO PLEASE TRY TO COME. R.S.V.P. to Pam or Sandy
     no later than the close of business hours on Monday. The
     reception will be over early, so if anybody has any suggestions
     for something to do afterwards, please let us know. In fact,
     we expect our social committee to handle this!!!

     Secretary Brennan will speak to the interns on Wednesday,
     July 24, 1974 at 3:30 p.m. in Room 459, OEOB.

     There will be a special tour of the Bureau of Engraving
     and Printing on Thursday, July 25, 1974. We will all
     meet at the Visitor's entrance on 14th. and C Street, N.W.
     at 9:45 a.m.

     Frank Zarb, the Associate Director of the Office of
     Management and Budget for Natural Resources, Energy, and
     Science has agreed to speak to the Interns on Friday, July
     26, 1974 at 10:00 a.m. in Room 459, OEOB. A biography will
     be sent next week.
```

That evening, Julie Eisenhower[105] was gracious enough to have a reception for the Interns in the residence of the White House. As I understand it, there have been fewer than ten

---

[105] Wikipedia contributors, "Julie Nixon Eisenhower," *Wikipedia, The Free Encyclopedia*, https://en.wikipedia.org/w/index.php?title=Julie_Nixon_Eisenhower&oldid=978638602 (accessed September 27, 2020), "Julie Nixon Eisenhower (born July 5, 1948) is an American author who is the younger daughter of Richard Nixon, 37th President of the United States, and Pat Nixon, First Lady of the United States, and is the wife of David Eisenhower, grandson of President Eisenhower."

receptions in the residence since the Nixon's have been in office, so it really was a treat.

The main area of the reception was in the Yellow Oval Room, directly above the diplomatic reception room on the ground floor. This is the Nixon's drawing room before one would enter their bedrooms. It is done in yellow and white and is absolutely gorgeous.

We were served iced tea with mint and an assortment of goodies. We all went onto the balcony overlooking the South Lawn and talked and enjoyed being elite for the short time.

Julie was gracious, but one could tell she was not totally at ease with the situation; perhaps the week's events had taken their toll on her. After a little while, she was kind enough to take us through the Lincoln Bedroom in which is housed the most beautiful bed that Mrs. Lincoln had purchased for the President but which he never slept in. Beside the bed, on a small table, was an enclosed hand-written draft of Lincoln's Gettysburg Address written by President Lincoln. <u>That</u> was impressive. Then, we sauntered into the Queen's Bedroom, also lovely, though not as appealing as the Lincoln Bedroom.

Downstairs we went to have our pictures taken with Julie and off we went—I to help Barb and Spank with a paper, and others out to dinn dinn.

Julie Nixon Eisenhower posed with the interns in the following photo (front row, left, holding the "W.H.I.P." [White House Internship Program] sweatshirt).

Saturday, July 27th

Am now in Ashland, VA dog sitting for Liz and Bill. But, again am overtaken by the events of the past week, and just witnessed a vote by the Judiciary Committee on the 1st Article of Impeachment, passed by 27-11. I was disappointed, believing as Congressman Sandman[106] does that, with the stakes as high as they are in this case, there must be concrete evidence, not circumstantial evidence, that links President Nixon with Watergate and the ensuing coverup. I haven't seen it, but would demand it.

During the past week, thoughts concerning impeachment have slowly eaten away at me. I have been unable to do constructive

---

[106] Wikipedia contributors, "Charles W. Sandman Jr.," *Wikipedia, The Free Encyclopedia*, https://en.wikipedia.org/w/index.php?title=Charles_W._Sandman_Jr.&oldid=948658225 (accessed September 27, 2020), "Charles William Sandman Jr. (October 23, 1921 – August 26, 1985) was an American Republican Party politician who represented New Jersey's 2nd congressional district in the United States House of Representatives and was the party's candidate for Governor of New Jersey in 1973. Sandman was on the House Judiciary Committee when it considered articles of impeachment against President Richard Nixon. He was the most vitriolic defender of Nixon in the hearings."

work and feel guilty about my neglect. The graveness of the situation has slapped me in the face. It is hard to be jovial at lunch with friends, hard to be ebullient on the phone and with the press, hard to motivate myself to work, and most unfortunately, a bit difficult to be jovial with Spank, whom I am very fond of.

I believe that I, more than most interns, feel the situation more fully—feel the depression more fully. If I were on the outside looking in, I know my attitude would be different, for the media with its "wink of the eye" bias and hatred for the President and in its search for the sensational, fills the minds of our nation's citizens. One can't say that the populous is "ignorant," but one can say that the biased and sensational tone of the media has affected the thinking of Americans. Yet, truly I believe that some Americans realize this and have fought this injustice.

I remember when I was in London last semester and news came out that the President had not filed the proper tax returns. I was livid and joined the resignation bandwagon. I continued to read about refusals by the President to turn over subpoenaed evidence and became more insistent for resignation.

Then, I began to realize that my attitude had been shaped by one paper—the International Herald Tribune published by the Washington Post and the New York Times in Europe. I began to slow down, to ponder more thoroughly the President's arguments for Executive Privilege and confidentiality. I began to realize that, regardless of his innocence or guilt, that he is entitled to proceed under due process, to take his case to the limits. I realized that resignation would truly weaken the Presidency and I felt President Nixon was sincere in this respect. Confidentiality is an absolute necessity; resignation by popular demand would have had an adverse effect upon this principle. The point—I realized that the media had duped me and had taken my emotions with it. In our fast-moving world when we reflect little upon our course or upon our past, the power of the media to form instant opinions of its clientele is immense and dangerous.

I don't know of the President's innocence or guilt. What frightens me utterly is that Congress doesn't either. I haven't heard one Congressman say that the President ordered the break-in, the hush money, the CIA, FBI involvement, etc. —<u>directly</u>. That's the evidence I need. Circumstantial evidence leaves me in complete doubt.

My contention is that when the stakes are as high as they are in the nation's second impeachment trial, when America is the world's most powerful, prosperous nation, when we face domestic challenges, and when the international scene is incessantly shifting, approaching crossroad after crossroad, the evidence to impeach President Nixon had better be damn conclusive. At this point, I don't see it.

In today's vote of 27-11, I would say that 50%—all Democrats—were totally politically motivated out of a deep dislike of the President and his former staff, and of a desire to make the road as rocky for him as possible; one fourth voted out of a combination of political motivation and sincerity; and one fourth voted as their "conscience" dictated.

It is discouraging to me that this nation, in time of a crisis as grave as this, is represented by such insincere, base individuals. Indeed, these are times that try men's souls. All of America is on trial, not just a President.

My Personal Diary of My White House Days

KEY FACTS: THE PRESIDENT RESPONDS TO THE HOUSE
JUDICIARY COMMITTEE

1. Cutting the impeachment knot: Responding to a subpoena for 42 Watergate conversations, President Nixon is providing the Committee with transcripts of all relevant portions of the conversations that were taped as well as other non-requested conversations bearing on the case. Thus, he has more than complied with the Committee subpoena.

2. Verifying the transcripts: The President has also invited the Chairman and ranking minority members of the Committee, Congressmen Rodino and Hutchinson, to listen to the tapes personally with the help of the transcripts to ensure that no relevant portions have been omitted from the transcripts and that the transcripts are accurate.

3. Answering further questions: The President has also reaffirmed his original offer to answer under oath interrogatories from the Committee and to meet personally with Messrs. Rodino and Hutchinson to resolve any problems.

4. Nothing to hide: Even though hostile elements will try to sensationalize elements of the conversations, the President wants the public to know that he has nothing to hide and to see the evidence for themselves. He has therefore directed that all of the transcripts given to the committee -- more than 1,300 pages in all -- also be made public -- another mark of courage in the President's long ordeal to combat rumors, hearsay, and unfounded allegations against him.

5. What the transcripts show: The key question is not how many tapes the President is turning over, but what the tapes themselves show. And the tapes reveal a President, suddenly confronted with tales of wrongdoing by his associates, trying to unravel the Watergate story and seeing that justice was done, fairly and according to the law:

> --On September 15, 1972, contrary to Dean's sworn testimony, the President showed that he had no awareness of an on-going cover-up and, again contrary to Dean, he did not praise Dean for "containing" it.

Monday, July 29th

My "rest" on days off in Virginia did no good. Didn't sleep well, as I sat on porch for hours that night smoking cigarettes with Bill; choking and coughing. That's a new one. Saw Wayne today. There was an article in the Post about the fact that Baroody is connected with impeachment and vote tabulation on the hill. Wayne is the "hit man" in the operation and has been doing quiet lobbying and support gathering for the President. Baroody didn't want the story to go any further at all—no further than the brief mention. He had been getting calls from (Carl) Bernstein[107] of the Post and Wayne got calls from (Bob) Woodward[108]. Bad. If Baroody were linked to the situation and Ford came in as President, Baroody would be bounced out. Also, if there was a general discovery of the situation in which Wayne was involved, he could really be smeared and tainted to look like another "cover-up or covert" operation, though I don't think he is doing anything illegal. And so, Wayne said for us to be careful with the Press in linking Baroody with impeachment—stay totally clear of it—and the press, if you can. I, after Friday, had resigned myself to abstain from press coverage of any sort.

---

[107] Wikipedia contributors, "Carl Bernstein," *Wikipedia, The Free Encyclopedia*, https://en.wikipedia.org/w/index.php?title=Carl_Bernstein&oldid=979538808 (accessed September 30, 2020), "Carl Bernstein (born February 14, 1944) is an American investigative journalist and author. While a young reporter for The Washington Post in 1972, Bernstein was teamed up with Bob Woodward; the two did much of the original news reporting on the Watergate scandal. These scandals led to numerous government investigations and the eventual resignation of President Richard Nixon."

[108] Wikipedia contributors, "Bob Woodward," *Wikipedia, The Free Encyclopedia*, https://en.wikipedia.org/w/index.php?title=Bob_Woodward&oldid=979403121 (accessed September 30, 2020), "Robert Upshur Woodward (born March 26, 1943) is an American investigative journalist. He started working for The Washington Post as a reporter in 1971, and currently holds the title of associate editor. While a young reporter for The Washington Post in 1972, Woodward teamed up with Carl Bernstein; the two did much of the original news reporting on the Watergate scandal."

My Personal Diary of My White House Days

John Rhodes was the House Minority Leader at the time of this article in the Washington Post.

Rhodes Suggests Nixon Take Case To People on TV

Haig Confident

By Carroll Kilpatrick and Morton Mintz
Washington Post Staff Writers

The White House chief of staff acknowledged last night that President Nixon's position has suffered "an erosion," but rejected assessments that impeachment by the House of Representatives is a sure thing.

"The case for impeachment is not there," Alexander M. Haig Jr. told an interviewer.

If the House were to impeach Mr. Nixon, would he resign to avoid the "trauma of a Senate trial?" Haig was asked.

"At this juncture, I see no value served in the interests of the people to have presidents driven out of office," he replied.

The White House staff chief appeared on the CBS television program "60 Minutes (WTOP). Mike Wallace had taped an interview with him in Los Angeles yesterday morning, only half a day after the House Judiciary Committee voted 27 to 11 to recommend the first impeachment of a President since 1868. Haig had been with Mr. Nixon in San Clemente, where Wallace also had interviewed him Friday night.

Wallace suggested that impeachment by the House seems "cut and dried," citing estimates by Democratic and Republican House leaders, the composition of the House—248 Democrats and 187 Republicans—and the vote of six of the 17 GOP members of the Judiciary Committee Sat-

'Only Possibility'

By David S. Broder
Washington Post Staff Writer

House Minority Leader John J. Rhodes (R-Ariz.) suggested yesterday that a full-scale television defense of Mr. Nixon's conduct in office is now the "only viable possibility" for the President to avoid impeachment by the House.

Rhodes offered that suggestion as House Majority Leader Thomas P. O'Neill Jr. (D-Mass.), House Deputy Whip John Brademas (D-Ind.) and Senate Majority Whip Robert C. Byrd (D-W.Va.) all predicted impeachment.

Byrd said it was "not an absolute certitude," but O'Neill said "only a miracle" can save the President, and Brademas agreed. Both talked of a margin of 70 votes or more in the 435-member House.

Rhodes said in a telephone interview that he would take his first formal head-count of House Republicans on impeachment this week. But he conceded that Saturday's 27-to-11 Judiciary Committee vote for the first count of impeachment, in which six Republicans joined the 21 Democrats, "is going to have some effect" in reducing House Republican support of the President.

"The imponderable is how much," Rhodes said.

During the interview, the Arizonan put forward his proposal that Mr. Nixon take his case directly to the nation.

Rhodes said he had not been asked for advice by the President, but "if he were to ask me, I don't know of anything I could tell him to do except to go on television and exhaustively explore and re-

Tuesday, July 30

With the Supreme Court decision out, the tapes have been housed in a room off of the cafeteria on the ground floor. There are three guards at the area—two on a desk and one at the door. Security around the building has increased greatly—I must show my pass to the guards even though I know them well. The mood is tense with the tapes. I did see St. Clair[109] (the President's personal attorney in the Watergate matter) coming down the steps today and wondered if he was heading into the room.

---

[109] Wikipedia contributors, "James D. St. Clair," *Wikipedia, The Free Encyclopedia*, https://en.wikipedia.org/w/index.php?title=James_D._St._Clair&oldid=877493662 (accessed September 30, 2020), "James Draper St. Clair (April 14, 1920 – March 10, 2001) was an American lawyer, and practiced law for many years in Boston with the firm of Hale & Dorr. He was the chief legal counsel for President Richard Nixon during the Watergate Scandal."

Wednesday, July 31

Had to do a crash project with Tom Eg in tracing the initiatives in the President's State of the Union message of 1974 and find out where they are located in Congress. Then, take them up to the Committee that Congressman Michel is heading to give to some PR person. I called all over the place to get ahold of someone who knew of this type of project, but no one had traced the initiatives. Unbelievable. I would think that they would be traced by more than one office—for PR purposes, at least. Got the job done, then to a seminar with Brennan[110], Secretary of Labor and a really funny, down-to-earth guy.

Thursday, August 1

Finally got the work on controls and decided to motivate myself to get the thing finished by the end of the weekend. Had 9-year-old Sarah Dahly who is a friend of Spank's to the White House for a tour, then Chuck Gagnier came and Spank was kind enough to show him the Oval Office and Cabinet Room and Roosevelt Room. Came back to office at 2:30 to work and missed Ray Price[111] at Seminar.

Friday, August 2

Worked all day on controls. Had a seminar with two Russians who were filled with B.S. I really didn't like the seminar—propaganda filled. But, just stared at them as Russians trying to think what life is like in Russia. It was a compulsory attendance seminar, and I left before it ended. Then, to a really nice English Tea in honor of some British students here in Washington and friends of an intern. The room in the E.O.B.—room 208—was beautiful and it was pleasant to hear the accents.

---

[110] Wikipedia contributors, "Peter J. Brennan," *Wikipedia, The Free Encyclopedia*, https://en.wikipedia.org/w/index.php?title=Peter_J._Brennan&oldid=971434656 (accessed September 30, 2020), "Peter Joseph Brennan (May 24, 1918 – October 2, 1996) was US labor activist and politician who was United States Secretary of Labor under Presidents Nixon and Ford."

[111] Wikipedia contributors, "Ray Price (speechwriter)," *Wikipedia, The Free Encyclopedia*, https://en.wikipedia.org/w/index.php?title=Ray_Price_(speechwriter)&oldid=953493096 (accessed September 30, 2020), "Raymond Kissam Price, Jr. (May 6, 1930 – February 13, 2019) was an American writer who was the chief speechwriter for U.S. President Richard Nixon, working on both inaugural addresses, his resignation speech, and Gerald Ford's pardon speech."

Monday, August 5

Turned in speech, which needs work yet—need to get away from rigid language. But, did the bulk of it. Needs Wayne's touch.

About 3:00, I went down to Baroody's office to chat with his great secretaries and the halls were filled with people—especially in front of St. Clair's office. On the way down, I saw many of the staff of the White House filing into the Briefing Room in the E.O.B.—a strange sight, indeed. Then, I saw Haig go in and I knew that something drastic was up—one gets sensitized around here for nothing but the worst, which has yet to come. On the way back from St. Clair's area, I ran into Barb (another intern), who was on her way to the West Wing to get some info on what was happening—whatever "it" was.

We got there and Spank gave us a press release by the President which, in short, indicated that he was involved in the coverup for two years and that three tapes will prove this, contrary to what he had been saying in his defense during the past 25 months. All as a result of the Supreme Court decision the weeks prior. I was spellbound—found it to be unbelievable. The press were scurrying around—Dan Rather[112] was in a tizzy. They had him—the clear evidence was there, something that I didn't think would exist at this late date. For so long, many had given the President the benefit of the doubt—and doubtful it was—in this case, I among them. But, in a sense, he confessed publicly, before it would come out bit by bit from the Special Prosecutor's office.

Well, I had had it with being despondent about the whole situation and resolved myself not to let this ruin an evening with Spank, as we needed to have a good time. It fell from my mind

---

[112] Wikipedia contributors, "Dan Rather," *Wikipedia, The Free Encyclopedia*, https://en.wikipedia.org/w/index.php?title=Dan_Rather&oldid=980712127 (accessed September 30, 2020), "Dan Irvin Rather Jr. (born October 31, 1931) is an American journalist and former national evening news anchor. In 1965 Rather served as a foreign correspondent for CBS in London and in 1966 in Vietnam. He served again as White House correspondent during the presidency of Richard Nixon. In 1970, he was also assigned as anchor for the CBS Sunday Night News (1970–73; 1974–75), and later for the CBS Saturday Evening News (1973–76). Rather was among those journalists who accompanied Nixon to China. He later covered the Watergate investigation as well as impeachment proceedings against Nixon in Congress."

for a while, but I knew that the ballgame was over. It is all over, as of today, August 5, 1974. I truly believe that it is the beginning of a fast end of the Presidency of Richard Nixon, a man who lived for his country, a man who has so gratefully given to his country, but who took his country and its people for granted. He is, in the classic sense, a tragic figure, a man with a flaw—the pursuit of power—who, like Macbeth[113], had a tragic flaw of ambition, which ultimately led to his demise.

The final chapter has been written, I'm afraid, and the episode will soon be history. My sympathy for his cause has vanished, to a considerable degree. I no longer can defend him in his fight against impeachment, for his fight against impeachment now is a fight against the American system and ideal of justice. He has lied to this nation for two years and has committed obstruction of justice. Painfully, I must say that he must pay the price. He must, by some avenue, leave office.

---

[113] Wikipedia contributors, "Macbeth," *Wikipedia, The Free Encyclopedia*, https://en.wikipedia.org/w/index.php?title=Macbeth&oldid=979185063 (accessed September 30, 2020), "Macbeth (full title The Tragedy of Macbeth) is a tragedy by William Shakespeare; it is thought to have been first performed in 1606. It dramatises the damaging physical and psychological effects of political ambition on those who seek power for its own sake."

First Hand

This is the press release that occurred after the "Smoking Gun" tape was released to the public.

FOR IMMEDIATE RELEASE   AUGUST 5, 1974

Office of the White House Press Secretary

THE WHITE HOUSE

STATEMENT BY THE PRESIDENT

I have today instructed my attorneys to make available to the House Judiciary Committee, and I am making public, the transcripts of three conversations with H.R. Haldeman on June 23, 1972. I have also turned over the tapes of these conversations to Judge Sirica, as part of the process of my compliance with the Supreme Court ruling.

On April 29, in announcing my decision to make public the original set of White House transcripts, I stated that "as far as what the President personally knew and did with regard to Watergate and the cover-up is concerned, these materials -- together with those already made available -- will tell it all."

Shortly after that, in May, I made a preliminary review of some of the 64 taped conversations subpoenaed by the Special Prosecutor.

Among the conversations I listened to at that time were two of those of June 23. Although I recognized that these presented potential problems, I did not inform my staff or my Counsel of it, or those arguing my case, nor did I amend my submission to the Judiciary Committee in order to include and reflect it. At the time, I did not realize the extent of the implications which these conversations might now appear to have. As a result, those arguing my case, as well as those passing judgment on the case, did so with information that was incomplete and in some respects erroneous. This was a serious act of omission for which I take full responsibility and which I deeply regret.

Since the Supreme Court's decision twelve days ago, I have ordered my Counsel to analyze the 64 tapes, and I have listened to a number of them myself. This process has made it clear that portions of the tapes of these June 23 conversations are at variance with certain of my previous statements. Therefore, I have ordered the transcripts made available immediately to the Judiciary Committee so that they can be reflected in the Committee's report, and included in the record to be considered by the House and Senate.

In a formal written statement on May 22 of last year, I said that shortly after the Watergate break-in I became concerned about the possibility that the FBI investigation might lead to the exposure either of unrelated covert activities of the CIA, or of sensitive national security matters that the so-called "plumbers" unit at the White House had been working on, because of the CIA and plumbers connections of some of those involved. I said that I therefore gave instructions that the FBI should be alerted to coordinate with the CIA, and to ensure that the investigation not expose these sensitive national security matters.

That statement was based on my recollection at the time -- some eleven months later -- plus documentary materials and relevant public testimony of those involved.

MORE

Such a tragedy as this has never occurred in this nation, but we must not let ourselves steep in the depression, not allow sympathy for the man to obstruct objectivity and rationality in deciding what is best now for the nation.

Having worked here for a brief, few months, I have seen what he has done for this nation domestically and internationally and I have become a strong advocate of his general actions, for they have been best for the nation and the world as well. Thus, with a loyalty to him in this regard, and a deeper sense of friendship with many in the White House, I realize that a decision to remove him from office has ramifications for the nation, but also painful ones for those whom I have come to know and respect within the White House. And, it pains me, as a mere intern, to realize that I now believe that President Nixon must leave office, for it is difficult to detach such a decision from my experiences in the White House. Yet, it is a decision made by careful consideration all summer of the evidence against him and possible, just ways by which he might remain as President...it is not a decision made off the cuff, on the spur of the moment.

Tuesday, August 6

Something that may have been left out of Aug 5 notes was that Rogers Morton[114] spoke to us yesterday and was excellent.

Today the mood was "just a matter of time" type. Resignation seems to be the most probable option of the two available, as nothing constructive could possibly be gained from a Senate Trial when the odds are insurmountable, as all concede them to be.

Yesterday, at Congressman Rhoades'[115] press conference when he said he would vote for impeachment, a reporter asked him if there were 25 votes against impeachment in the House. He said, "I don't know."

If the Minority Leader of the House isn't sure there are 25 votes for the President's case in the House, it is a "foregone conclusion" that not only will he be impeached in the House, but convicted in the Senate by a substantial margin.

Spoke briefly with Wayne today and he said that if he were a Senator, he would vote for impeachment. Not very reassuring news from one who has worked so strenuously on Watergate in tabulating and keeping record of House reaction. Sat in his chair as he said that it wasn't worth it to begin tabulation on the Senate.

The ball-game is over. While there, I glanced through the transcript of the three tapes between the President and Haldeman.

The atmosphere is that of a fine line between sinking and sunk.

The President had a Cabinet meeting and there was much stir outside concerning his resignation, but those here felt that he was

---

[114] Wikipedia contributors, "Rogers Morton," *Wikipedia, The Free Encyclopedia*, https://en.wikipedia.org/w/index.php?title=Rogers_Morton&oldid=970592570 (accessed September 30, 2020), "Rogers Clark Ballard Morton (September 19, 1914 – April 19, 1979) was an American politician who served as the U.S. Secretary of the Interior and Secretary of Commerce during the administrations of Presidents Richard M. Nixon and Gerald R. Ford, Jr., respectively."

[115] Wikipedia contributors, "John Jacob Rhodes," *Wikipedia, The Free Encyclopedia*, https://en.wikipedia.org/w/index.php?title=John_Jacob_Rhodes&oldid=966280249 (accessed September 30, 2020), "John Jacob Rhodes Jr. (September 18, 1916 – August 24, 2003) was an American lawyer and politician. A member of the Republican Party, Rhodes was elected as a U.S. Representative from the state of Arizona. He was the Minority Leader in the House 1973-81, where he pressed a conservative agenda. Rhodes was elected, by acclamation, to be House Minority Leader on December 7, 1973, succeeding Gerald Ford when Ford became Vice President."

telling them of his position not to resign. He wants to wait a few days or perhaps longer to gauge reaction after the initial bomb was dropped. Reaction will not get any better however. Things have fallen apart so rapidly and are continuing to fall apart at a rapid pace.

Every morning at 7:00 a.m. the President would be given a News Summary such as this one to keep him up to date on the 'big news stories' of all the different networks.

NEWS SUMMARY

August 6, 1974
(Mon nets,wires,papers)

The major stories are:

-- AP leads: "Conceding he w/held some WG evidence from Hill and his own lawyers, RN made public a t'script showing he authorized attempt to thwart FBI WG investigation".... UPI leads: "RN acknowledged/shortly after WG break-in he acted to slow FBI investigation knowing it'd protect his re-election Comm. and w/held this from Judiciary and Supreme Court."..."RN stunned the country" and caused a "storm" in DC, led NBC...."The Nixon Presidency is virtually being overtaken by events," led CBS, citing resignation calls and RN statement.....Also led ABC w/13-17 mins. on all shows.

-- All nets noted RN acknowledged info may further damage his case, that he accepted full responsibility and apologized w/deep regret for keeping data from lawyers, Hill and public, and that he regards impchmnt as foregone conclusion. But, all shows also noted, RN doesn't feel the evidence in its entirety or in perspective justifies extreme step of impchmnt and removal.

-- T'scripts show RN was aware of WG connection w/campaign and CRP financing and that CIA was being pressed to set up a cover, said ABC....RN was aware of plan to use CIA as cover for his campaign workers, said NBC....Whether it's smoking pistol or just a potential problem is being left to Senate, said CBS. RN's throwing himself on Hill's mercy, said ABC....All nets quoted same section from t'script where HRH said FBI was getting into problem areas and RN told him to get CIA to tell the FBI to "stay the hell out." CBS focused on concern over CRP money links; ABC/NBC noted RN concern w/Hunt and all that he knew.

-- UPI leads: "VP, the man who'd succeed RN if he were removed, took himself out of impch debate and indicated there'd be trial in Senate." As noted by ABC/CBS, VP said "public's no longer served by my expressed belief that, on basis of all known to me and public, RN's not guilty of impchble offense.... Inasmuch as add'l evidence is forthcoming... I intend to respectfully decline to discuss impchmnt..." Jones of CBS saw the new t'scripts as giving VP all he needed to "jump ship" and to "abandon his defense."

Wednesday, August 7

Did two pieces for Wayne concerning friends who are trying to get government employment. The Post was just literally covered with Watergate and even had six pages of surplus on Watergate. Even they can't keep up with the chain of events. Went to the University Club for lunch with Mike and had a swim and relaxed.

In afternoon, I spoke with Mr. Baroody about my future and he was very encouraging to the fact that he would do all he can to assist me in getting a good job. He said that, when I do get out of Colgate, that he would look about the White House, in particular his "shop," to see if there would exist a place for me. Now, that triggered off thoughts galore in my little head. I came to the conclusion that I would like to stay at the White House now, rather than lose the momentum. I will approach him with the possibility of that and taking courses at Colgate or Georgetown.

My Personal Diary of My White House Days

NEWS SUMMARY

August 8, 1974
(Wed nets,wires)

The major stories:

-- The question in DC shifted from whether or not RN would resign to how and when, led Chancellor.....The capital was seized by resignation fever, began Mudd....Rumors of RN's imminent resignation swept DC and the world led ABC. ...Hill was seething w/rumors, speculation and gossip that RN was to resign, said NBC....AH/VP were responsible for much of the confusion, said CBS w/all nets noting the unplanned meeting, called by AH.

-- Goldwater on all nets in lead stories said he, Scott and Rhodes were "extremely impressed" at session to which RN invited them w/RN's putting best interests of US uppermost in his mind. RN's made no decision yet and they didn't suggest resignation -- neither that nor immunity came up. They told him Hill situation's "gloomy" and "very distressing." On CBS, Scott said RN was in entire control of himself, serene and amiable. On ABC, Rhodes said RN was in good spirits and good health as "4 old friends" discussed something that's "painful for all" of them.

-- RN's reconsidering whether to resign, step aside temporarily or sit tight, said Rather and several WH aide expect decision before end of wk, probably Thurs. RMW/BT and Steve Bull all deny resignation's imminent, said Rather, but CBS noted one of factors contributing to the fever was the less than iron-clad denials by WH. ABC also noted WH stopped short of outright denial. And NBC reported Rabbi Korff said RN will resign unless there's sudden flood of support. There was none, said Chancellor. On NBC film, Korff described RN as one of strongest men he's ever seen; only a man of his strength and caliber could've achieved peace as he has...."Very unsettled and tense" was how NBC described WH, but there's no feeling USG is about to halt altho WH seem to have halted....A WH legal staffer told ABC defense preps are at literal standstill w/RN not expected to force trial. Defense has all but been abandoned, this source said....Brokaw said RN's now "actively considering" resignation.

Thursday, August 8th, 1974

On the 8th of Aug—Interns met w/ V.P. Ford at 8:30. JU got to work early & went upstairs to Veep's office—7:30-7:45 & saw HAK (Kissinger) leaving Ford's office.

Ominous sign—turns out that in all likelihood, Ford & HAK conferring re: resignation later that day. (Note: In front of the Vice President's suite of offices always stood at least stood one Secret Service Agent. This morning, when I reached the top of the stairs looking left at the Vice President's office doors, and when Kissinger walked out, both he and the Secret Service Agents quickly gave me a glare, which signified to me "who the heck are you and what are you doing up here.")

Met with Ford—got our pictures taken with him.

But, because of resignation, pics went to Nixon Archives.

Very historic—we 20-22 yr. olds meeting with man who knew he was to become President within 24 hours.

He was very gracious, calm, but a quick meeting. He held the appointment so as not to bring awareness to schedule change.

My Personal Diary of My White House Days

Feeling that Nixon was about to resign, I wanted to thank Julie Eisenhower for having us up to the residence for the reception back on July 26th. Here is the note I sent her. Knowing she may not receive this before the Nixon family left the White House, I had it couriered to the East Wing anyway.

THE WHITE HOUSE
WASHINGTON

August 8, 1974

Dear Julie,

    This is a belated note of thanks for the delightful reception which you held for the Interns on July 26th. Indeed, it was a great privilege for all of us to have met you and to have been with you that evening.

    We all have thought of you often and wish you the very best in the future.

    Again, thankyou so very much.

Sincerely,

John Unland

John Unland
Summer Intern for Mr. Baroody

At 11:00 A.M. we met with Father McLaughlin, the famed defender of the President's language and Special Assistant to the President. The entire seminar was relaxed, informal, lengthy, and centered totally around the impending resignation. We talked of the ramifications of a Senate Trial which would begin around Labor Day and there would be a three-month ordeal of just calling witnesses, cross examining, etc. to get the trial organized.

The case is so complicated and so intertwined that St. Clair and his staff could proceed to draw attention to every conceivable detail and force debate and vote on a myriad of technicalities to draw it out to the finest legal points of the President's guilt. There would be thousands of objections. Father M. suggested that the President's case itself could be drawn out to ten weeks at a minimum—then further with cross-examination...the case could be finished by July, 1975.

What would be at stake would be the nation—no less—and possibly the state of the world, to degrees. Government would come to a certain standstill—the Presidency certainly would be shut down, with Haig running the show as well as he could; the House would be "inoperative," for it cannot function without the Senate, which would be totally consumed with the case and be totally inoperative. Then, the Supreme Court would be dysfunctional to a degree without the Chief Justice, who would preside over the Senate Trial.

On top of this, the morale of the nation would be something to worry about for there would be no movement or the spinning of wheels without movement. The governmental bureaucracy would carry the load on its own momentum, which occurs to a large degree.

Economically, it would be difficult to see how a 7-month trial and governmental stagnation would aid the current economic difficulties we now face.

Political affects—people would become apolitical, defecting from the two-party system, perhaps.

The media would sensationalize the whole affair—a zoo-like atmosphere. It was offered that the media would suffer as a result in a backlash, but that is questionable.

Internationally, the whole affair would be damaging to democracy as the trial is transmitted throughout the world. Leaders of foreign nations would say, "So this is democracy?" and laugh.

Nixon would save his own skin and dignity if he did resign, but getting immunity from his enemies will be difficult if resignation transpires. He would sacrifice his due process in thinking of the national interest. Saved the nation from an incredible ordeal and immunity would be fair play in such a circumstance. Immunity in the exchange for national interest is fair.

Then talked of drawbacks of resignation. Nixon would be surrendering his mandate, the most popular mandate in history. Enfeebling the office?

Going forward with the trial—showing all how almost impossible it is to remove a man from this office.

People will think Nixon is guilty of serious charges and suspect him of other things.

My impression of McLaughlin is that he favors resignation without flatly stating. He has tried to say flatly that he favored resignation and it is tough to swallow, but I can tell that that is his feeling, as well as the feeling of others. The mood was quiet but firm, favoring resignation among the Interns.

Then he moved into discussion about the uniqueness of the case itself. The evidence was insupportable—strange case.

Asked about the speech-writing staff writing a resignation speech, he replied that "a number of things are under foot."

First Hand

To follow is a memo detailing the check-out procedures for the summer interns: By this time, I had made arrangements with Mr. Baroody to stay on the White House staff for an indefinite period of time and had made arrangements with my college, Colgate University, to take courses at Georgetown University and transfer those credits in order to get a degree from Colgate. Thus, I did not resign and leave with the rest of the interns.

THE WHITE HOUSE

WASHINGTON

August 8, 1974

MEMORANDUM FOR THE WHITE HOUSE SUMMER INTERNS

FROM: SANDY LAUGHLIN

SUBJECT: <u>Resignation and Check-out Procedures.</u>

Attached are the proper check-out procedures that must be followed before you leave this summer.

Please note that numbers 3, 6, 7a., 7 are not applicable to you therefore you need not check with these offices.

<u>It is essential that you notify me no later than Tuesday August 13, 1974 when you plan to resign.</u> You will not receive you final paycheck until you have done so.

All the instructions are self explanatory, but if there are any problems, give me or Pam a call.

<u>Finally, Pam wants to receive all yours final reports by the end of next week.</u>

IN ORDER TO RECOVER YOUR WASHINGTON D.C. TAX, YOU MAY PICK UP A FORM AT ANY PUBLIC BUILDING OR POST OFFICE. THIS MEANS THAT YOU CAN RECOVER YOUR FULL TAX IF YOUR YOUR APPOINTMENT WAS FOR NINETY DAYS OR LESS.

My Personal Diary of My White House Days

August 8, 1974, continued

3:30 PM, went to the East Wing—last day in President Nixon's White House. Walked by reporters who stared at me as I was with my head down and in a subdued mood. Into East Wing upstairs to Spank's office where I found Wayne chatting with Patty Matson (Spank's immediate boss in the First Lady's press office) and Spank. Answered some press calls, our spirits were boosted by a few funnies by it all, but very quiet in there and sad. Very quiet in Helen Smith's office (the First Lady's press secretary). Stayed for about half an hour, then walked through Richard Nixon's White House—his last official day and his last official night. It was so still—so hushed. Not even did the Secret Service nod nor respond to my presence, nor I to them.

Walked by the library, where I had written a leadership speech supporting the President, all was dark and closed up. Then past the Diplomatic Reception Room where I had, on several occasions, seen him come and go and where I had been and had once felt the awe and the excitement of walking in the White House where the President had walked.

Then, through the double doors at the end of the hall, out another set of doors to the left, and onto the covered walk which is next to the Rose Garden, off to the right, 20 yards away, sits the Oval Office, The doors—both sets—were open and the lights from the office were bright yellow against the dusky grey afternoon. Television crews were there setting up the cameras for the President's speech—his last. I stood alone by the bushes knowing that the Secret Service was watching me, but transfixed in sadness—I couldn't move—my mind filled with thoughts so confusing as not to make sense. I was staring at the Oval Office—the office where Presidential power will be transferred from Richard Nixon to Gerald Ford tomorrow via a resignation.

I waited for about three minutes, then went on through the doors, past the press office, down the stairs, and down the corridor on whose walls hang the beautiful pictures of the Mid-East trip and the Russian summits—pictures worth a thousand words as are those which portray the President in his greatest moments—in foreign diplomacy. Passing the guard, I walked through the doors outside—having passed through the White House on the day of President Nixon's resignation.

It is a vacuum day—a day of unbelief, shock, and waiting—waiting for 9:00 p.m.—for the President's resignation speech. I came up to my office in an attempt to organize some work, but could do nothing.

On leaving the White House proper, I walked toward the crowds assembled on Pennsylvania Avenue which had gathered there and been in position since Monday. I walked towards them wanting to mingle and gauge their mood. I was on one side of the fence and they, looking at me, were on the other. I passed through the gate and could feel the eyes on me, though obviously they knew I was no one important. Yet, they asked me questions: "Will he resign?" "Is it all over?" Knowing that it was not official, I said nothing. But I could sense a change in atmosphere—that those gazing in were not aware of the affection and the closeness of the White House staff to each other and to the President, they did not feel the impact of the situation as gravely. People were listening to radios, chatting, carrying signs pro and con for resignation, and milling around also waiting.

I returned to the gate, stared at the White House, and walked in. As I walked by Secretary Kissinger's entrance, I noticed some activity at the doorway. The black limo and security car pulled up to the door and out came Kissinger carrying a bundle of papers. This is the man to whom the President must resign. He sped away and I walked back into the E.O.B.

I went into Mr. Baroody's office to see Maureen and Loraine and I asked them to dinner. Maureen went, as they had to take shifts. Spirits were uplifted by companionship and drinks. We ordered two dinners for Mr. & Mrs. Baroody and left at 8:00 to go back to Mr. Baroody's office suite. On the way out, I ran into Mr. St. Clair alone in the dimly lit hall. I had seen him several times, but this time I stopped, introduced myself, and said, "Sir, I truly appreciate all your efforts and wish you the best of luck." To which he said, "Son, I appreciate that," with a smile.

My Personal Diary of My White House Days

First page of White House press release announcing that the President will resign tomorrow morning, August 9th, 1974, and the reasons why.

```
FOR IMMEDIATE RELEASE                           AUGUST 8, 1974
           OFFICE OF THE WHITE HOUSE PRESS SECRETARY
_____

                         THE WHITE HOUSE

                    ADDRESS BY THE PRESIDENT
                    TO THE AMERICAN PEOPLE

                         THE OVAL OFFICE

        9:01 P.M. EDT
```

Good evening.

This is the 37th time I have spoken to you from this office, where so many decisions have been made that shaped the history of this Nation. Each time I have done so to discuss with you some matter that I believe affected the national interest.

In all the decisions I have made in my public life, I have always tried to do what was best for the Nation. Throughout the long and difficult period of Watergate, I have felt it was my duty to persevere, to make every possible effort to complete the term of office to which you elected me.

In the past few days, however, it has become evident to me that I no longer have a strong enough political base in the Congress to justify continuing that effort. As long as there was a base, I felt strongly that it was necessary to see the constitutional process through to its conclusion, that to do otherwise would be unfaithful to the spirit of that deliberately difficult process, and a dangerously destabilizing precedent for the future.

But with the disappearance of that base, I now believe that the constitutional purpose has been served, and there is no longer a need for the process to be prolonged.

I would have preferred to carry through to the finish whatever the personal agony it would have involved, and my family unanimously urged me to do so. But the interest of the Nation must always come before any personal considerations.

From the discussions I have had with Congressional and other leaders, I have concluded that because of the Watergate matter I might not have the support of the Congress that I would consider necessary to back the very difficult decisions and carry out the duties of this office in the way the interests of the Nation would require.

First Hand

And then the speech at 9:00. To hear all the commentators chatter was a bit irritating—sounded as though they were giving info about a space flight.

The speech was what we all expected, but it was different in so many ways: it was so human, so warm, such a normal flow of words—and, his appearance was so dignified. He was strong and forgiving so that his country could again be strong and forgive him in return.

He had tried, by every conceivable means, to stay in his chair as President, but he knew he could no longer remain. And credit must be given to him for resigning, for, as he said, he did so for the national interest. He did not say goodbye or farewell to his people, but left with a look of uncertainty and gloom on his face.

There was no need to hear the commentator; no need to discuss the speech; no need to ask others how they felt or what they thought of the resignation. Just a need for unwanted, uncomfortable silence in which to reflect upon his success as President and this bizarre, unique event.

There were tears, but most had accepted the fact and were quietly realistic about the situation.

We sat and chatted lightly for a few minutes, then I went into Wayne's office to call home. I briefly spoke to mom and then spoke to dad. When the tears came and the sadness mounted, I couldn't hold back.

I then walked outside along the fence up to Pennsylvania Avenue where the crowds—thousands—were assembled. The sight and sound of what I heard silenced my heart—as did the crowd at the Supreme Court after its fateful decision weeks ago. Pennsylvania Avenue had been closed off in front of the White House as the crowd had spilled over onto the street. There was much cheering, honking of horns, screaming, and dancing. Camera lights in Lafayette Park cast quite a scene upon the crowd at the front of the White House.

Nothing is sacred—not even a man's peace on his last evening of service to his nation.

Well, I left with Spank and Barb, both of whom had taken the events in stride. We fought our way through the traffic to Clyde's (a bar we frequented) where we had a drink. I couldn't rebound and left to sleep at 1:00.

For the first time in years I said a prayer to someone to watch over President Nixon and for our own people to treat him with compassion and warmth and to forgive him.

My Personal Diary of My White House Days

Friday, August 9th

Got to the White House very early, 7:00 am, with the Post under my arm which had the large headline, "Nixon Resigns" to arrive in Mr. Baroody's office.

President Nixon was due to give his farewell remarks to the Cabinet and White House staff at 9:00, so we all lingered and waited to go to the East Room. We left at 8:50 and waited outside the Diplomatic Reception Room until the Cabinet members and Senior Staff had been escorted upstairs.

The music began and we all trotted up to the East Room where a podium was set up flanked by the American Flag and the Presidential Flag. The Cabinet was seated to the left of the podium as one faced it and they all were in attendance—Kissinger and wife, (William) Simon[116], Brennan, Morton, Schlesinger and wives. Suddenly, they burst out singing "Hail to the Chief" and applause began to ripple from the front North Hallway into the East Room. The President, Mrs. Nixon, their children and husbands walked in and stood on the podium.

The President was given a lengthy, loud ovation for about six minutes until he said "Thank you" and the applause ceased. He looked somber—a bit uneasy. He had no prepared remarks and began to speak on a philosophical—emotional level.

He spoke of his gratitude to his Cabinet and staff saying that the greatness of a President and the Presidency depends upon the greatness of its staff. He was gracious to all.

He then moved into remarks a bit distant from the current events, as tears filled his eyes. He did not stare at faces for the pain would have been unbearable. He stared in a daze to his lower left at the floor and spoke of his parents—his "old man" who held a menial job, but an important one and his mother

---

[116] Wikipedia contributors, "William E. Simon,' *Wikipedia, The Free Encyclopedia*, https://en.wikipedia.org/w/index.php?title=William_E._Simon&oldid=978294104 (accessed September 30, 2020), "William Edward Simon (November 27, 1927 – June 3, 2000) was an American businessman, a Secretary of Treasury of the U.S. for three years, and a philanthropist. He became the 63rd Secretary of the Treasury on May 9, 1974, during the Nixon administration. After Nixon resigned, Simon was reappointed by President Ford and served until 1977 when President Carter took office. He also served as the first Administrator of the Federal Energy Office. From December 4, 1973, Simon simultaneously launched and administered the Federal Energy Administration at the height of the oil embargo. As such he became known as the high-profile 'Energy Czar', and represented a revitalization of the 'czar' term in U.S. politics."

"who was a saint." The President's voice waivered many times and, while he spoke of his mother, I felt he would break down.

He came out of it by saying that greatness is built from getting through rough spots; one who has been in the lowest valley can truly appreciate the highest mountain. He also spoke of hatred—there will be those who will hate you, but they will not win...unless you hate them back and then, gesturing to himself, he said that in hating them back, you destroy yourself also. And, he said thank you to all of us and left amidst a grand ovation.

I then walked onto the porch of the South Portico and found a place next to the White House Chef to watch the President and his family board that beautiful helicopter. The President stopped as he boarded, turned around and did his classic wave.

The blade began to churn and the fumes of exhaust filled the stale air. Slowly the helicopter began to rise away from the red carpet and the Vice President and his wife.

Slowly but steadily did the helicopter fly past the Washington Memorial and by the Jefferson Memorial.

Slowly but surely did Richard Nixon leave the White House for the last time as I stood there on this humid, gray day on what once was his porch. And I, with others, brushed away the tears that had been welling up.

My Personal Diary of My White House Days

As I often did, I had my camera with me, and though I felt it almost inappropriate to take the following photo—it was a historic moment—so I did it anyway. (As you can see, standing next to the White House Chef, we had a side view of President Nixon leaving on the helicopter)

First Hand

Press Release of President Nixon's resignation speech on August 9th, 1974

FOR IMMEDIATE RELEASE   AUGUST 9, 1974

        OFFICE OF THE WHITE HOUSE PRESS SECRETARY

THE WHITE HOUSE

REMARKS OF THE PRESIDENT
TO THE
MEMBERS OF THE CABINET
AND
WHITE HOUSE STAFF

THE EAST ROOM

9:36 A.M. EDT

    Members of the Cabinet, Members of the White House staff, all of our friends here:

    I think the record should show that this is one of those spontaneous things that we always arrange whenever the President comes in to speak, and it will be so reported in the press, and we don't mind because they have to call it as they see it.

    But on our part, believe me, it is spontaneous.

    You are here to say goodbye to us, and we don't have a good word for it in English. The best is au revoir. We will see you again.

    I just met with the members of the White House staff, you know, those who serve here in the White House day in and day out, and I asked them to do what I ask all of you to do to the extent that you can and, of course, are requested to do so: To serve our next President as you have served me and previous Presidents -- because many of you have been here for many years -- with devotion and dedication, because this office, great as it is, can only be as great as the men and women who work for and with the President.

    This house, for example, I was thinking of it as we walked down this hall, and I was comparing it to some of the great houses of the world that I have been in. This isn't the biggest house. Many, and most, in even smaller countries are much bigger. This isn't the finest house. Many in Europe, particularly, and in China, Asia, have paintings of great, great value, things that we just don't have here, and probably will never have until we are 1000 years old, or older.

    But this is the best house. It is the best house because it has something far more important than numbers of people who serve, far more important than numbers of rooms or how big it is, far more important than numbers of magnificent pieces of art.

                          MORE   (OVER)

My Personal Diary of My White House Days

White House Press Release of remarks by President Ford who was sworn in just hours after the departure of President Nixon.

```
FOR IMMEDIATE RELEASE                          AUGUST 9, 1974
            OFFICE OF THE WHITE HOUSE PRESS SECRETARY
```

THE WHITE HOUSE

REMARKS BY GERALD R. FORD
UPON BEING SWORN IN AS
38TH PRESIDENT OF THE UNITED STATES

THE EAST ROOM

12:05 P.M. EDT

Mr. Chief Justice, my dear friends, my fellow Americans:

The oath that I have taken is the same oath that was taken by George Washington and by every President under the Constitution. But I assume the Presidency under extraordinary circumstances, never before experienced by Americans. This is an hour of history that troubles our minds and hurts our hearts.

Therefore, I feel it is my first duty to make an unprecedented compact with my countrymen. Not an inaugural address, not a fireside chat, not a campaign speech. Just a little straight talk among friends. And I intend it to be the first of many.

I am acutely aware that you have not elected me as your President by your ballots, and so I ask you to confirm me as your President with your prayers. And I hope that such prayers will also be the first of many.

If you have not chosen me by secret ballot, neither have I gained office by any secret promises. I have not campaigned either for the Presidency or the Vice Presidency. I have not subscribed to any partisan platform. I am indebted to no man, and only to one woman -- my dear wife -- as I begin this very difficult job.

I have not sought this enormous responsibility, but I will not shirk it. Those who nominated me and confirmed me as Vice President were my friends and are my friends. They were of both parties, elected by all the people and acting under the Constitution in their name. It is only fitting then that I should pledge to them and to you that I will be the President of all the people.

Thomas Jefferson said the people are the only sure reliance for the preservation of our liberty. And down the years, Abraham Lincoln renewed this American article of faith asking, "Is there any better way or equal hope in the world?"

I intend, on Monday next, to request of the Speaker of the House of Representatives and the President pro tempore of the Senate the privilege of appearing before the Congress to share with my former colleagues and with you, the American people, my views on the priority business of the Nation and to solicit your views and their views. And may I say to the Speaker and the others, if I could meet with you right after these remarks, I would appreciate it.

MORE

First Hand

SIDE STORY: At 9 am on August 9th, Richard Nixon bade farewell to the White House staff and walked through the South Lawn to the helicopter that took him and Mrs. Nixon from the White House for the last time. At noon that same day, Vice President Ford was to be sworn in as President. Soon after he was sworn in, I walked through the West Wing and through the corridors of the White House and noticed that all the pictures of President Nixon had been removed from the walls and new photos of President Ford and his family had been hung in their place.

There were now pictures of President and Mrs. Ford with their kids, President Ford skiing, pictures of Liberty (their dog); and within a matter of hours, it was as though a dark cloud had been lifted from the building—replaced by a sense of freshness and new beginnings.

My Personal Diary of My White House Days

First Hand

Final seminar notice for the interns

THE WHITE HOUSE

WASHINGTON

August 12, 1974

MEMORANDUM FOR THE 1974 WHITE HOUSE SUMMER INTERNS

FROM: PAM POWELL
              SANDY LAUGHLIN

SUBJECT: Seminars and other Events.

Mr. John C, Sawhill, the Administrator of the Federal Energy Administration, has agreed to speak to the Interns on Wednesday August 14, 1974 at 3:30 p.m. in Room 459, OEOB. A biography is attached.

Patrick J. Buchanan, a Special Consultant to the President, has agreed to speak to the Interns on Thursday August 15, 1974 at 11:00 a.m. in Room 459, OEOB. A biography is attached.

Mr. Bryce Harlow, formally Counsellor to the President, has agreed to speak to the Interns on Thurday August 15, 1974 at 3:00 p.m. in the Roosevelt Room. We will meet promptly outside the West Wing Basement at 2:50 p.m. A biography and last year's speech to the Interns is attached.

The Final banquet for the Interns will be held at Blackie's House of Beef. The cost will be approximately be $ 7.95 per person. Cocktails will be served starting at 7:00 p.m. If you really want to find out all the summer's gossip and what your leaders think about you, you would be well advised to attend. More details will be forthcoming.

Mr. Howard Callaway, the Secretary of the Army, has agreed to speak to the Interns on Friday August 16, 1974 at 11:00 a.m. in Room 459, OEOB.

My Personal Diary of My White House Days

Final communique with the White House interns indicating that our photos with then-Vice President Ford taken the morning of August 8th are the property of the Nixon Archives since President Nixon was President at that time; though only for 24 more hours.

THE WHITE HOUSE

WASHINGTON

October 8, 1974

MEMORANDUM FOR THE 1974 WHITE HOUSE SUMMER INTERNS

FROM: PAM POWELL
                 SANDY LAUGHLIN

Attached is an updated list of all the current addresses that we had on file before you left. We hope you will find it useful in keeping track of your fellow interns.

Also enclosed are the remarks that were made by President Ford at his swearing-in cermony on August 9, 1974. It is a great souvenir for a most historic occasion.

We would like to hear from you from time to time so please drop us a line sometime in the near future, and be sure to include your most current address and any interesting news that you might want us to pass along to the others.

First the good news. The official intern certificates have finally arrived and are waiting for signature at this time. You should be receiving them in a couple of weeks.

Now the bad news. The photographs that were taken with then Vice President Ford on August 8, 1974 were taken by the Nixon Archives people and can not be located at the present time. We realize how disappointed you must be, however we selected some excellent candid photographs of the President and are having them signed for you. We realize that it is a poor substitute, but little else can be done right now.

If there are any future news items that might be of interest or if there is any special requests that we can help you with, please do not hesitate to call on us.

First Hand

As I have indicated, I did not want to leave the White House and wanted very badly to stay on the staff of Mr. Baroody. To follow is a list of suggested work/duties that I said I could do for him and the office. I presented this to Mr. Baroody and he decided to keep me on the staff indefinitely.

    A. Coordinate meetings, serving as a central focal point in funneling meeting requests, keeping the staff posted on meeting schedules, setting up the meetings, etc.

    B. Maintain a file on all meetings - Tuesday at the White House, Wednesday Meetings, and Field Conferences - as Mr. Baroody has desired. This would entail obtaining the appropriate materials from staff members in charge of each meeting.

    C. Handle the new telephone requests which now are a part of our office duties.

    D. Serve as a home-base contact with those advancing the Field Conferences of still be a member of the advance teams to the Conferences.

    E. Maintain a current scrapbook of Mr. Baroody's activities - i.e.: newspaper interviews, etc., as he has requested.

    F. Assist in your backlog correspondence and other dutues with which you might need assistance.

My Personal Diary of My White House Days

This is the press release announcing me into my new position..

JOHN L. UNLAND
Biographical Data

John L. Unland, age 23, currently is a Research Assistant for the newly established Office of Public Liaison at the White House. The Office of Public Liaison is responsible for providing liaison with major non-governmental organizations in the private sector including farm, labor, veterans, business, civic, academic, ethnic, consumers, youth, senior citizens, and professional groups. Mr. Unland was formerly a White House Summer Intern in 1974. He joined the White House staff permanently in September, 1974.

Prior to coming to the White House, Mr. Unland served as an intern in the Department of the Treasury, Office of the Secretary, during the summer of 1973, working closely with the Office of Revenue Sharing. During the summer and fall of 1972, Mr. Unland served on the campaign staff of former Governor of Illinois Richard B. Ogilvie.

Mr. Unland also is currently enrolled at Colgate University, Hamilton, New York, where he is in his final year of study for his B.A. in American Studies, concentrating in Colonial American History. In the spring semester of 1974, he attended classes at the London School of Economics where he did research on America's Puritanical Heritage.

Mr. Unland was born in Peoria, Illinois.

First Hand

An example of my job is this memo below: I had to research several topics and issues for Mr. Baroody and our staff during my tenure and then present my findings to Mr. Baroody and others in the White House.

MEMORANDUM

THE WHITE HOUSE
WASHINGTON

May 21, 1975

FOR: MR. BAROODY
FROM: JOHN UNLAND

Regarding the effect of the Railroad Revitalization Act on the Chicago and neighboring areas, I spoke with Gary Broemser of DOT. He said that there are no areas of the legislation that are singled out at the Chicago area. Yet, there are some specifics that you may want to be aware of:

> A. The Bill does not drastically change the status of rail abandonments, but leaves it basically at its present status quo. Rail abandonments occur most often when a RR will abandon a branch line in a rural area such as rural Illinois. Yet, the Bill does improve the situation by requiring RR's to give a year's notice to the affected communities rather that pulling the branch line out from under them quickly.
>
> B. The Bill outlaws State tax discrimination against RR's. States often tax RR's higher than other businesses. This is not a big problem in Illinois, but is in neighboring states.
>
> C. The Bill encourages the consolidation of RR's lines to provide for better management and better service. An example of this: there are at present 5 or 6 lines from Chicago to Omaha. The Bill encourages better management to perhaps cut the number to two or three and allow the non-owning lines access to the beds.
>
> D. The overall emphasis of the Bill is to encourage competition within the private sector and to allow the market to play a greater part in changing prices to a level more commensurate to the costs of hauling goods. In some cases the prices will rise and in many cases, prices will fall.

My Personal Diary of My White House Days

"OUR OFFICE'S CHARTER WITHIN THE WHITE HOUSE"

During my years on the Ford staff I continued to work with Mr. Baroody and the staff of that office, including Wayne and the fantastic administrative assistant who ran the show and with whom I got along very well. One of the things that we did and devised was to get this new president out around the country so that all of America could become more familiar with him. Our strategy was not necessarily to get him into large markets like New York City, Chicago, Los Angeles, and other big markets, but to get him into medium markets; cities like Cincinnati, Ohio, Portland, Oregon, and others.

Since the country did not know him well, we put together what were called White House Domestic Economic Affairs meetings; which were day-long conferences to which stakeholders of communities were invited. For example, we held a day-long conference in Cincinnati. Those in the educational community around the state were invited to attend. Those from the labor community were invited to attend, as well as other important stakeholder organizations such as the American Medical Association.

The meetings were set up so that they would begin at 9:00 o'clock in the morning and run until 4:00 or 5:00 in the afternoon. We would bring in cabinet members to speak about their respective areas of responsibility. For example, we would bring in the Secretary of Labor to talk to an audience of perhaps a thousand people, maybe more, who were invited to attend from that region. Then the Secretary of Education would speak for a while. And these cabinet members and key administration officials would not only talk to the large audience, but would come in the day before and meet privately with stakeholders in their respective areas. During their time in these cities, we also set up interviews for them with local television, radio stations, and newspapers.

The point here is that the Ford administration was interested in what their community was doing, were paying attention, and more than anything, we were listening to that local market and their respective concerns about certain issues and departments of the government.

At the end of these conferences, we would schedule the President to come in and spend an hour to close out the day-long session. For example, he would come in at 4:00 o'clock, have a few interviews and then speak at 5:00 o'clock to close out the session. That's how these meetings worked.

My role in the office was an advance person's role. I went out ahead of the actual conference, helped make sure that the hotel arrangements were set, that the interviews were organized, and attended to logical issues. I was then 23 years old.

"THE PORTLAND, OREGON CONFERENCE"

I recall very, very vividly going out to Portland, Oregon, to the first conference, which was held in on October 7th, 1974. I went out with some of the Secret Service agents to do some advance work. We started the meeting around 9:00 a.m. and then the President flew in to close the meeting out—around 4:00 o'clock or so—I can't remember. But I do clearly remember him climbing up to the podium. And this was only two months after he had become President of the United States. I remember the audience leaping to their feet and gave him what seemed, at least to me, to be a 15-minute standing ovation.

I was standing down on the floor looking up at him not far away as he wiped tears from his eyes. He was overwhelmed at the reception. And, I am going to guess, overwhelmed at his new position.

On a given night in February of 1975, prior to our office going to Hollywood, Florida for a conference we had organized—one of our daylong conferences—I was in my office.

I remember it being cold and miserable and raining that night when my telephone rang and I answered the phone "Office of Public Liaison, John Unland." I heard on the other end of the phone, "This is Warren Rustand in the Oval Office" Terry was the scheduler and a very important figure in the West Wing. In a very stern voice he said, "the President is leaving tomorrow to go to your conference in Florida and he does not have a briefing memo around the trip or who will be there. I need a memo over here in an hour."

Now, I was alone in the office. All the staff had left and it was around 5:00 p.m. Mr. Baroody had left for the evening and I called the White House operators and asked if they would patch me into his car. He had a driver, as did many of the senior staff, and they were always accessible day and night; where ever they were. It was definitely 24/7, 365 for senior staff to be accessible by the White House. In this instance, I was patched into Mr. Baroody's phone in his car and I said, "Mr. Baroody, Warren Rustand from the Oval Office just called and said that the President doesn't have a briefing memo for closing out our conference in Florida. What should I do?" and his response was "Well, write it."

So, there I sat, by myself, knowing I had to write a memo and get it to the Oval Office in an hour. Now, at that time there were no computers—we only had IBM Selectric typewriters with what was called 'auto-erase.' Which meant that if one made a mistake typing a letter, you would push this button and a white ribbon would appear and then you could type over the mistake with the same wrong letter(s) and it would "white it out"—not be visible.

SPECIAL INSTRUCTIONS -- PREPARATION
OF PRESIDENTIAL PAPERS

1. Presidential Signature Letters - Memoranda going outside of White House to other Departments/agencies - Final preparation of Letters (transmittal) to the Congress - Proclamations Executive Orders, etc., etc. - See Style Manual available from the Correspondence Office. (We do NOT prepare in this office.*)

2. Material specifically prepared in the Writing/Research area.

    SAMPLES - Instruction/and Actual attached

3. Hints and advices of assistance

    a. Liquid white-out is NOT allowed.

    b. KO-REC-TYPE (IF erasure does not show) IS allowed.

    c. Word division

        (1) Be sure correct - See your GPO style manual and word-division dictionary.

        (2) Division of word carried from one page to next is a "no-no."

    d. It is also a "no-no" to carry the last half-line of a paragraph to the next page.

4. TRY to -- in drafts -- where possible to put full paragraphs on a page even if some pages are shorter. This permits the President (in his speeches), or the editor to delete the full text of paragraph or play with revision as a whole.

5. Margins and space guidance. (Samples are quite specific)

    a. Always begin work 6 lines from top of page (See samples)

    b. Margins should be generous -- especially on Presidential speeches - to allow his marginal write-ins. Try for 6-lines top/and bottom on all material prepared. (Aim for the "a framed picture" look

---

* Should you find yourself faced with the need to know how and to prepare, consult Secretarial Manual or if not available call the Correspondence Office for assistance.

My Personal Diary of My White House Days

When writing a memo to the President, there were strict rules and in sending a memo to the Oval Office, white-out was not permitted. A memo had to be cleanly typed with absolutely no mistakes or any evidence of a white-out.

So, there I sat, 23 years old, knowing I had to not only draft a memo to the President in terms of its content, but then I had to type it perfectly and get it to the Oval Office within an hour.

I wrote a draft of the note on a yellow legal pad, typed it up perfectly in one try, pulled it out of the typewriter, read it to Mr. Baroody in his car (and he approved it), made a copy, and walked it into the West Wing and up the steps to the Oval Office.

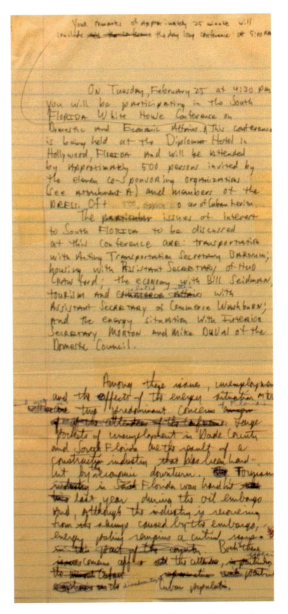

Terry took the memo and went into the Oval Office where the President was sitting with his feet on the desk, smoking his pipe. I saw Terry hand the memo to the President and he took it and began reading it— I about fainted right there in the hallway and then scampered back to our offices.

First Hand

All of this happened within 90 a heart stopping, 90-minute timeframe and was one of the highlights of my working at the White House.

THE WHITE HOUSE

WASHINGTON

February 24, 1975

BRIEFING PAPER FOR THE PRESIDENT

PERPARED BY: JOHN L. UNLAND
               OFFICE OF PUBLIC LIAISON

SUBJECT: <u>White House Field Conference
               Tuesday, February 25, 1975
               Hollywood, Florida</u>

On Tuesday, February 25, at 4:30 p.m. you will be participating in the South Florida White House Conference on Domestic and Economic Affairs. Your remarks will conclude the day-long conference at approximately 5:00 p.m. This conference is being held at the Diplomat Hotel in Hollywood, Florida, and will be attended by approximately 600 persons invited by the eleven co-sponsoring organizations (see attachment) and members of the press. Of the 500, approximately 150 are of Cuban heritage.

The issues of interest to South Florida to be discussed at this conference are: transportation with Acting Transportation Secretary Barnum; housing with Assistant Secretary of HUD Crawford; the economy with Bill Seidman; tourism and related matters with Assistant Secretary of Commerce Washburn; and the energy situation with Interior Secretary Morton and Mike Duval of the Domestic Council.

Among these issues, unemployment and the effects of the energy situation on tourism stand out as two predominant concerns of Floridians. Large pockets of unemployment in Dade County and South Florida are the result of a construction industry that has been hard hit by the economic downturn. Tourism in Florida was hard hit last year during the oil embargo and, although the industry is recovering from the slump caused by the embargo, energy policy remains a critical issue. Most Floridians strongly oppose any fuel rationing policy and support your anti-rationing position. Both of these concerns affect the attendees, especially the disadvantaged Cuban population.

The entire conference will be open to the press and, for the first time at a White House conference in the field, live television and radio coverage is expected.

My Personal Diary of My White House Days

A request to increase my daily travel per diem from $25.00 per day (including hotel, meals, and other travel expenses.

November 15, 1974

MEMORANDUM FOR: JERRY JONES

FROM: BILL BAROODY, JR./S/

I have a young researcher on my staff, John Unland, who has been helping out with the advance preparation for the White House field conferences. He is on travel status for approximately 3 days for each of these conferences.

I understand that John's travel quoto is $25.00 a day. It is necessary for John to stay at the hotels where the conferences are being held. Hence, his hotel bill alone is running in excess of $25.00 a day.

I would appreciate it if special arrangements can be made so that John does not end up paying money out of his own pocket to cover these trips. Give me a call if you envision any problem.

Thank you.

COPY FOR: JOHN UNLAND

First Hand

A request for $50 to send boxes from Washington, D.C. to Ft. Lauderdale for a Conference.

THE WHITE HOUSE

WASHINGTON

February 19, 1975

MEMORANDUM FOR: JERRY JONES

FROM: BILL BAROODY

SUBJECT: Transportation of Materials to Ft. Lauderdale Conference

My office has four boxes of materials to send to Ft. Lauderdale on Thursday, February 20, via commercial airliner at the approximate cost of $50.00.

If approved, a member of my staff, John Unland, will need the money in cash from Wilbur Jenkins to pay National Airlines tomorrow evening.

Your consideration of this would be sincerely appreciated.

OK JCH 2-20-75

My Personal Diary of My White House Days

March 21, 1975

Had a talk today with Dolf Droge, Deputy Director of The ACTION Agency, who was very conversant about all the issues in Southeast Asia and, in particular Vietnam. I have read with concern the accounts of the Cambodian, Vietnam, and Thailand situation. My concern has been centered on several factors: our potential re-entry of combat troops, our moral obligation to Indochina,[117] and our image on the international scene in keeping our commitments abroad. Day after day, I have clipped out stories on the eventual doom of Indochina—the hourly disintegrating situation in Cambodia, the relinquishing of commitments in S. Vietnam, and the message from the Thai government that our presence in Thailand within the year will be unwanted.

From about every angle of thought on the subject, the situations in these countries points to an unfavorable situation for America. For years, we spent billions of dollars on aid, military assistance, and food, in that area, fighting a war which could have been won, but was never fought to have been won—thus, our presence was ugly and futile, to a large degree. And the bill? —50,000 American men dead and hundreds of thousands wounded.

Today, the situation is ugly. In 1973, Congress refused to allocate aid to Indochina Vietnam of substantial amounts to ensure its security. This was undoubtedly looked upon by the N. Vietnamese as a signal that America was not going to live up to her commitment to S. Vietnam in being the guarantor of its survival.

The North Vietnamese look at this situation, seeing America's refusal to commit a small amount of aid to Cambodia. They now

---

[117] Wikipedia contributors, "Mainland Southeast Asia," *Wikipedia, The Free Encyclopedia*, https://en.wikipedia.org/w/index.php?title=Mainland_Southeast_Asia&oldid=973622080 (accessed September 30, 2020), "Indochina" redirects here. Mainland Southeast Asia (or the Indochinese Peninsula) is the continental portion of Southeast Asia. It lies east of the Indian subcontinent and south of China and is bordered by the Indian Ocean to the west and the Pacific Ocean to the east. It includes the countries of Cambodia, Laos, Myanmar (Burma), Peninsular Malaysia, Thailand and Vietnam. The term Indochina (originally Indo-China) was coined in the early nineteenth century. It emphasizes the cultural influence on the area of Indian civilization and Chinese civilization. The term was later adopted as the name of the colony of French Indochina (today's Cambodia, Vietnam, and Laos)."

realize—through this American inaction and the 1973 minimal aid allocation to Vietnam—that America is not a nation that will live up to its commitment and will have nothing to do with Indochina. They see us as a slumbering entity, void of might, and, in their assessment of the situation, launch an all-out invasion of the South—an invasion which was planned in a later year. But the time was right. America would not heed the most desperate calls from Cambodia and is perceived as a country who will not live up to its commitment. Thus, now, S. Vietnam has lost five provinces and many strategic areas. It's not that the N. Vietnamese are better soldiers, but that they perhaps are better organized and have aid from the communist nations that they wed—USSR/China. And, Thailand, watching U.S. inactivity, decides to awaken and play its cards right and snub the U.S. from its borders.

Of course, we are not totally to blame—that is the Congress. The USSR/China, as guarantors of the peace of '72, have flagrantly violated the peace accord by arming N. Vietnam, Khmer Rouge, and the insurgents. But, they too, under the veil of detente, see the U.S. weakening its own role in the world—see us as a nation of non-commitment—and are taking advantage of our inaction.

While this takes place, HAK (Kissinger) is in Israel trying to persuade Israel to accept a peace agreement with Egypt.

What do the Israelis think of our abilities to hold to a treaty and commit ourselves to them as Cambodia and S. Vietnam are falling into Communist hands? Admittedly, the theme of U.S. non-commitment can easily be overstated and over-dramatized, but it is now becoming an increasingly important factor to these nations—the so-called "3rd World Nations"—a factor which they are going to weigh with increasing anxiety. If the Israelis believe that, after HAK's attempt at further withdrawals and concessions, that the U.S. will be reluctant to live up to its word, they may feel that now is the time to strike or provoke an attack with the Arab nations while they are supposedly strong enough militarily. If that were to occur, the U.S. would be the likely victim of an oil embargo that would be very drastic and damaging—perhaps lead us into an economic tailspin and depression of incredible depth.

In essence, much rides upon U.S. credibility in the world, least of which is our own self-interest and survival. To paraphrase Senator Moynihan[118]: "The time has come now for the U.S. to stand in opposition to nations of the 3rd World who are shifting toward totalitarianism. We are at a crossroads in international diplomacy." Will we continue to be sedate, taking it on the chin, making smaller gains than the Communist/Socialist/Totalitarian regimes, or reassert our principles on the international scene, especially within the 3rd world, using our affluency and technology as weapons to seek needed partnerships to preserve democracy and liberty? We live in an environment of increasing interdependence; we cannot afford to sit back. We must become more understanding of the 3rd World as the entire world shifts in attitude against the U.S. and assert our interests and principles strongly in order to seek the world we wish to live in.

---

[118] Wikipedia contributors, "Daniel Patrick Moynihan," *Wikipedia, The Free Encyclopedia*, https://en.wikipedia.org/w/index.php?title=Daniel_Patrick_Moynihan&oldid=977080807 (accessed September 30, 2020), "Daniel Patrick "Pat" Moynihan (March 16, 1927 – March 26, 2003) was an American politician, sociologist, and diplomat. A member of the Democratic Party, he represented New York in the United States Senate and served as an adviser to Republican U.S. President Richard Nixon. In 1969, he accepted Nixon's offer to serve as an Assistant to the President for Domestic Policy, and he was elevated to the position of Counselor to the President later that year. He left the administration at the end of 1970, and accepted appointment as United States Ambassador to India in 1973. He accepted President Gerald Ford's appointment to the position of United States Ambassador to the United Nations in 1975."

First Hand

I just had to have a radio in my office—and here is a copy of the requisition I sent to the communications office so I could get one.

MEMORANDUM

THE WHITE HOUSE

WASHINGTON

May 16, 1975

MEMORANDUM FOR WACA COMMANDING OFFICER

FROM: JOHN UNLAND
        OFFICE OF PUBLIC LIAISON

I am housed in Room 198, EOB and would be most appreciative if you would furnish me with an AM/FM radio for my office.

Thank you.

My Personal Diary of My White House Days

This is a request by my bosses for me to have a White House pass which allowed me access to the West Wing and the White House Complex.

July 22, 1975

MEMORANDUM FOR: JANE DANNENHAUER

FROM: TED MARRS

John Unland has recently joined my staff and since the major part of his responsibilities will lie in organizing the TUESDAY AT THE WHITE HOUSE Program, it will be necessary for him to acquire a White House pass. In addition to this requirement, it will be necessary for John to assist in arranging our Presidential meetings held in the White House.

October 17, 1975

I have known for about three weeks that I will be leaving the immediate White House staff, but it wasn't until last evening when I chatted with Mr. Baroody that I found that I would not be given access list status which means that I will not be coming to the White House at random.

Throughout the evolution of staff cuts, I had been promised that I would be taken care of and that there would be no problem with keeping me on. I worried little, but as events unfolded and as the demands were increasingly made upon Mr. Baroody, I found that I was going to have to be shifted onto another roll. A deal was worked out between Mr. Baroody and Virginia Knauer's[119] office whereby I would be a consultant on their regional meetings with availability to Mr. Baroody.

In talking with Loraine several times, I understood that to mean that I would be on the Access List and that I would be spending time here, doing WJB's work, trying to continue as before. Last night I ascertained that this arrangement would not be possible, for if I were on the access list, I would be classified as a detailee, which is forbidden and would look like "subterfuge" to Congress. Thus, I leave the building, and my privileges here entirely and work for the Consumer Affairs Office with some contact with the staff here.

I am not bitter except for the fact that I found out bit by bit what my status would be and that I will not be working here under any arrangement. This is the fault of no one that I am aware of; it only saddens me and irritates me that my departure came about so sloppily after inflated expectations that something might be worked out.

---

[119] Wikipedia contributors, "Virginia Knauer," *Wikipedia, The Free Encyclopedia*, https://en.wikipedia.org/w/index.php?title=Virginia_Knauer&oldid=905194101 (accessed September 30, 2020), "Virginia Harrington Knauer (née Wright; March 28, 1915 – October 16, 2011) was an American Republican politician. She served as the Special Assistant to the President for Consumer Affairs and Director of the U.S. Office of Consumer Affairs (1969–1977 and 1981–1989)."

I left Mr. Baroody's office dismayed to run an errand to Jerry Jones's[120] office and to Mr. Cannon's[121] office. I decided to pass by the Oval Office, which I have done and love so frequently when the President is away. The entrance to the office is roped off, guarded by EPS (Executive Protective Service, which became the Secret Service in 1977). I chatted with the guard, entranced as I always am by the sight of the President's desk and his working area, and by the history within the oval walls. The guard began talking with another lady who needed to go through the office onto the portico by the Rose Garden and he let her through. I followed and while they were outside searching for a Magnolia tree that Andrew Jackson[122] planted, I walked about the office alone.

It was a rainy, chilly October evening and dark outside. The President was in the residence preparing to go out to dinner. I observed his artifacts: His pipes through the office, pictures of his family, the grand picture of Ben Franklin[123] near the door and of Abe Lincoln[124]; and the bust of Harry Truman[125] by his desk,

---

[120] Wikipedia contributors, "Jerry H. Jones," *Wikipedia, The Free Encyclopedia*, https://en.wikipedia.org/w/index.php?title=Jerry_H._Jones&oldid=979736974 (accessed September 30, 2020), "Jerry H. Jones (born June 13, 1939) is an American political aide who served as White House Staff Secretary from 1974 to 1977 during the Ford Administration."

[121] Wikipedia contributors, "James M. Cannon," *Wikipedia, The Free Encyclopedia*, https://en.wikipedia.org/w/index.php?title=James_M._Cannon&oldid=928850742 (accessed September 30, 2020), "James M. Cannon (February 26, 1918 – September 15, 2011) was a historian, author and former Assistant to the President of the United States for Foreign Affairs during the Gerald Ford administration."

[122] Wikipedia contributors, "Andrew Jackson," *Wikipedia, The Free Encyclopedia*, https://en.wikipedia.org/w/index.php?title=Andrew_Jackson&oldid=979729373 (accessed September 30, 2020), "Andrew Jackson (March 15, 1767 – June 8, 1845) was an American soldier and statesman who served as the seventh president of the United States from 1829 to 1837."

[123] Wikipedia contributors, "Benjamin Franklin," *Wikipedia, The Free Encyclopedia*, https://en.wikipedia.org/w/index.php?title=Benjamin_Franklin&oldid=980761292 (accessed September 30, 2020), "Benjamin Franklin (January 6, 1705 – April 17, 1790) was an American polymath and one of the Founding Fathers of the United States. Franklin was a leading writer, printer, political philosopher, politician, Freemason, postmaster, scientist, inventor, humorist, civic activist, statesman, and diplomat."

[124] Wikipedia contributors, "Abraham Lincoln," *Wikipedia, The Free Encyclopedia*, https://en.wikipedia.org/w/index.php?title=Abraham_Lincoln&oldid=980983849 (accessed September 30, 2020), "Abraham Lincoln (February 12, 1809 – April 15, 1865) was an American statesman and lawyer who served as the 16th president of the United States from 1861 to 1865. Lincoln led the nation through the American Civil War, the country's greatest moral, constitutional, and political crisis. He succeeded in preserving the Union, abolishing slavery, bolstering the federal government, and modernizing the U.S. economy."

[125] Wikipedia contributors, "Harry S. Truman," *Wikipedia, The Free Encyclopedia*, https://en.wikipedia.org/w/index.php?title=Harry_S._Truman&oldid=981167740 (accessed September 30, 2020), "Harry S. Truman (May 8, 1884 – December 26, 1972) was the 33rd president of the United States from 1945 to 1953, succeeding upon the death of Franklin D. Roosevelt after serving as the 34th vice president."

papers about his desk with his pen left on top of it. I sat on the arm of the sofa where so many important individuals have been and absorbed the warmth that the pale-yellow rug gives to the mahogany desk and the white walls. It was so quiet and pleasant and so awesome. I thought of leaving the staff and thought that this room is what all my work has really been about; I was so lucky to have worked at the White House and for this President in particular at this time. History has provided me with such an experience and a valuable time to have worked at the White House. I had a slight, almost insignificant thought that perhaps someday I will return in a greater capacity and will sit in this office again alone, behind the desk. Life is so filled with unexpectancies that one just never knows. I have no designs on the office and at my age it is utterly trite and foolish to say that I would, could, or might. But, one just never knows what events will take place. The President two years ago did not think that he would be here. The five minutes I spent alone in the office of Presidents was worth the disillusionment received from my departure. It was incredible to me in my own way.

I left the Oval Office to return to my office, grab my coat, and walk out into the rainy, cold evening as the Presidential motorcade swept past me. It was a rewarding time.

My Personal Diary of My White House Days

Here is my farewell note to Mr. Baroody for whom I had enormous esteem and also gratitude for having me on his staff.

THE WHITE HOUSE

WASHINGTON

October 30, 1975

Mr. Baroody:

I can't thank you enough for all that you have done for me during the past year and one half. As I sit here typing this note, I think of the first day here as an Intern in June, 1974 a bit nervous about what my work would entail; I think of the many times that I have trotted into your office to run errands; and I think of how your staff and you have been adopted by me as my second family.

Words just are impossible to express my gratitude to you for such a wonderful opportunity which I have relished every minute and what a wonderful example you have provided me by which to lead my life and tax career. I always will have such fond memories of these days and I thank you from the bottom of my heart.

With best wishes in all of your endeavors,

First Hand

This is a letter to my parents that I typed up on my last day at the White House.

THE WHITE HOUSE

WASHINGTON

October 31, 1975

Dear Mom and Dad:

This is my last letter from my trusty typewriter in Room 198. Just returned from a most special party given in my honor by Mr. Baroody. Enclosed is a song the staff wrote for me which is sung to the tune of " From the Halls of Montezuma". I guess each staff member had a hand in writing it and it was quite touching and amusing; a wonderful tribute to go out on. Thought you might want a copy to read.

Must go . Sad to leave.

Love you both,

Log

Log

My Personal Diary of My White House Days

At lunch on my last day, I was asked by Mr. Baroody to come into his conference room, which was an unusual invitation because usually we met in his private office not his conference room. I opened the door and there stood the entire office staff—who broke into a very warm round of applause—surrounding a nice-sized cake in the middle of the table. Then, to the tune and cadence of "From the Halls of Montezuma," they sang these words about me and our working relationships. [Go ahead, take a minute and run through the melody in your head and match up the words. It's quite fun!] I was completely surprised and thrilled that the dozen or so staff members planned such an event on my behalf. This truly was a great end and quite a crescendo to so many months of working with an incredible bunch of people.

THE WHITE HOUSE
WASHINGTON

SONNET TO JOHN UNLAND

```
FROM THE HALLS OF EOB TO THE DOORS OF BAROODY
HE EXUDES BOYISH GOOD LOOKS AND YOUTHFUL PURITY.

    AS HE WHISTLES DOWN LONG CORRIDORS,
      AND TELLS EVERY GIRL "GOLLEE"
    PEKIN SMILES AND FLIRTS WITH YOUNGER JAWS,
      BUT RETURNS TO OLD SPANKY.


    HE'S A CHEERFUL, HELPFUL, NOBLE KNIGHT
      WHO WILL RESCUE ALL IN NEED.
    WHETHER TRANSCRIPTS, MEETINGS, TELEPHONES,
      HE'S A WALKING BOY SCOUT CREED.


    FROM ALL THOSE WHO'VE GROWN TO KNOW HIM WELL
      AND RESPECT THESE QUALITIES,
    COMES THANKS AND LOVE, AND KEEP IN TOUCH
      WITH YOUR OLD WHITE HOUSE CRONIES.
```

                                        October 31, 1975

The Proposal

Take three months—from the middle of July to the middle of October. I knew Spank as a good friend and fellow intern. She was good looking and seemed to be fun. I asked her out only to have a good time for an evening—to the National Gallery and Hogate's. I was relaxed the entire evening but thought all along that I was out of my league—that this girl was too worldly for me—was much more the gal about town and the extravert than I was. She seemed so solid—so much of what I have always wanted and what I have always wanted to <u>really</u> be.

Now, three months later, after fighting for her—mentally—and after having been through some—several—difficulties, I am comfortable with her and, in many ways, am in love with her. In three months—coming from absolutely nothing—we have built together a base that we fought for and that we knew we could build—a base of friendship personified—of light and enjoyable love. We are <u>working</u> on a relationship that we feel will work and hope will work.

Whatever develops between us from here on out may take as much effort and develop slowly. But, God willing, we will appreciate it as much as we have the beginning.

On March 25th, 1976, Linda and I were sitting on the terrace of the Shoreham Hotel in Washington, having gin and tonics, and though I had not really planned the following 100% for that evening, after 2 of those gin and tonics, and feeling their impact and feeling happy, I asked Linda to marry me—proposed to her right on that terrace.

I knew that I wanted to marry her, but I sure did not organize my asking her for that night. It just happened. She nearly fell off her chair she was so shocked. I, too, was surprised at my boldness. Initially, most likely because of the 2nd or 3rd gin and tonic she had consumed, she said, "Yes," but then told me that she wanted some time to think about it because she was so taken off guard.

Well, she slept on it and the following day she confirmed that she wanted to get married. Whew!

My Personal Diary of My White House Days

June 13, 1976

After some time, I decided to again resume what once was a most refreshing and rewarding personal experience—maintaining a personal log/journal of thoughts and movements. One frequently wonders exactly why one feels guided to do such; the answer, I suppose, lies within the makeup of the individual.

For me, keeping a diary has many important aspects: to maintain a daily log of activity, which I have found to be most valuable for a country boy to do in Washington, especially while working at the White House; to coalesce my feelings and emotions and whatever intellectual thoughts I might scratch upon this paper; to practice the wonder of the English language; and to give the members of my family (present and, in the years forthcoming) a record of what at least one of their relatives was up to while he visited his wonderous planet for so short a time. Thus, I continue and if thoughts do not seem to portray continuity in subject or time, it is due to both the nature of the keeper and his neglect for over a year to maintain such a log.

Today, I began a new phase of my life. Having awakened early, I sat about the house in Pekin with Mom and Dad while Jim slept his needed ten hours. Dad and I drove to the country club and played seven holes of golf, as it was too blasted hot to continue and our games were both undesirable. Having finished, we all had lunch at 622 Washington Street (our home) and Jim and I packed the car and at 3:00 headed for Chicago. To him, such a journey was routine; to me, it would be my last trip to Chicago where I have spent time since February.

I am, tomorrow, to pack up a U-Haul truck and move back to Washington where Linda and I will begin our married lives. I felt a great deal of sadness having left Pekin this time, for in the very near future the many times I will be leaving will be as a husband as well as a son to my home.

Life is rapidly taking a changed direction for me and, having decided to return to Washington and this being the last trip to Pekin before moving back, I felt the past slide reluctantly and too rapidly by and the newness of my to-be-changed life thrusting itself upon me again, too quickly. My grandfather once told me that the one thing that never stops is time. I felt it today; it passes and approaches too rapidly.

I am confident in all of my decisions, but must confess a degree of discomfort in the unknown which will present itself soon. I have had the most comfortable and loving childhood and young-adulthood as one can have. I am familiar and know what I leave behind; I am unfamiliar and unknowing what lies ahead for me in married life. I am not scared, I am not undesirable of it, I will never, hopefully, shirk it, but it is the unknown and a very, very large step in one's life. For those reasons, I am uncomfortable, as one is uncomfortable with anything unknown to a degree. My leaving Pekin should not be overly symbolized, but it was symbolic of my next steps in my life.

Yesterday was Jim's 26th birthday and we celebrated in a rather low-key manner at the farm with Susan, Bobby, Dr. Bill, Laverne, and the four Unlands. The evening was cool and all enjoyed the food and fellowship, especially Dr. Bill who does love to be with his very good friends and family.

During the day of the 12th, Dad, Jim, the Dog, and I played golf and Jim and Gene barely beat Dad and I. Jim was super, with a 37 on the front nine. We all truly enjoyed the day. Amy (nickname for my Mom) and I then went out to VAL's to look at possible shower gifts for friends to purchase for Linda and I when she is in Pekin for the second week of August.

All in all, it was, as it always is, just terrific to be home with my family and friends and, though I begin a new life soon and am moving to Washington, Pekin and "622" will always be my home. They have provided me with an upbringing full of the most marvelous memories and sound values that any person could ever wish for. I love my family and home so very much.

Chapter Fifteen: Some Final Stories

When President and Mrs. Nixon left Washington, Linda stayed on the staff of the First Lady who, within a matter of minutes, was Mrs. Ford. Linda is shown in the preceding photo in a red patterned dress at a White House party and in the following photo in the background at an event with Mrs. Ford on the South Lawn.

First Hand

"LOCAL NEWSPAPER PRESS COVERAGE—NIXON'S RESIGNATION DAY"

As I mentioned, I am from a relatively small town in Illinois where our family was well-known; and my work at the White House was of interest to several local news reporters—including the Editor of the Pekin Daily Times, our hometown newspaper.

When President Nixon resigned on August 9th, the paper ran this photo and article about me. (transcription follows on separate page)

Some Final Stories

Pekin Times, Friday, August 9, 1974

"Pekinite John Unland Present When Nixon Bade White House Staff Goodbye This Morning" By SHIRLEY COFFEY

John Unland, son of Mr. and Mrs. James Unland of Pekin, a Colgate University senior working as an intern this summer in the office of William Baroody, special consultant to the President, has been in the thick of the historic activities which have taken place the past few days in the White House.

Inevitably, those working in the executive office building where Unland's boss has his headquarters, have experienced numerous traumatic emotional experiences since last Monday afternoon when events, Unland says, began to occur so rapidly that "we have had all we can do to keep up morale and to function in our jobs." Baroody, who serves as a special consultant to the President in establishing liaison among all business, farm and labor organizations thruout (sic) the country, has his office just doors away from the room in the executive office building where

First Hand

the former President spent a great deal of time.

Unland saw Mr. Nixon Wednesday as he was coming from the oval office in the White House, and said he appeared calm.

The consensus of opinion that resignation of the President was imminent became apparent about noon Thursday to those in the White House and the executive office building, Unland said.

At 9:30 a.m. (EDT) today, Unland was present in the East Room when Mr. Nixon gave his last speech as President of the United States, a farewell address to his entire Cabinet, to members of the White House senior staff, and to others.

"It was a deeply emotional experience for all of us, as well as for the President, whose voice wavered several times. There were tears in the eyes of everyone listening to Mr. Nixon. However, members of the first family, seated on the podium, were composed, as was the President," Unland said in a telephoned conversation with the Times shortly afterward.

Altho (sic) Unland had not yet seen Gerald Ford this morning, he was with him for about 20 minutes Thursday morning. The then Vice-President did not at that time mention the impending resignation of the President and said nothing about the circumstances which later in the day culminated in Mr. Nixon's announcement that he would address the nation on television Thursday evening.

Overall reaction in the White House and executive office building today is one of relief and disbelief, Unland noted. "It gives one an eerie feeling to walk thru the White House on Mr. Nixon's last day here...to look from the rose garden toward the windows of the oval office, knowing that it will be the scene very soon of the transfer of power of the President of the United States from one man to another. Thursday I saw Gerald Ford as Vice-President and today I will see him as President."

Unland said he heard this morning that the swearing-in ceremony, to be conducted by Chief Justice Warren E. Burger, probably would take place in the oval office, which necessarily would limit the number of persons who could be present.

"I imagine it will be confined to family members and perhaps a few other persons," Unland said.

In summing up the feeling engendered among White House

staff members and others who have worked in close association with Mr. Nixon, Unland observed: "It is a time when all of us must pause very briefly, take deep breaths and move forward as strongly as we can, whether we're in the White House, in Illinois, or elsewhere thruout (sic) the country, in support of President Ford's goals and in support of him personally as President of the United States. I think he will be a very fine and strong President, for he has many great assets. All of us in the White House are being strong, and I hope the nation will be strong," he concluded.

Caption under photo reads: JOHN UNLAND, interning this summer in the office of William J. Baroody, special consultant to the President, has been close to developments in the White House which led to Mr. Nixon's resignation of the office of President. In a telephoned interview this morning, he gives his observations about reaction to this momentous event in the history of the United States. Photo by Frank Johnston Courtesy of The Washington Post

Some Final Stories

"UNEXPECTED PRESIDENTIAL ENCOUNTER"

As previously mentioned, I was rarely without my camera during my White House internship days. To follow are a few photos I snapped on a weekend as I strolled the White House grounds. On this occasion, I happened to catch President Ford leaving the Oval Office.

First Hand

Some Final Stories

When I was on the staff in September of 1975, there were two assassination attempts on the President. After one such attempt (on September 5th, 1975), he returned to the White House where all of us—the entire staff— were there on the South Lawn to greet him when his helicopter, Marine One, landed. For me, and for everyone, it was quite an emotional few minutes as he stepped off the helicopter. In his usual calm and casual way, he made the following remark: "It's nice to be home..." Considering that a woman from the Charles Manson "family" had just pointed a .45 caliber handgun at him recently, we thought that was quite an understatement. But it was a great way to break the tension of the moment and everyone broke into laughter and cheers at the remark. (See press release to follow)

First Hand

"FORD'S HUMOR EASES TENSION"

FOR IMMEDIATE RELEASE   SEPTEMBER 5, 1975
           OFFICE OF THE WHITE HOUSE PRESS SECRETARY

                          THE WHITE HOUSE

                    ==REMARKS OF THE PRESIDENT==
                    ==UPON HIS ARRIVAL==
                    ==FROM SACRAMENTO, CALIFORNIA==

                          THE SOUTH LAWN

10:50 P.M. EDT

           ==It is nice to be home.== (Laughter) It is especially really good to see Betty and Steve and Jack and to see all of you.

           We had a great trip--just a fraction of a second or two that disturbed things--but everything else was superb, and I am most grateful that you all came out here. I don't know why all the bother. (Laughter)

           It was a very successful visit in Washington, Oregon, California and Sacramento, particularly the people were wonderful, and just a single incident I don't think we should feel was a distraction in the overall things that were done in a very affirmative way.

           I want to thank the Secret Service and the other law enforcement people. I particularly was impressed with the wonderful reception we got in California and in Sacramento, especially.

           I wouldn't, under any circumstances, let one individual's efforts to undercut the warmth that we felt from the people of California.

           Let me say with emphasis, we are going to be among the people in all of our States because I think it is highly important that a President has that opportunity to meet people from all parts of our country and to let them have an opportunity to express to me their views, whether they agree or disagree.

           This is one of the greatest assets, I think, in a country such as our own.

                          END   (AT 10:53 P.M. EDT)

Some Final Stories

To follow are some details of two assassination attempts upon President Ford as described by Wikipedia.com:

"Assassination attempts[126]

Ford was the target of two assassination attempts during his presidency. In Sacramento, California, on September 5, 1975, Lynette 'Squeaky' Fromme, a follower of Charles Manson, pointed a Colt .45-caliber handgun at Ford and pulled the trigger at point-blank range. As she did, Larry Buendorf, a Secret Service agent, grabbed the gun, and Fromme was taken into custody. She was later convicted of attempted assassination of the President and was sentenced to life in prison; she was paroled on August 14, 2009, after serving 34 years.

In reaction to this attempt, the Secret Service began keeping Ford at a more secure distance from anonymous crowds, a strategy that may have saved his life seventeen days later. As he left the St. Francis Hotel in downtown San Francisco, Sara Jane Moore, standing in a crowd of onlookers across the street, fired a .38-caliber revolver at him. The shot missed Ford by a few feet. Before she fired a second round, retired Marine Oliver Sipple grabbed at the gun and deflected her shot; the bullet struck a wall about six inches above and to the right of Ford's head, then ricocheted and hit a taxi driver, who was slightly wounded. Moore was later sentenced to life in prison. She was paroled on December 31, 2007, after serving 32 years."

---

[126] Wikipedia contributors, "Gerald Ford," *Wikipedia, The Free Encyclopedia*, https://en.wikipedia.org/w/index.php?title=Gerald_Ford&oldid=979044716 (accessed September 30, 2020)

President Ford with his dog, Liberty.[127]

[127] Wikipedia contributors, "Liberty (dog)," *Wikipedia, The Free Encyclopedia*, https://en.wikipedia.org/w/index.php?title=Liberty_(dog)&oldid=964150361 (accessed September 20, 2020), Honor's Foxfire Liberty Hume (February 8, 1974 – 1984) (AKC Registration Number SB578950) was the Golden Retriever Presidential pet of Betty Ford and Gerald Ford. Liberty was born February 8, 1974 and given to the president as an 8-month-old puppy by his daughter Susan Ford and new White House photographer David Hume Kennerly in the fall of 1974."

Some Final Stories

During Linda's tenure at the White House, she had a terrific boss by the name of Patty Matson who was the assistant press secretary to the First Lady, Mrs. Nixon, and then Mrs. Ford. Through Linda, I became friends with Patty and the three of us had a great relationship and a great deal of fun. Often, I would wander over to the East Wing just to say 'Hello' and there usually was a great deal of laughter. Linda and I at that time each had a golden retriever. Linda (Spank) had a golden by the name of Kirby and I had a golden by the name of Molly. The first family's dog was a golden retriever by the name of Liberty. Patty took the picture shown here with the President petting Liberty and then had copies made and framed. She also took Liberty's paw, placed it on an ink pad, and then gave us an 'autograph' on these photos for Linda and me. How adorable is that?

To Spank and Kirby Smith
With best wishes,

To Molly and John Unland
With best wishes,

"SON, I LOVE YOUR LONG HAIR"

When President Ford became president on August 9th of 1974, that left the vice-presidency open. And there was lots of chatter about who was going to become his vice-president, who he wanted to pick. Of course, he picked Nelson Rockefeller who was a liberal Republican. When Rockefeller was confirmed, he came to the White House and occupied the suite of offices that then Vice-President Ford had occupied just months before; offices that were directly above my office and where I had walked by several times. I would see the Vice-President, the new Vice-President, in the hallways often. And at this time, I still had my long hair.

There were times he would stop me in the hallway and grab my hair—and give it a good yank! And he would say, "Son, I love your long hair." That happened probably two or three times. I remember vividly being in his private elevator—which I used sometimes without authority—and he would walk in going up to his offices. We would chat for a minute and on the way out he'd tug on my long hair and tell me how much he loved it. I thought that was the most hilarious thing.

First Hand

"MISTER SPEAKER, THE PRESIDENT OF THE UNITED STATES!"

In 1975, our office was tasked with reaching out to hundreds of people to brief them on the content of the President's State of the Union Address. It was my responsibility to send this message out to all of the invitees.

MAILGRAM

THIS IS TO INVITE YOU OR YOUR ~~DESIGNATE~~ Designated Representative TO ATTEND A ONE AND ONE HALF HOUR WHITE HOUSE BRIEFING AND DISCUSSION ON THE PRESIDENT'S STATE OF THE UNION MESSAGE. THE BRIEFING WILL BE CONDUCTED BY THE PRESIDENT'S TOP ECONOMIC AND ENERGY ADVISERS AND HELD IN ROOM 450 OLD EXECUTIVE OFFICE BUILDING AT 17TH AND PENNSYLVANIA AVENUES, N.W., DIRECTLY ADJACENT TO THE WHITE HOUSE.

THE BRIEFING WILL BE HELD ON FRIDAY, JAN. 17, 1975, AT 10:00 AM. PLEASE PLAN TO ARRIVE ABOUT 30 MINUTES EARLY AT THE 17TH STREET ENTRANCE, E.O.B., TO ALLOW TIME FOR CLEARANCE INTO THE BUILDING. IF YOU OR YOUR DESIGNATE WISH TO ATTEND PLEASE NOTIFY MY STAFF AT (202) 456-1414 AND CONNECT ONLY WITH EXTENSIONS 573, 574, 575, AS SOON AS POSSIBLE.

WILLIAM J. BAROODY, JR.
ASSISTANT TO THE PRESIDENT

Some Final Stories

Though it doesn't say it, I was the one responsible to provide all the materials for the roughly 1,200 attendees for these briefings.

January 9, 1975

MEMORANDUM FOR: ROLAND ELLIOTT

FROM: BILL BAROODY

In conjunction with the President's State of the Union Address, my office will be conducting six briefings between January 21 and 24 with approximately 1,200 representatives from many organizations.

Due to the increased amount of work to be done in preparation and followup for these briefings, I am requesting authorization for a person skilled in clerical typing work to aid my office between now and the end of January.

I would sincerely appreciate your help.

First Hand

This is the cover of the packet that I put together for the 1,200 attendees; which had 7 or 8 items each that had to be collated and distributed accordingly. Since I only had about 5 or 6 days to accomplish this, I pulled in every friend I knew of to help me, including Spank. We would stay at the White House until 9 or 10 at night, every single night for days. Needless to say, this entire task just about killed me! But on a positive note, as a reward, Mr. Baroody got me an invitation to the State of the Union Address at Congress, which—of course—I attended.

THE PRESIDENT'S 1975

STATE OF THE UNION MESSAGE

including

ECONOMY

and

ENERGY

Some Final Stories

"WILL IT PLAY IN PEORIA?"

In April of 1975, my father was on the board of an organization called the Dirksen Center, which housed the papers of Senator Dirksen during his time in public service, both as a congressman and as the minority leader of the United States Senate. Being on the board of the Dirksen Center, the board was dedicating a new building that housed the papers. At this time, during his tenure as minority leader of the United States Senate, Gerald Ford was the minority leader of the House of Representatives.

Photo courtesy of Tom Paullin

And given that the board of the Dirksen center had built a brand-new building housing the Senator's papers, they wanted President Ford to come out to the dedication in August of 1975. I was working in the White House for Mr. Baroody, and as we held our conferences on domestic and economic affairs around the country, I thought it might be worthwhile to mention to him that perhaps we should hold such a conference in Peoria, Illinois—which is only nine miles from Pekin.

Now, during the Nixon administration, John Ehrlichman and Haldeman created a saying: "Will it play in Peoria?" Meaning that if a certain policy would play in Peoria, which was then demographically considered a cross-section of the country; if a policy would generally be accepted in Peoria, then chances were high that the administration could promote such a policy around the country and gain support even during Watergate. So, the expression, "Will it play in Peoria?" became sort of a moniker of the Nixon Administration in terms of floating policy ideas around such a community.

So, one day in April of '75 I was in the men's room in the old Executive Office Building standing next to Mr. Baroody. And I just decided to ask him right then and there. I blurted out, "Mr. Baroody, my dad is on the board of the Dirksen Center and Congressman Michel is interested in getting the President to come and dedicate this center. The Mayor and others think it would be appropriate for President Ford, having known Senator Dirksen so well[128], to come for the dedication. One idea would be to have one of our Domestic and Economic Affairs town halls in Peoria and we could tie that into the expression "Will it play in Peoria?" so that we bring the President to Peoria to close out our day-long session with labor leaders, education leaders and all the key stakeholders of Central Illinois. What do you think of that idea?"

---

[128] Wikipedia contributors, "Gerald Ford," *Wikipedia, The Free Encyclopedia*, https://en.wikipedia.org/w/index.php?title=Gerald_Ford&oldid=979044716 (accessed September 30, 2020), "As Minority Leader in the House, Ford appeared in a popular series of televised press conferences with Illinois Senator Everett Dirksen, in which they proposed Republican alternatives to [President] Johnson's policies. Many in the press jokingly called this 'The Ev and Jerry Show.'"

Some Final Stories

This is the schedule proposal sent to Warren Rustand, who was in charge of the President's daily schedule. This proposal was written by me and delivered to the West Wing in hopes that the President's schedule allowed him to come to Peoria on August 19th, 1975.

THE WHITE HOUSE

WASHINGTON

SCHEDULE PROPOSAL
DATE: May 12, 1975
FROM: William J. Baroody, Jr.
VIA: Warren S. Rustand

MEETING: White House Conference on Domestic and Economic Affairs

DATE: Tuesday, August 19, 1975 -- Open

PURPOSE: To allow the President to meet with local leaders and to close the White House Conference on Domestic and Economic Affairs

FORMAT:
- location: Peoria, Illinois (exact location undecided)

- participants: Ten to Fifteen business, agriculture, labor, civic, educational and press associations have expressed an interest in sponsoring this Conference. Participating will be about 500 persons invited by the co-sponsoring organizations.

- length of participation: 60 minutes in total

SPEECH MATERIAL: To be prepared by Paul Theis' office

PRESS COVERAGE: The entire meeting will be open to all legitimate press with potential for live television coverage

CABINET PARTICIPATION: At least six senior Administration officials from various departments and agencies

STAFF: Jeffrey P. Eves, Director, White House Conferences, Office of Public Liaison

Well, it turned out that for the President to come out only for the dedication of the library itself wasn't going to happen. But once the idea of holding a conference on domestic and economic affairs became part of the possible agenda, the President's staff agreed to have him fly out to Peoria, close up our day-long conference, and then motorcade from Peoria down to Pekin for the dedication. So, in a very real way I played a major role in getting the President to come to our hometown to dedicate this library.

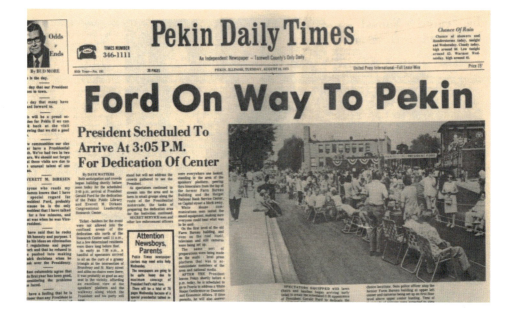

Some Final Stories

Interestingly enough, one of the ads on the following page was for my father's insurance agency—Unland's Insurance Agencies.

First Hand

Some Final Stories

Another thing I remember is that I wanted to ride in the motorcade. I was in Peoria working on the conference and I wanted to ride in that motorcade.

So, I sent a memo through to the person in charge of the motorcade asking if that would be possible. And it turned out that after the end of our conference, I went out with the President's personal entourage and Secret Service agents and jumped in a car and road from Peoria to Pekin with all the sirens and the advanced motorcade, and so forth, and arrived at the Dirksen Center—which had already been set up for the President's dedication. My dad was on the board for the Center, as I had mentioned, and he got to sit on the dais right next to the Presidential podium.

Well, when I got out of the limousine, the car I was assigned to that day—I got out at the corner of Fourth Street and Court—all of my friends were on the corner, all of my age group who lived in Pekin—and I stepped out of the car and they all yelled "John Logan!, John Logan!" as loud as they could and completely embarrassed me in front of my boss and all of my staff who knew very well that this was my hometown. It was as if I was a bigger celebrity to them than the President! That's a fun memory I have of that particular day.

Then I got to watch the President dedicate the museum with my father sitting very close to him. How surreal that was as well.

When the dedication was over, my boss, Mr. Baroody, took me by the arm and took my dad over and introduced my dad to the President, which I thought was—well, didn't introduce him, but they spent some time together. I thought that was very nice.

And again, on the dais with my father was Senator Baker, Senator Dirksen's son-in-law, Bob Michel, minority leader of the House, and other dignitaries.

But the fun thing for me is that the President would not have gone at all if only to dedicate the library, or he may have only come in for a half an hour, but he ended upcoming because of our Domestic and Economic Affairs day-long session, and to tie it up in front of all the major stakeholders in Central Illinois.

So, from my standpoint, that was a great memory of working in the White House, largely because it tethered my father and I together around politics and around that event.

Some Final Stories

This is the White House press release of the President's remarks in Pekin.

FOR IMMEDIATE RELEASE　　　　　　　　AUGUST 19, 1975

OFFICE OF THE WHITE HOUSE PRESS SECRETARY
(Peoria, Illinois)

THE WHITE HOUSE

REMARKS OF THE PRESIDENT
AT THE
DEDICATION OF THE DIRKSEN WING
OF THE
ILLINOIS PUBLIC LIBRARY

PEKIN, ILLINOIS

AT 3:26 P.M. CDT

　　　　Howard Baker, my dear friend Louella, Senator Chuck Percy, Senator Jennings Randolph, Senator Roman Hruska, Governor Walker, my very good and dear friend, Charlie Halleck and, of course, my long time friend and great helper, Les Arends, Mayor Waldmeier, distinguished guests, ladies and gentlemen:

　　　　As one of the many, many Americans who knew and loved Everett Dirksen, obviously I am pleased to be in his hometown for the dedication of this great building in his honor.

　　　　I wanted to be here in a very special capacity, not as President of the United States, not as a former President of the United States Senate, but as the spokesman for a very exclusive fraternity -- Minority Leaders of the House of Representatives and the United States Senate.

　　　　How delighted Ev would be that the dedication coincided with your third annual Marigold Festival. This city really looks beautiful today with so many thousands of Ev's favorite flowers in bloom.

　　　　And as I said a moment ago, I did want to be here representing Minority Leaders. Unfortunately, as Charlie Halleck and I both know, our fraternity has been overwhelmingly Republican in recent years, though we keep trying to recruit more Democrats every day. (Laughter)

　　　　We take some comfort, however, in the obvious fact that leading the Minority in the House or the Senate is a much more demanding job than leading the Majority and, if ever a Minority Leader could be said to dominate either body, the House or the Senate, that man was Everett Dirksen.

　　　　He was a power to be reckoned with, and he did it not by the numbers of his Minority, but by the sheer power of his unique personality, his persuasiveness, his profound gift for friendship and his consummate legislative skills.

MORE

First Hand

"A GIFT FROM THE FIRST LADY'S STAFF"

As part of the first lady's staff, there were several people who specialized in caligraphy for invitations to state dinners, name cards for table placements, etc. When I returned from Peoria, a staff member of our office sent this portion of the Presidnent's speech to the caligraphy office to be written in caligraphy for me. I still keep it hanging in my home since I am so fond of this passage from his speech— particularly the very last line.

> Freedom, in my judgment, is more than a word. It is a way of life, a vital living thing, and each generation must strengthen and renew it or it will surely perish, as we have seen all too often elsewhere in the world.
>
> The time is now for our generation to keep this idea alive. We must make sure that our first 200 years as a free people, glorious as they have been, will only be the beginning of the American success story.
>
> Together let us prove to the entire world that the American dream is best realized when we are wide awake.
>
> President Gerald Ford
> Peoria, Illinois
> August 19, 1975

Some Final Stories

"THE SADAT VISIT TO THE WHITE HOUSE"

In October of 1975, Egyptian President Anwar Sadat made a visit to the White House in order to "seek economic and military help from Washington and to explain his policies to the American people."— according to a *New York Times* article published October 27, 1975.

A digitized version of the article is available at this link: https://www.nytimes.com/1975/10/27/archives/new-jersey-pages-sadat-in-the-us-in-quest-for-arms-and-economic-aid.html

WHITE HOUSE CUSTOMS FOR THE ARRIVAL OF VISITING DIGNITARIES

Welcome to the White House.

During the playing of Honors for the President and the Visiting Dignitary, it is customary that White House guests observe the following:

- *Stand at attention during the playing of Ruffles and Flourishes (Musical Salute).*
- *Stand at attention during the playing of Hail to the Chief.*
- *During the playing of National Anthems, salute by placing your right hand over the heart. If gentlemen's hats are worn, the hat is held over the left shoulder with the hand over the heart.*

PROGRAM

10:55 a.m. *His Excellency the President of the Arab Republic of Egypt and Mrs. Sadat arrive at the President's Park (Ellipse) and proceed by car for the White House.*

11:00 a.m. *Arrival at the White House where the President and Mrs. Sadat will be greeted by the President of the United States and Mrs. Ford, the Secretary of State and Mrs. Kissinger, Chairman of the Joint Chiefs of Staff and Mrs. Brown, the Dean of the Diplomatic Corps and Mrs. Sevilla-Sacasa, and other officials.*

Military honors are rendered.

When a head of state visited the President in Washington, almost always there was what was called "an arrival ceremony" where the President would greet the visiting dignitary, and the U.S. Marine Band and Color Guard would perform. In these photos, President Anwar Sadat of Egypt came to the White House and I attended the arrival ceremony on the South Lawn and, true to form, brought my camera.

Some Final Stories

President Ford speaks at the podium with the Old Executive Office Building in the background, where our offices were located.

"THE '76 CONVENTION"

During my Ford years, in 1976, President Ford ran for reelection, or election, depending on upon how you look at it because he was not elected president in 1974.

The Republican National Convention was held in Kansas City that year, in 1976, and Ronald Reagan entered the race to compete against the President for the nomination. I very much wanted to go to the convention and I worked it out so that I got a press pass by reporting for my local hometown newspaper, the Pekin Daily Times. They hired me to cover the convention on their behalf where I wrote an article every day for the newspaper, which was printed. And through that assignment, I was allowed to get a press pass, which got me onto the convention floor.

I remember so clearly the bitter fight between Reagan and Ford in terms of accumulating enough delegates to receive the nomination. I was on the floor when heads of delegations were trading delegates. And if I recall correctly, the state of Missouri delegates were heavily in play between Reagan and Ford, and it was a rather tense few days as to who was going to get the nomination. There was a great deal of activity and competition,

to say it mildly. And at the end, President Ford did acquire enough delegates to win the nomination. And on the evening of his victory, he got up to the podium, and I was standing just beneath him and the podium and he gave a speech. After he gave the speech, he waived to Ronald and Nancy Reagan who were sitting up in the balcony to come down and join him in a moment of unity to raise hands together. Reagan did not come down. He stayed in his seat for what seemed to be two or three minutes with the President waiving once or twice for Governor Reagan to come down and stand on the podium with him.

I personally thought that was a bit rude, though I could understand the Governor's disappointment. He finally did come down on the podium and they raised their hands in unity—and of course the crowd erupted. Needless to say, it was a very exciting couple of days for me to be on the convention floor and watching what was one of the more historic battles for a nomination for the presidency.

To follow are some personal photos and other items that I dug out of my archives from my trip to Kansas City for that historical moment in politics.

Some Final Stories

Congressman Bob Michel

Senator Howard Baker

First Hand

Vice President Nelson Rockefeller

Mrs. Reagan was with her son, Ronnie, and I was in such a rush that I failed to stand still long enough to get a good photo of them in the stands. Such a shame, but such a great lady that I wanted to include her photo in my book—no matter how blurry it is.

Some Final Stories

Though a bit grainy, this is obviously a photo of Ronald Reagan that I managed to take at the convention in 1976.

First Hand

Some Final Stories

"THE CRAZY COINCIDENCE"

Now, this is a story pertaining my office mate, Michael Mulligan, during my White House internship days in 1974.

Thirty years after we all separated and Michael went back to Middlebury College, and most of the other interns returned to their respective colleges, I stayed on President Ford's staff for another year; completely engrossed in my job. I loved every single second.

After leaving the White House in 1975, Linda and I lived in New York City and Philadelphia, and we had two boys, Logan and Tyler. Logan went to a boarding school in Newport, Rhode Island, and competed with several schools on the East Coast, including a school called GDA. This school happened to be Michael Mulligan's alma mater—and I remembered this from my White House days.

While Logan was at this boarding school, I promised him in his senior year that I would drive from Philadelphia to Newport to see every lacrosse game in which he was playing. There were games on Wednesday afternoons and Saturdays. And on one particular Saturday Logan's school was playing Michael Mulligan's alma mater, GDA, up in the Boston area.

I drove up there to watch him play and I remembered Michael telling many stories about his time at GDA. So, I walked into the development office and asked if they had ever heard of a guy by the name of Michael Mulligan and, indeed they had. When I asked them if they had any contact information of his, they were gracious enough to give me his e-mail address and phone number. Now, this was in 2002. Michael and I had not been in contact at all since 1974.

So, I went back to my office in Philadelphia, picked up the phone and dialed his number. At that time Michael was the headmaster of a school by the name of Thatcher School. A receptionist answered the phone and I asked for him. When he picked up the phone he said, "Oh my God, John Unland. Holy cow!"

We talked for maybe 15 minutes and then he asked a question I have never asked of anyone. Knowing that Linda (Spank) and I were married (remember Michael was an intern with both Linda and me at the White House in 1974), he asked, "So, where do you guys vacation?" Which I thought was a strange question to ask of anyone who hadn't seen someone for about 30 years. So, I mentioned to him that we go to Colorado and had a place in Vail. And then I mentioned to him that we have some land in Idaho which we bought as an investment and we go out there once a year or so to camp and take the kids and just sleep in tents.

And then he asked the ultimate question: "Where in Idaho?" And I paused—because no one has usually ever heard of the town in which we have this property. But I told him where it was, "It's in Driggs, which is a town of about 1,000 people." And then he said, "Where in Driggs?" And this time I was like, "Wow, where are we going with this conversation?" But I continued on by explaining, "Well, we have property about three miles outside of town." He followed that up by asking, "Well, do you have any pictures that would give me some bearings of the Teton mountains so that I can understand where you are?"

Now at this time, in the early 2000's, the Internet allowed people to send photos with the dial-up internet. So, I got a photo of our view from our property of the Teton mountains and sent it to him with all the screeching through AOL. It wasn't long before he was calling me back saying, John, "I downloaded the picture onto my laptop and I took it home to have my wife, Joy, look at it. And I said to her, Joy, where was this picture taken? And she said, well, that's off our back porch."

So, it turns out after more than 30 years of not being in touch with each other, somehow we managed to purchase property in the same small town within a 20-minute walk from each other; which means that three interns from 1974 in the Nixon White House now live within 20 minutes of one another on the east side of the Teton mountains.

Epilogue: What We Did in Our 20s

We were young men in our 20s: Lt. McDowell, my dad, and me; and each of us were involved in our way in some of this country's major historic eras and events. In a way, we chose to insert ourselves into these history-making situations on purpose: The Revolutionary War; where Lt. McDowell joined the 1st Pennsylvania Regiment in 1778, at the age of 28; World War II, where my dad participated in that conflict through his involvement with the ROTC[129] and subsequent appointment to Lieutenant in the U.S. Army at the age of 23; and the White House/Watergate scandal, where I was a first-hand witness to the historic transition of presidential power by resignation because of my internship and subsequent position on the White House staff, also at the age of 23.

I think most would agree that there is a general eagerness to be independent during that decade which encompasses our 20s. There also exists an air of invincibility in our 20s which allows us to take on and even seek out challenges; to act upon our subconscious desires to take risks and succeed.

Clearly in the lives of Lt. McDowell and my dad this was true, since at times they faced life-threatening challenges on an hourly basis—and I'm willing to bet they went into it knowing it wasn't going to be a 'Sunday school picnic.' No matter what was happening around them, they had to believe that they would survive; and somehow would garner the fortitude to do so. And in the thick of it all, both of them knew that they were witnessing history in the making—at least I know my dad felt that way.

My situation was different, of course, though there are some parallels. Certainly, I had the traits of a 20-something striking out to be independent; seeking challenges and trying my best to meet them and to succeed while consciously (or subconsciously)

---

[129] Wikipedia contributors, "Reserve Officers' Training Corps," *Wikipedia, The Free Encyclopedia,* https://en.wikipedia.org/w/index.php?title=Reserve_Officers%27_Training_Corps&oldid=983214468 (accessed October 27, 2020), "The Reserve Officers' Training Corps (ROTC) is a group of college and university-based officer training programs for training commissioned officers of the United States Armed Forces."

developing confidence in myself. And I most definitely knew that I was watching history unfold—first-hand—right before my eyes. Of course, I do not equate my situation with the daily, and sometimes hourly, life-threatening situations of my father or Lt. McDowell. The pressure under which they describe finding themselves is quite extraordinary. The mere fact that they survived each hour, each day, each week, and each year certainly is remarkable—and certainly brought them a confidence that they otherwise would not have had.

For me, being 23 years old and succeeding in handling the intense pressures of my job while working in what might be characterized as one of the most tumultuous times in the White House in recent history certainly gave me a boost of self-confidence I otherwise would not have had. Everything is relative.

As I mentioned in the prologue of this book, it is unusual for a family to have three first-hand diaries/memoirs of historic events such as these of our country's history—and for reasons unknown, these three young men in their 20s took the time to capture the essence of their experiences.

Speaking of time, thank you for giving me some of yours, and I do hope that you've enjoyed reading these "chronicles." I further hope that they—written through the lens of first-hand experiences—in some way lend insight and perspective to these events and eras of our country's past, especially around the creation of our nation and its constitution; around the sacrifice of defending freedom and our constitution; as well as around its fragility in terms of how it can be abused to the detriment of each of us.

If there is one thing I took away from all the articles and mementos I looked through, it was finding—and being reminded of how much I love—this quote from President Ford at our Peoria, Illinois conference: "...the American dream is best realized when we are wide awake."

All my best,
John Unland

--The End--

Back Cover Photo Credits:
Top photo; Wikimedia Commons contributors, "File:Washington Crossing the Delaware by Emanuel Leutze, MMA-NYC, 1851.jpg," *Wikimedia Commons, the free media repository,* https://commons.wikimedia.org/w/index.php?title=File:Washington_Crossing_the_Delaware_by_Emanuel_Leutze,_MMA-NYC,_1851.jpg&oldid=438393555 (accessed October 26, 2020)
Middle photo; John & Linda Unland on a personal trip to Europe
Bottom photo; John Unland during his internship at the White House, circa 1974

Made in the USA
Columbia, SC
18 November 2020